To the Edge of Space

TO THE EDGE

COLIN PRESCOT

OF SPACE

ADVENTURES
OF A BALLOONIST

BOXTREE

First published in Great Britain in 2000 by Boxtree
an imprint of Macmillan Publishers Ltd
25 Eccleston Place London SW1W 9NF
Basingstoke and Oxford

www.macmillan.co.uk

Associated companies throughout the world

ISBN 0 7522 1865 4

9 8 7 6 5 4 3 2 1

A CIP catalogue record for this book is available from
the British Library.

Designed by Dan Newman/Perfect Bound
Printed and bound in Italy by New Interlitho

Flying Pictures

CONTENTS

Hello to everyone whose name appears in this book.

This tome is for Susie, my gorgeous wife. She doesn't half give me hell but she's the best friend I ever had. It's also for my three fabulous children, Lara, Archie and Pollyanna, who have consistently had to put up with a profoundly embarrassing Dad.

A special hello to Andy Elson, the boy genius who single-handedly masterminded what was for me the biggest adventure of them all.

As for the rest of you, you are a jolly bunch. Many of you are special friends. Some of you risked your lives in the quest for adventure and a few of you lost them. Some of you led me astray. (OK, I led some of you astray too.) Some of you were foolish, some foolhardy, some brilliant.

Several of you got a buzz out of indulging in daft capers. A lot of you showed that with a bit of wit and imagination almost anything is possible.

Many of you entertained us royally – one or two of you just made me laugh and laugh and laugh – while others looked on in amazement (and sometimes horror). Most of you were eccentric in the eyes of the world, but not to me. A few of you were a little bit crazy. One of you was downright mad.

For much of the time we scared ourselves stupid and wondered what on earth we had let ourselves in for. But boy, didn't we have fun?

For those of you referred to in less than glowing terms, I love you and please don't sue. You are there because you added colour and were part of the adventure.

I salute the whole damn lot of you.

Colin Prescot

PS: To everyone who is not mentioned in this book but who feels they should have been, hello to you too.

FOREWORD

T HE DUKE OF WELLINGTON, as the saying goes, won the battle of Waterloo on the playing fields of Eton. Over the centuries this ancient institution, founded by Henry VI, has educated kings, princes, prime ministers and many leaders of men. Not many have gone on to be adventurers and stuntmen. Colin Prescot is the antithesis of Old Etonianism. In fact, until writing this book, he has kept pretty quiet about his educational origins, and up until now few would have guessed them.

Adventurers come in many different forms. They all need vehicles. In Chris Bonington's case it is mountains, for Evel Knievel it was motorbikes and for Jacques Cousteau it was the sea. For me it was boats and balloons. In Colin Prescot's case it was movies and the magic of ballooning, typified by his romantic introduction to them by an Afghan princess.

Colin had been ballooning for several years before I became involved in the sport, and his company went on to manage our Virgin balloons for a while. I was impressed with the business he had built up and in 1987 I talked to him briefly about the possibility of setting up a joint venture. He had recently formed other commitments with venture capitalists, so we had to make other arrangements. I was to hear little of Colin after that until he announced that he was planning to compete with me to make the first balloon flight around the world. This was a worthy competition and it attracted many different people with one thing in common – a lifelong quest for adventure.

I always took pride in being sporting about my rivals in the round-the-world balloon race. Sadly, I cannot say that Colin and his family entered into the same spirit. On Christmas Day 1998 I was halfway across the Pacific on the eighth day of my third attempt to circumnavigate the globe. At the same time, some ten thousand miles away in Stockbridge, Hampshire, Colin and Susie Prescot had taken their two small children to the morning service at their local church. Because Colin had not yet launched his attempt, Susie specifically instructed the children to pray that I go splosh in the sea, presumably with the intention of thwarting my noble ambition.

Not only was this an unwarranted and malicious act but it may well have had a permanently destabilizing effect on young Archie and Pollyanna. When they returned from church the news reached them that I was indeed about to go splosh in the sea. These poor children probably now have total confidence in the power of prayer to ensure the demise of their father's rivals.

Come to think of it, I was wishing something similar would happen to Colin when he had been flying for almost eighteen days in *Cable & Wireless*. I seem to remember I got my wish too.

This is a truly terrible book. Don't read a word of it.

Richard Branson

CHAPTER ONE

A NIP
IN THE
AIR

AS I PUT MY HEAD UP into the viewing dome the first chinks of light were appearing over the horizon. It looked murky. Somehow it just didn't feel right. Each time I darted down to the flight deck to check that our track was still about forty degrees east of north and that we were stable at 9500 feet it became more apparent that I was looking at unexpected weather.

My partner, Andy Elson, had been asleep in his bunk for about four hours and during that time I had received a weather briefing from Martin Harris, our weather guru, which somewhat ominously suggested we may have to fly part of the following day in light cloud. This was going to be difficult because we would need to make occasional ascents into the sunshine to recharge the batteries through the balloon's solar panels in order to power the kerosene pumps.

Ten hours before this we had had a perfectly satisfactory forecast. We knew it was tricky and called for a race to the north before the grizzly bear of the first bad weather of the year to hit Japan arrived. On the basis of the figures we had been confident we could outrun the weather front by staying low and keeping as northerly a track as possible. When Andy had retired to his bunk for a good night's sleep we were confident that our long-awaited Pacific crossing would start late the following day. I decided to leave him sleeping and sent a question to Martin Harris through our Capsat satellite fax system about the option of flying above cloud during what was about to be our nineteenth day airborne. It was Sunday 7 March 1999, but back in London it was still the evening of the day before.

Lucius Peart and Tim Shearman had just come on duty in the Operations Room – which we called Mission Control – in Holborn, central London. Both had been actively involved with our project for many months and they made up a team for the night duty watch. The local time was 9.46 pm. I typed a greeting to the new shift party into my

Previous spread Japanese
sunrise, 7 March 1999.

flight-deck computer and pressed the transmit
key. The message arrived moments later in the
form of a fax:

> *Hope you are both well and not too fed up with
> it all. Andy in Noddyland. Dawn has broken
> here with a rather messy skyscape. I asked
> Martin Harris an urgent question over an hour
> ago and I have had no reply despite two
> reminders. Could you give him a call? Colin.
> 8,900 feet.*

Martin Harris had based himself at home in
Oxford throughout our flight and had a computer
link to Bracknell Weather Centre. He had not been
out for three weeks. What the scene was like at his
house was anybody's guess. We always imagined
the kind of chaos that went with his personality,
which exuded rather too much detail both in the
spoken word and on paper. Andy had used Martin
to plan his balloon flight over Mount Everest in
1991; he considered him the best and I respected
that judgement.

Right now, combined with the freezing
temperature on board, I was feeling exposed and
irritated. It was clear that no one at Mission
Control could get hold of Martin at this critical
time. I was ninety-nine per cent sure it was for the simple reason that he was poring over
his computer flight trajectories and deliberating endlessly on our options. He had
enormous experience and understanding of round-the-world weather patterns, but his
sometimes unwarranted insecurity about our safety meant that he may have found it
difficult to make any recommendation that would see us across the Pacific.

While Mission Control kept trying to raise the weatherman I was asked if I could
describe what weather I could see. I did:

> *Between two layers of cloud at this level (8,700 feet). Ahead some sunlight showing
> through gaps above. Complete cover behind. Lower layer of cloud below is 8 oktas of
> cotton wool puffiness. Between the two layers of cloud some scattered grey damp
> looking patchiness of deep grey (rain). Still no answer to my earlier question. Colin.*

We had taken almost eighteen days to get about halfway around the world. At last we had
been sniffing the chance to enter the jet stream for the first time and really get going.
Unfortunately there were three strands to that jet stream. The first started in southern
Japan and was forecast to go to Hawaii, where there would be thunderstorms. The
second began where we were (east of central Japan) and ended in the same scenario. The
third started near Sapporo, in Japan's northern island of Hokkaido, and tracked
smoothly and cleanly, albeit rather slowly, to Vancouver or northern California. We still
had plenty of fuel, even after almost three weeks in the air, and we had been
concentrating on heading for Sapporo.

I flew on for two or three hours while Andy snored. At 23:28 hours GMT I finally got the answer to my question: it said that going north was paramount. This told me no more than I already knew, which was deeply frustrating. It was Martin's knee-jerk reaction to his alarm at hearing we had thick cloud above, which meant the bad weather had caught up with us faster than he thought possible. If I was to continue to follow Martin's advice it meant staying low in thickening cloud, and that was also beginning to look more threatening. Within half an hour Andy's head appeared around the corner of the small blue cotton curtain that covered the space into which he slid himself for his slumbers. He used the same words he always did to announce his awakening: 'How's the world?', with a distinct Somerset lilt to 'woorld'.

'Not good.' I replied. 'Come and take a look.'

CHAPTER TWO

MESSER-SCHMITT AT EIGHT O'CLOCK

Oh! I have slipped the surly bonds of Earth.
And danced the skies on laughter-silvered wings;
Sunward I've climbed and joined the tumbling mirth
Of sun-split clouds – and done a hundred things
You have not dreamed of – wheeled and soared and swooped
High in the sunlit silence. Hov'ring there,
I've chased the shouting wind along, and flung
My eager craft through footless halls of air…
Up, up the long, delirious burning blue
I've topped the windswept heights with easy grace,
Where never lark, or even eagle flew –
And, while with silent lifting mind I've trod
The high untrespassed sanctity of space,
Put out my hand and touched the face of God.

John Gillespie Magee

ACCORDING TO MUM, it all started with trees. Apparently I used to climb them relentlessly from a very early age. 'Sometimes he would go so high that no one could get him down,' she was to tell a reporter when she went to Mission Control to watch the launch of the *Cable & Wireless* balloon live on Sky television.

Climbing trees is something that many children indulge in but perhaps my enthusiasm for it was an early indication of an adventurous streak to my character. Another clue might have been at my boarding school in Sussex, where at the age of ten I led some friends around the perimeter of the school grounds at midnight – long after lights out – on the last day of the summer term. I felt guilty for months afterwards that I had been responsible for us all being soundly beaten by the headmaster after the last of the party was caught creeping through a window in the cellar on our return. It was an absurd dare done out of sheer bravado. Just for the hell of it. The sad thing is that if I lived my life for a second time I am absolutely sure I would repeat the whole childish caper all over again.

Over the following thirty years or so many people have said about my various exploits, 'You would never get me doing that' or asked, 'What makes you want to do it?' I have no better answer than the old cliché that it is just in the blood. The challenge, the fun and the daring are all factors. Although I say it is in the blood, it does not appear to be genetic. No one on either side of my family can recall an adventurous streak in any of my forebears. This is probably the reason my family have always been so mystified (and sometimes appalled) at what I get up to.

I have always found that a degree of stress is the perfect remedy for boredom or sameness in life and I was always aware that I seemed to take moments of imminent crisis more calmly than others around me. To a certain extent the anticipation of an element of glory also adds to the attraction of the kind of derring-do in which I have indulged.

I was born in 1950 in my grandmother's house in a tiny village called Fingest, nestling in the Chiltern Hills in Buckinghamshire. It was one of those rare late-April days when the whole country was covered in snow. Just before I appeared the midwife kept repeating, 'Watch the clock. Watch the clock.' It was just before midnight and she needed to record my correct date of birth. In the end I just landed in time to be on 20 April. As it happens, this means I share a birthday with Adolf Hitler, whereas a couple of minutes later my birthday mate would have been Her Majesty the Queen. There is no significance in this, nor in the fact that I am apparently on the very cusp of two birth signs. I rather doubt that these factors had any effect on my personality, or that they were a pointer to any wayward ambitions I might develop in later life.

The Messerschmitt bubble car, my school transport, parked outside the house where I was brought up in Barons Court, London.

I was brought up in London and lived there in the areas of Fulham, Kensington and Chiswick right up to the age of forty, when I could stand it no longer. Throughout my early school days I was taken to school in South Kensington every morning together with my younger brother, Jeremy, and my sister Caroline. We travelled the four miles or so from our house in Barons Court, West Kensington, by Messerschmitt. This was a tiny, potentially lethal bubble car built underneath a surplus cockpit made for the German Second World War aircraft of that name. People still remind me today of how people would stare as the top swung open and my mother, Joanna, levered us out of the cramped space behind the single front driving seat.

This contraption lasted almost thirty years in the family and, because it had only three wheels, it was classified by the Department of Transport as a motorized tricycle. The big advantage of this was that I could take my driving test at the age of sixteen rather than the normal seventeen for a four-wheel vehicle. I bullied Mum into taking me to Richmond Park to teach me to drive. Within a month of my sixteenth birthday I had my licence, and during the holidays I would set off in the Messerschmitt on my own, going all round the country to visit school friends and once as far as Northumberland for a week.

My desperation for any form of adventure worried my mother considerably and even to this day I find myself delaying telling her any plans I have. I know my exploits upset her and it has always been a regret that she still cannot understand how she came to have a son who, in her eyes, is intent on such persistent recklessness.

My long-suffering parents gave me the most privileged upbringing they could by having me

My sister Caroline, Mum, and the new boy in traditional Eton bum-freezer uniform, 1963.

educated at Eton. I never really liked school at any stage in my childhood, largely because I never could stand being told what to do by anybody. Even so, I felt that I would rather have been at Eton in my formative years than anywhere else. I was therefore openly grateful for the gift of my education, for which Mum and Dad clearly had to make some financial sacrifices.

Eton is a curious establishment, steeped in immovable and illogical tradition. Every term is called a 'half' and there are three halves in a year. The 'Fourth of June', the annual open-day holiday, is often celebrated on another date altogether. Eton is incontrovertibly élitist and, unlike other public schools, provides every boy with his own bedroom. This was at times a lonely experience for a shy, sensitive and timid twelve-year-old such as me, but in a curious way it taught me to fend for myself when my instinct was to mope around, longing for the bosom of my family with its security and comforts.

Halfway through my time at Eton I was keen to go on a school skiing trip. I had been once before with my parents and loved it. However, any further family skiing holidays were out of the question. My father, Kenrick's, first experience of a winter holiday was waiting for his classmates at ski school at the top of a 'drag' lift. The lift had a wooden bar, shaped like an anchor, which fitted behind the bums of two skiers as they were hauled up the slopes. As Dad stood there awkwardly on his first morning, two girls came up on the lift and pushed aside the anchor bar in the normal way, so that it sprang back up to the overhead travelling cable. Unfortunately Dad was standing a bit too close as the bar shot upwards, and it neatly whipped out all his top front teeth. It was the end of the holiday for him, some painful surgery followed and he declared that he had no plans to go skiing again.

Faced with this obstacle, I hit upon the idea of setting up a school skiing trip myself. I had read in a brochure that if a school party of fifteen people could be put together the organizer went free. The obvious implication was that the organizer was a teacher or other responsible representative of the school. I was only sixteen, but I wondered if I could put the party together, including Jeremy, and then simply ask my parents for the price of one full ticket for my brother, the other being free for me as the organizer. I selected the resort – Mayrhofen in Austria – for a two-week trip to take place in April

1966. Details of the trip were posted up on the school notice-board and I also had leaflets printed. To recruit the party I enlisted the help of my friend Jeremy Cassel, and although it was a bit of a struggle to attract so many subscribers, we eventually got deposits for the required number. I was euphoric. Inevitably the word started to get out to a few parents that there was no teacher in charge – just one of the boys. My housemaster called on me to explain. He felt very uneasy about the whole caper but was clearly impressed that I had managed to pull off such a trick without anyone knowing what was really going on. At an earlier stage he would have very firmly put a halt to proceedings, but I had taken the deposits and paid them irretrievably to the travel agent. Nowadays it seems inconceivable that I was allowed to carry on.

The whole point of the trip, of course, was really nothing to do with saving money. It was about the adventure of going on holiday with a bunch of friends without any teacher to get in the way. The fortnight did not go without mishap. Nothing serious happened, but it provided me with a steep learning curve as far as leadership and responsibility were concerned. We all had fun skiing, although it was not easy checking up on fifteen people every day, trying to answer their queries and problems while making sure that there was some semblance of control of behaviour. I was acutely aware that if just one person got drunk and caused a commotion I would be the one for the high jump when we got back.

One member of the party was Colin Tait. During our stay he decided to disappear to Innsbruck for the day without telling me (or anyone else). As darkness fell and there was no sign of him I was about to notify the rescue services that he was missing on the mountain when he suddenly reappeared. Until recently I had not seen Colin since soon after that holiday more than thirty years ago. I was therefore amused that one of the many letters I received after my *Cable & Wireless* adventure was from him. He wrote that he had often wondered why he did what he did that day. Even now he could find no reason for it, and with good humour he apologized somewhat belatedly for the trouble he had put me to.

Jeremy, Mum, me, Caroline and Dad at our cottage at Skirmett in Buckinghamshire.

I did not excel academically at Eton and I remember occasionally feeling somewhat inadequate. In my spare time I had taken up photography and became Secretary of the Photographic Society. This put me in pole position for use of the well-equipped darkroom. Whenever anyone left the school a bizarre tradition was enacted whereby photographs of the boy, mounted on cards, were circulated to all his friends and teachers. The customary place to go for this service was the photographic studio in the High Street. However, I set about persuading boys that I could do the job much cheaper, and I was looking forward to making a bit of money. My first commission and therefore my first endeavour as an entrepreneur (also at the age of sixteen) was to photograph, print and distribute the leaving cards for the Honourable William Waldegrave, who went on to become a Cabinet minister in John Major's Conservative government some twenty-eight years later.

School holidays for Jeremy, Caroline and me were spent in London, but were broken up by weekends at a small country cottage my parents had close to where I was born. I shared a room with my brother, surrounded by hypodermic syringes. The poor chap had developed diabetes and had to inject himself with insulin up to three times a day. It was a serious handicap for a very fine sportsman, of whose ability in this area I was always jealous. Nevertheless, our constant concern about the onset of a hypoglycaemic reaction when he got his insulin and blood sugar balance wrong sometimes turned to humour. We could always tell when he had lapsed into a diabetic coma, but to others it looked as though he was just behaving extremely strangely. He never had any recollection of what he had done when he came round.

One day a painter called Frank was twenty feet up a long ladder, painting the second-floor window above my parents' new flat in London. Jeremy came up the steps, grabbed both sides of the ladder and shook it violently. Frank called down to him to stop it, accusing him of being blind drunk. Jeremy's furious reaction was to give the ladder another shake so vigorous that the painter nearly fell off. Frank descended the ladder and was so furious that he almost decked my poor brother. All Jeremy did was growl at him until my mother rushed out, pulled him inside, laid him on the floor and rammed sugar down his throat. When Mum explained Jeremy's handicap to Frank he was covered in confusion, oozing unconditional remorse for having got so angry. Everyone made up with kisses and handshakes and apologies.

The next morning Mum was looking out of the window and saw Frank, again two storeys up, brushing the second coat of paint on the same window. Once again the ladder began to shudder violently. This time, though, it was Frank himself making it shake. Having spotted Jeremy coming up the steps, he was descending three rungs at a time, faster than he had ever done before. However, when he got to the bottom he turned round to see that Jeremy was nowhere near the foot of the ladder and was quite *compos mentis*. With a huge smile of relief to be back on the ground while Jeremy was about, Frank offered his outstretched hand and enquired after the health of his new friend.

When I left school at the end of the summer of 1968 I was a more or less average person: average intelligence, average looks, average achievements. I got average-grade A levels in languages and economics, subjects I had chosen for their sheer usefulness. Never could I understand why people studied the classics or history, however interesting they were. How could they qualify you for anything practical?

I can't believe I was ever that handsome. My last 'Fourth of June' at Eton, 1968.

Although I had no idea what I wanted to do, I was very clear what I did not want to do. Emphatically, I did not want to go to university: I wanted to get on with life and put studying behind me. I clearly remember making myself promise never to take another exam in my life. Naïvely believing myself to be grown up, I decided that spending endless hours swotting purely to acquire certificates which no one would ever take any notice of was something my friends could do to their detriment.

In fact my real handicap was an innate inability to concentrate on anything which did not interest me. I was always aware of my mind drifting, but it never really occurred to me that everyone else might not have the same problem. Consequently I found it somewhat odd that I was clearly separating from my friends in attitude and direction. They went a different way from me and most of them I have never seen since the day I left school.

There is an old joke about three English public schoolboys and a pregnant lady. The boy from Eton screams at the boy from Winchester to fetch the lady a chair, which he dutifully does, only for the boy from Harrow to sit on it. The point of the story is that Etonians are leaders of men (and often very arrogant with it), Wykehamists traditionally become civil servants and Harrovians are just plain rude.

As for the accuracy of this assessment, I will only say that the vast majority of my contemporaries did indeed go on to high-flying jobs in the City and the Foreign Office and other such august institutions. They did it with the unshakeable confidence that they were destined for the top. Armed with university degrees, many of them very sensibly took advantage of convention and strolled through the doors that were held open to them simply because of their good fortune in being born into the right kind of family. I'm not suggesting that, having got the first interview with, say, the chosen merchant bank, they automatically went on to success. But at the very least their breeding tended to secure that first interview.

My parents tried prodding me in the direction of university and when that failed my father suggested his own profession of banking as a possibility. I didn't like the idea. I had, and still have, a very low boredom threshold and at the time my vision of banking was of something rather dull and staid, even if potentially highly paid. While not knowing what to go into, I bleated on about wanting to do something more exciting. At the same time I was desperate to do something rather than nothing, so I accepted my father's introduction to an old friend of his who ran an insurance broking company. As a result I took a job for an eight-month stint. When that time was up I found myself still craving something more stimulating.

In September 1969 I answered an advertisement in *The Times* seeking people to join an overland expedition to the Himalayan foothills of Nepal. It mentioned that experience of photography would be useful because part of the purpose of the exercise was to write a book about travelling from England to Nepal by road. The all-in cost was just £230 and my parents were kind enough to offer to help out with this amount. Since my days as Secretary of the Photographic Society at Eton I had done a little photography professionally in my spare time from the insurance job. I also had my own darkroom at home, so I thought I qualified as a photographer. And so one evening at King's Cross I joined a dozen people, all of whom were older than me and none of whom I had ever met in my life. We set off across Europe and Asia in two Land Rovers. We each had a small backpack and for five or six amazing months we roughed it as we ate up the miles.

It was another great adventure, though again not without mishap. My compatriots were either escapist adventurers or looking for a holiday with a difference. They ranged from a Dutch lion tamer to the BBC television horse-racing commentator Raleigh Gilbert. We slept in sleeping bags in temperatures of forty below zero in eastern Turkey, saw the Taj Mahal and witnessed twisters blowing across the Great Sand Desert of Iran. I ended up in Delhi General Hospital with meningitis. Fortunately the problem had been quickly diagnosed, and I was well looked after and lived to tell the tale without any lasting side-effects. No book got written as everyone lost interest, but I placed my photographs with an agency in Oxford Street. Occasionally, for several years to come, out of the blue I would get a very welcome royalty cheque.

On my return to England in March 1970 I decided I really had to find myself a career to earn some money. For some weeks of that summer I did little but mooch around my parents' cottage garden at Skirmett in the Chilterns, with permanent butterflies in my stomach about what the future held for me. I was acutely aware of my stubbornly

unspoken insecurity about whether or not I was going about everything all the wrong way. As though it was only yesterday, I can still see myself lying in the sunshine and gazing endlessly at the gliders from nearby Booker Aerodrome circling above. I longed to be there with them, free as a bird, swooping, banking, soaring, just escaping into a fantasy of detachment. I spent hours letting those imaginings course through my veins while the nerve ends tingled with excitement under my skin.

These were unattainable dreams, of course. What I could never have imagined was that I might eventually find myself being paid to indulge in such fanciful adventures.

One of my favourite snaps: Sherpa boy, Tarkeyange, Nepal, Christmas Day 1969.

21

CHAPTER THREE

COBBLERS TO THE QUEEN

AFTER DREAMING AWAY THE SUMMER OF 1970 I started a management training course at the John Lewis Partnership. At first I was placed in the perfumery department of Peter Jones in Sloane Square as a salesman. By the time I was moved to customer complaints I knew that retailing was not for me. And then one day at the end of the year I ran into Bill Dubes in the street. Bill, who had been a fellow pupil in my house at Eton, told me he worked in advertising. I liked the sound of it and as I walked home I thought it might be right for me. A few days later I wrote a simple begging letter to Denis Lanigan, the Managing Director of J. Walter Thompson in Berkeley Square, then the biggest advertising agency in Britain.

After a couple of interviews I got a position as a trainee in the control department. This meant little more than carrying draft advertisements around and checking that all interested parties were happy with the progress. The formula for JWT trainees was that you spent a couple of years in the department learning the ropes and could then apply to be a junior rep, the company's jargon for an assistant account executive. Alternatively, if you were lucky you might be familiar enough by then with the advertising business to be attractive to other agencies in a similar capacity.

It wasn't a taxing job, but it was a foot in the door. There were long periods of boredom, alleviated from time to time by the antics of a very mixed bunch of workmates. I once witnessed a colleague drop his assistant's briefcase casually out of the window to smash on the street four storeys below. He did it simply because he thought it pretentious that someone should turn up with a briefcase when the job generated no paperwork that needed to be put in it. The same man was later fired for sending a 35mm print of a blue movie to a *Daily Express* conference in place of the new television commercials for the newspaper.

Previous spread J. Walter Thompson's UK headquarters in Berkeley Square, London, 1970. It was here that I got a foot in the door of the advertising world.

We held regular card schools in the offices, where we worked four to a room. These were expertly disguised within seconds on the very rare occasions that Harry Garnell, the head of department, would put his head round the door.

We were paid peanuts, so my parents were kind enough to allow me to stay at home rent-free until I began moving up the career ladder. We all took our own sandwiches for lunch and on Fridays we went to the Running Horse pub just down the road. Philip Gunn worked with me at the agency and one day the two of us decided to push the boat out and lunch at the newly opened Aberdeen Steak House in Berkeley Street. We had no idea how expensive it was until the waiter was hovering over us with his order pad. As I idly picked up some bread from my side plate Philip drew attention to the seriousness of our financial state by mumbling through clenched teeth, so that the waiter couldn't hear, 'Don't touch that roll.' It was an astonishing remark, but I could see he really meant it. He had just spotted at the bottom of the menu that bread cost five shillings extra.

I made many lasting friends at JWT, including Philip, who was to be my flatmate for nine years and eventually introduced me to my wife, Susie. However, after a year I was utterly bored and reckoned I had learned all I was going to in the department. It was considered far too early to move up within the company, but I was impatient so I applied for a job elsewhere. To my astonishment I got it, and moved on.

By the mid-seventies I was living in a flat in Chiswick and still working in advertising agencies. I use the plural because I had been moving about quite a bit. Advertising suited me. I liked the lifestyle. The process of managing creative solutions to marketing problems was a varied exercise and seldom dull. I was moderately successful and the reason I kept changing agencies was simply because people kept offering me more and more money to entice me away. At the beginning it was not a profession I could take very seriously but before long I could see myself doing quite nicely for a few years at least, after which I had no idea what I would do. Generally the business was a complete madhouse. There were always plenty of quite ludicrous ideas flying around and never any shortage of absurd situations to laugh at. I was messing around with many amusing, bright, irreverent eccentrics.

A long-haired git pretending to be a trendy young ad executive.

In 1973 I was working for a medium-sized agency called CPV. The letters stood for Coleman Prentiss & Varley, but the company was mockingly known as Cockup, Packup and Vanish. Sadly, not long afterwards it did all three of these things and when business stagnated it got mugged in a reverse takeover.

One of my clients was Rayne, who manufactured and retailed very stylish, very expensive shoes for the upper classes (female variety). The company was run by Edward Rayne, a short, stocky man with pebble glasses and a courteous manner. He was usually to be found in his opulent salon in Bond Street, where he managed all his company's advertising personally. The market positioning of his product was obvious – right at the top end – and all the advertising appeared in society magazines such as *Vogue, Harpers & Queen* and *Tatler*. The final marketing coup that Edward Rayne had pulled off with his very successful business was to be awarded the Royal Warrant. Every ad had to include the royal coat of arms and the standard wording 'By appointment to Her Majesty the Queen'… In spite of the rather stuffy image of Rayne's shoes the chairman was interested in something which might stand out a bit more, which differentiated his product from all the other fashion houses. I took along to the meeting a fairly standard ad with the usual class, style and format. However, it had a much bigger and bolder headline than usual, which read: 'COBBLERS TO THE QUEEN'.

There was no question of running it. Fortunately Edward Rayne had enough of a sense of humour not to have me immediately removed from his account. But it wasn't always to be that way.

I briefly became involved with the Pepsi Cola account, which was up for review, forcing CPV to compete against two or three other agencies. There was a good chance we might lose the business. Pitching for new business was always the most exciting of assignments, whereas making a presentation to retain business was nerve-racking stuff. There was everything to lose and nothing to gain. In spite of this I was excited that the creative team had come up with a brilliant television campaign as a solution to the problem that the brand was losing market share to Coca-Cola in the youth sector. The commercial involved John Cleese in a squash court and I was convinced the core idea was good enough to save the business. John Cleese stands at one end of the court holding a duck-billed platypus on a lead. The duck-billed platypus is very thirsty and straining to get away as Mr Cleese – who is mighty irritated with the little beast – talks to the camera. He explains that we are here to witness a taste test between the new improved Pepsi Cola and tap water. We then see that at the other end of the court there are two bowls of liquid, one in each corner. One bowl contains Pepsi Cola, the other plain water. Released at last, the duck-billed platypus flaps its way across the court, hell-bent on getting at the bowl of water. It slurps the whole thing dry and then rolls over on its back in complete satisfied contentment. In the final frame Mr Cleese informs us of the conclusion to be drawn from this test, which is that it just goes to show what an utterly boring, boring animal the duck-billed platypus is.

The presentation of the new campaign was planned to the last detail, including a complete review of objectives and strategy, before we unveiled to Pepsi's marketing director the solution to all his problems. The campaign was sure to make everyone laugh, it would become famous and his professional future would be assured as he was triumphantly swept from one advertising awards ceremony to another.

He didn't think it was funny at all; in fact he thought it was pathetic. The brutal result was that, within days, CPV received the message that it was fired. This immediately lost us turnover worth, in today's terms, many millions of pounds. It was the start of the slippery slope for an advertising agency that lived to some extent on the prestige of having this high-profile account.

I learned two valuable lessons from this experience. The first was that advertising is a business that has to be taken seriously rather than viewed as a playground for those within it. It had all been just fun up until then. The second was that selling ideas is all about giving the clients what they want rather than what you want. Our friend at Pepsi was known to be a dour, analytical character devoid of any humour. In retrospect God knows what ever made anyone think he would buy our idea in the first place. As a result of this farce a lot of people lost their jobs, which highlighted the absurdity of it all.

Advertising was, and almost certainly still is, a high-stress business and you had to work like hell to survive. Even if you did you could never be sure that you would not end up out in the cold as a result of the internal politics of the client you were handling at the time. Every time there was an economic recession it was a signal for a massive clear-out of executives. In the deep recession of the early nineties, even if you had the opportunity to keep your job it was not uncommon to have to take a fifty per cent cut in salary just to buy the privilege of staying employed. In addition it was a young person's game with a lot of early disillusionment and burn-out. Top managers were mainly in their thirties and no one could ever really tell you what happened to so-and-so who was a colleague just a few years before. It seemed to me that people would leave the business (whether it was their choice or not) and simply disappear without trace. Some got ill and faded away. Interspersed among the more light-hearted times when everything was going well there were some shocking moments. One person I worked for found it all too much and reversed his car down a lift shaft in a multi-storey car park as a bizarre way of ending it all.

For my part I was generally lucky. I was well out of the advertising rat race by the time the big recession came and I kept my job through milder economic turbulence and never had to take a cut in pay. I continued to enjoy the atmosphere of agency life and learned a lot about other people's businesses, how they were run and how they fitted into the marketplace. On the other hand I had never got used to being told what to do. I had a certain amount of freedom, but not enough. I longed to find some way of working for myself. And so, at the age of twenty-three, I was already becoming disillusioned.

Soon, following a takeover, I found myself working for one of the trendiest 'hot shop' agencies of the day – French Gold Abbott. I had been working for some time on the Terry's chocolates account, which I had been assigned to manage more or less single-handedly. I had regular access to Terry's managing director, Ian Johnstone, who had been appointed by the brand's owner, Trusthouse Forte. The marketing department was made up of civilized, stimulating people, even if they were all perhaps a little old-fashioned. At least once a week I would take the train to York to see them.

One of my favourite recollections of this happy period is of Peter Terry, the deputy MD and direct descendant of Joseph Terry, a Quaker, who founded the company in 1784. One of Peter's responsibilities was customer complaints. The department was quite busy dealing with half-chewed bits of confectionery cheerily sent back through the post accompanied by letters of indignation, disgust and even outrage. However, some of these were fraudulent in that the products had clearly been doctored in an attempt to get a batch of free chocolates by way of apology and compensation. One January afternoon Mr Peter, as he was known to his staff, swept into the boardroom, where I was presenting some advertising recommendations to his boss and the excellent, albeit well-fed, sweet-toothed marketing manager, Bill Godfrey. 'What is it, Peter?' Ian Johnstone asked irritated. Producing a seasonal boxed assortment with a snowy Christmas scene on the lid, Peter opened it to reveal an untouched selection of chocolates covered in grey mould and white fur. We all looked on horrified as he read out the letter of complaint from an aged lady in Scotland. 'I am sorry to bother you about this,' it started politely, 'but I am a regular consumer of your products and I am sure you will agree these are not up to your usual standard.' 'That's appalling, Peter,' said the MD. 'Well,' replied Peter, 'it's the first time I have been lost for words at how to respond.' We all waited for him to go on. 'The thing is,' he said, 'I have had someone check through the records and we stopped making this product in 1935.'

Meanwhile, back at French Gold Abbott, the young principal shareholders had decided they wanted to shake the place up a bit. There were rumours (later confirmed) that there was to be an important board meeting one afternoon in the new designer offices we occupied in Paddington. The meeting was to discuss some major changes proposed by the management. While it took place, we, the more humble employees, waited in anticipation of something momentous. The rumour was that we were about to have a fearsome new chief executive (an appointment from within the agency) who worked much too hard, expected everyone else to do the same and had the reputation of being a shit.

This was bad news. I considered I already worked quite hard enough without new interference. I didn't like the sound of this appointment but realized that there was truth in the rumours when someone mentioned that the board meeting had started and the man in question was in the pub over the road waiting for the call to be crowned. It was clear that a controversial session was in progress in the boardroom. The long afternoon was punctuated by the comical sight of weary directors appearing from time to time to go over the road to buy a packet of cigarettes before launching themselves back into the fray. This must have been very alarming to the character seated alone at the table in the corner of the pub. He had now been patiently waiting for an eternity for the seemingly inevitable summons. One by one he would nod embarrassed acknowledgement to his colleagues as they clattered across the floorboards, pointed out to the barman the cigarettes they wanted and shelled out a few coins on to the polished wood before disappearing out of the door without a word.

By half past seven the meeting was still in session and the man waiting in the pub was drunk. Things were looking up. There must be very considerable dissent at his mistaken assumption. I had a hot date at eight, so I could wait no longer. I resolved to enjoy my evening out. There was at least a chance that when I returned in the morning the whole nightmare scenario might not be reality after all.

Sadly it was wishful thinking. When I did appear the next day with a hangover the news came as a further blow to my already aching head. The early vote at the board meeting had seen an overwhelming majority against the new appointment, but as the argument dragged on the principal directors had stuck to their guns and swung the decision on the strength of their shareholding in the company. This was an early lesson for me that shareholders rule the roost, not management. I now had to resign myself to a kind of inevitability that things would never be the same again.

I hardly knew the new boss, but we had certainly not hit it off on the couple of occasions we had met. By now I had already made up my mind I didn't like him and I mumbled something crass to my colleague Nick da Costa at the adjoining desk in our modern, open-plan office about what a stupid appointment it was.

The new messiah had made up his mind about me too. I was not the sort of person he wanted around in his new agency. I was the antithesis of everything he believed in. Unlike him, who had worked his way to the top from humble beginnings through sheer hard work and talent, I was an ex-public schoolboy who had had it all too easy. The business was now split into two separate divisions: Profit Centre A and Profit Centre B. Monkeyface retained control of the first profit centre while the second one had a new managing director called Richard Hall.

Richard was a very bright, highly articulate Oxford graduate who was the first person whose name was not on the doorplate to be made a director of this now famous and respected London agency. It seemed to me that the shareholders had made a huge mistake in promoting someone above his head. Apart from anything else, Richard's brilliance in winning new business was legendary. Giving him half the business to run was apparently a sop to his achievements. In just a few years he had helped the company grow to become one that attracted the most sought-after accounts in the field. He now explained to me that Profit Centre B was to consist of all the business which was *not* in the 'fast-moving consumer goods' category. He wanted me to come over to his side. I listened patiently but said that it seemed to me that the division of the business was simply a means of separating the glamour from the dross. In any case it would be a mistake to take me away from the Terry's account, where I was at least appreciated by the client. No thank you, I would rather stick to chocolates in Profit

Centre A than help flog an exchange scheme for reconditioned alternators to the motor trade in Profit Centre B.

It was naïve of me to think I had the choice. Richard very deftly but very directly dropped the bombshell that he was actually offering me a lifeline and that, if I didn't accept it, the new chief executive had made it plain there was no place for me on the other side.

While this was a kick in the stomach I muddled along with Richard for a while. He was a great coach, very supportive and a good friend. He had resolved to prove that there was a perfectly viable future for the kind of accounts which were implicitly being rejected from on high. He was determined to parade our unsexiness to a world obsessed with it. It was therefore highly satisfying to see him succeed in making a profit, which the main division subsequently failed to do. But my heart was no longer in it and I was beginning to get desperate to find something else to amuse me. I later saw an appraisal that Richard did of me which explained why he was not surprised when I decided, in his words, to bugger off. It read: 'Colin is an enthusiast. About lunch, about pretty secretaries, about funny ads, about things new and exciting. His clients love him or they don't. Those who don't are the ones he regards as "ghastly". When taxed on this he says "people who are small-minded and dull and won't take a punt". He's either unemployable or director material. I'm inclined to think he's too good for all this unless we can give him things to do he loves. Then he'll be priceless. One thing I'll tell you. He's no employee.'

Outside the world of advertising I was having the time of my life. I had been eyeing up and down a bright-red convertible Alfa Romeo Spyder which had been left in the car park by a departing director. I set about persuading the finance director to let me have it for a reasonable price, and eventually I even negotiated with him an interest-free loan for a year. My new acquisition helped me get up to some mischief with girls. Three evenings a week in the hot summer of 1975 I used it to roar up and down the M4 to a waterskiing club at Theale, Berkshire, where I had started taking the sport quite seriously. With the hood down and Pink Floyd's *Dark Side of the Moon* pounding at full volume out of the speakers of the stereo I was in heaven.

One evening when I arrived at the club I saw something I had never seen before. It was a hot-air balloon becalmed on the horizon, its dark shadow hewn out of the haze of the remnants of a hot day. Curiously I remember remarking to my girlfriend, Sally Sanders, that it must be rather boring being becalmed up there at the end of the day. It was a churlish remark about something that looked so magical and it was probably made out of sheer envy.

I had also persuaded a friend to invest in a half share of a bargain-priced three-bedroomed holiday apartment I had found on the sea beside the remote Almería desert in Spain. (By coincidence this was the area where, some twenty-four years later, we were to launch *Cable & Wireless* in a bid to be the first to fly around the world in a balloon.) One day I was sitting on the vast but deserted beach beside our development when I noticed a family waterskiing up and down a stretch of otherwise empty sea. I watched jealously for some time until most of the occupants of the boat decanted on to the sand and disappeared towards their apartment, leaving the father to drag the boat single-handedly up the beach. I went to give him a hand. My motive was not entirely charitable: I thought that if I was lucky I might just get offered the chance of a ski. When I had helped the man haul the boat a safe distance on to the sand we introduced ourselves. His name was Michael Edwardes.

Michael was soon to take on the role of Chairman and Chief Executive of British Leyland and was widely acclaimed for his ultimately successful attempts to beat off Derek 'Red Robbo' Robinson and his fellow militant trade unionists and thereby save the British car industry from complete self-destruction. He was extremely friendly and I did indeed get the chance to waterski. Michael and I soon struck up a friendship in spite of the fact that I was some twenty years his junior.

The stress of managing Britain's most politically important issue of the late seventies was clear to see, not just in private, but in the interminable high-profile battle of brinkmanship Michael had to wage with the unions in the press and on television. Therefore I was flattered that he used to suggest that we go to Spain for the occasional

With Philip Gunn on the way to the beach from the apartment in Spain. (God knows what was in the briefcases.)

 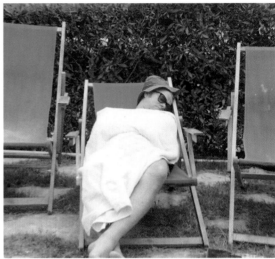

Above left *Sally Too*, the waterskiing boat I bought with Michael Edwardes.
Above right An exhausted Captain of Industry. Michael Edwardes takes a break from battling with the unions.

long weekend or longer holiday of tennis and waterskiing while he tried to relax a little before launching himself back into the fight. Sometimes he would be accompanied by his family and I by my girlfriend, and sometimes we just went on our own. I recall one evening when he appeared on the tennis court after a lengthy telephone call. He announced that it was a truly significant day. It was the first in many years that not one of the seventeen unions he dealt with had any of its workers out on strike.

In spite of the heavy load that Michael had on his mind he still managed to display a wicked sense of humour. When we ended up jointly buying a new waterskiing boat it was during a break Sally Sanders and I had taken at Easter. Sally was the replacement for another girl with the same name who had been there with me the year before. I had been discreet about this fact but need not have bothered. Without consulting his co-owner Michael had arranged to have the new boat delivered with its new name emblazoned on the side. He had decided it should be called *Sally Too*.

Michael was a fascinating man to know in those days and he still is. He even found time to help me through my micro-crisis of obsession in starting my own business, the Hot Air Balloon Company. A few years later I was to ask the newly knighted Sir Michael Edwardes to join my own company's board in a non-executive capacity. He accepted with the words that he had always wondered why he had never been asked before. He had run some of the biggest companies in Britain and overseas – British Leyland, Chloride, Dunlop, ICL, Minorco – and it had never occurred to me that he would want to be part of something so tiny in comparison. In fact the request had seemed a little cheeky. Nevertheless, he is still fulfilling that invaluable role at my company, Flying Pictures, and several times over the years when we needed additional finance he was always the first to put his own hand in his pocket by way of example. I have never known him to this day to miss a single board meeting, an act of amazing goodwill which he continues to perform ungrudgingly for a mere pittance in fees.

And as I write, Richard Hall from my days at French Gold Abbott, who became a client of mine after I started my own company, is now chairman of the board of Flying Pictures. Richard had gone on to become marketing director of a big toy business before rejoining Richard French (of French Gold Abbott) in a new advertising venture. They later sold their successful agency to Euro RSCG, Europe's largest advertising agency, where Richard Hall became deputy chairman. I caught up with him after a long

gap when I heard that his lovely wife, Caroline, had died suddenly after twenty-two years of marriage. He said he would be delighted to join us and that he thought he could make a difference, which he did.

Which all goes to show, I suppose, that in spite of all the change and turbulence of the intervening years, I am back to where I was in the first place. I am still surrounded by the same terrific people who were big enough to give my crazy dreams of adventure a chance of success.

Full circle. Richard Hall still trying to keep a semblance of control over young Prescot in April 2000, twenty-five years after we first worked together.

CHAPTER FOUR

THE PRINCESS AND THE BIRDMAN

MY BIG BREAK IN BALLOONING came in the form of a chance meeting with a charming Afghan princess in late 1975. One Saturday afternoon that winter I went beagling with my father in the Cotswolds. God knows what I was doing because, although it was a passion of Dad's, I hated it. Beagling appeared to me to be a social pastime with a degree of exercise thrown in. Just how much running around is done is up to the individual. One of the other regular members of the Dummer Beagles who partook of these murderous pursuits was a friend of Dad's, Françoise Gevers, the very pleasant daughter of the Dutch ambassador in London. She had brought with her as a guest a charming friend to whom I was introduced. Her name was Safia Tarzi and she had the striking angular beauty that could only have been moulded from royal Afghan ancestry.

Françoise's friend immediately struck me as a rather enigmatic girl from a country with a romantic history but also all the problems of modern-day political and social upheaval. Afghanistan had hit the headlines in 1973 when centuries of tradition ended as the king, Mohammed Zahir Shah, was deposed.

As I engaged Safia in conversation it emerged that she lived in London. She had a daughter living in Wimbledon who was studying for her bar exams and, most unlikely of all, she revealed that she herself was a hot-air balloonist. She went on to describe how she had been introduced to the sport by a British friend. Having trained with ballooning clubs, she studied for the relevant exams and finally got her pilot's licence the previous

Previous spread This extraordinary lady got me into all this. Safia Tarzi, 1975. **Above** Safia in traditional Afghan costume.

year. Now she had her own black and white hot-air balloon, called *Jammy*, after her sister Jamila.

Hot-air ballooning in its modern form was then still in its infancy. For most people the sport evoked either the romantic stuff of fairy tales or a centuries-old and still primitive form of air transport. I had seen a balloon in the far distance earlier in the year, but most people had never set eyes on one of any kind.

Safia Tarzi was born on 15 November 1936 in Kabul, the capital of Afghanistan, the second youngest of seven children. The royal blood flowed through to her from Mahmud Tarzi, who in the early part of the twentieth century was one of the most illustrious reformers in the country's history. Soon after the birth of his sixth child Safia's father became the first Afghan ambassador to Japan when diplomatic relations were set up in 1934, and in 1946 he became the first ambassador to China when relations were formalized there. Therefore Safia was educated and spent her childhood in Japan and China before returning to her native land in her teens. By all accounts she was an extraordinary girl with a nomadic, tomboy character, always rebelling and forever seeking adventure. Until just a few days before I met her she had never even heard of beagling. Here again was something new and she was intrigued to find out what it was that attracted her friend Françoise to this minor sport. Safia's insatiable quest for new horizons did not sit easily with the Muslim culture of her native land at the time. Afghanistan was a noble country steeped in traditions which effectively excluded independent-minded women. In spite of this she always yearned after her homeland and the Afghan people, whom she loved deeply.

At the age of seventeen Safia married an Afghan aristocrat named Ibrahim Seraj and their lovely daughter, Amelia, was born the following year, when Safia was barely eighteen. Although she was devoted to her child, the frustration of her mental imprisonment was left unassuaged. Before long she talked to her husband about leaving Afghanistan. She wanted him to come with her to a new life, but he could not bring himself to do so. And so in 1955, with a one-year-old daughter in a basket, Safia departed to make a brave new start in America. Amelia was not to see her father again for thirteen years.

Before settling in England in 1968 Safia had remained close to her daughter throughout the ever-changing times. At the same time the strictness of Amelia's upbringing was the result of Safia's determination to act as both mother and father to an unsettled and highly gifted child of a single parent. Before she could set Amelia free as an adult in her own right Safia had clearly wrestled with the guilt of taking her small child away from her father and of abandoning her country of origin and its strict religious values. Nevertheless, although she retained close ties with her compatriots she was by no means persuaded of the value of all that they traditionally considered both decent and mandatory. She eventually decided that the best education for Amelia was at a Catholic boarding school in France run by Dominican nuns, where the girl was blissfully happy. And yet, paradoxically, just a few months before I met Safia she had felt the need to make the hajj, the pilgrimage to Mecca that all Muslims are expected to undertake at least once in their lifetime. Whether this was a self-imposed brake on her rebelliousness, a mark of genuine spiritual respect or just another adventure is unknown, even by her daughter. It just added to her mystery.

In between her attempts to arrange some form of stability in her daughter's life Safia was finding outlets for her passion for adventure. She had become an excellent photographer and her work was widely published. In addition she was a parachutist, a scuba-diver, a horsewoman, a practitioner of karate and a fine shot, and had even been a motor-racing driver. Giving up this last indulgence was the one major sacrifice she had made for the sake of her daughter.

In 1967 Safia completed an archaeological course at the Louvre in Paris and started giving lectures far and wide about Afghanistan. She decided to make one of her occasional visits to her native country, where she had already opened a clothes boutique in Kabul. She reached her destination by driving a Land Rover all the way to the capital. It had always been her dream to participate in the native Afghan sport of buzkashi and she was determined to use this visit to realize that dream.

The magnificent but dangerous game of buzkashi consists of two extensive teams of horsemen who strive to snatch the carcass of a beheaded calf from a circle marked out in chalk. This is then galloped with over a predetermined course before being hurled back into the circle. The rules are complex and to a Westerner an explanation of this hugely popular national pastime is likely to prove as baffling as a description of cricket to an Afghan horseman.

Before the king was deposed, buzkashi was traditionally played in Kabul on 14 October, his birthday. It was played in a formal manner with specially preselected teams. In the north of the country it is still played, but as a wild game in which up to three thousand riders gallop through the dusty desert plains in pursuit of the prize.

Northern Afghanistan, 1967. Noble horsemen preparing for the game of buzkashi, in which Safia participated and took the photographs.

Safia travelled to this region and after talking to some of the participants she managed to wangle her way into a game practised exclusively by men. She asked a horseman if she could mount his wild and nervous charge. Assuming that she wanted simply to pose for a photograph, he readily agreed. Once mounted, she asked the owner if she could ride the horse a short distance. Initially surprised, he eventually waved his hand in assent. Safia was soon in the heart of the game, which became rougher and rougher as riders got closer to the beheaded calf. She emerged from the furious mêlée with no more than minor injuries and described it as the most extraordinary and unforgettable adventure she had ever had.

Now, in 1975 on a windswept hill in the Cotswolds, I was riveted at meeting a real live balloonist. My unrestrained enthusiasm prompted Safia to invite me to a small gathering at Marsh Benham, near Newbury in Berkshire, after Christmas.

She picked me up from Chiswick and we travelled down together. When we arrived

The buzkashi chalk circle from which the beheaded calf is snatched…

she introduced me to her friends Jean Costa and his beautiful American wife, Sharon. Jean turned out to be the aristocratic Comte Costa de Beauregard and his wife was a former New York model. They lived in the grand château at Meaux, east of Paris, and had a pied-à-terre in the capital. I was starting to wonder if I was getting slightly out of my depth in such distinguished company and wished momentarily that I was in the relative security of my flat in Chiswick. It had not occurred to me that ballooning was a sport of royalty and titled dignitaries, reeking of the unearned income that oozed from every pore.

I need not have worried. The balloonists I was to meet that weekend were a broad spectrum of social class and means. I just happened to have struck the top of the pile. My new friends could not have been nicer and the Gallic charm poured forth from the Count throughout the weekend. I was to go on seeing Jean and Sharon for a year or so and once I even dined in their sumptuous apartment in the Avenue Foch in Paris. Thereafter I lost all contact with both of them. For some reason they fell out in a big way. During a serious incident a shot was fired and although Sharon survived without serious injury, Jean ended up in prison. He spent about a year running the prison library, from where he corresponded regularly with those fellow balloonists who were loyal enough to keep in touch.

As Safia and I checked in with all the other balloonists and their crews at the Halfway Inn near Newbury on that Friday night, the start of my first weekend of ballooning, I had no inkling that I was approaching a major turning point in my life. The Icicle Meet convened at Marsh Benham the following morning. As we all assembled under the archway clock in the damp drizzle of David Liddiard's farmyard I listened to the official briefing. I had been concerned that I might be somewhat underdressed and self-conscious in my black jeans and jumper. Although Safia was an elegant lady with exquisite taste, the only thing she had asked was that I should be dressed in the same black and white colours as her balloon. Some of the other balloonists were clad in plus fours, tweed jackets and other such sporting garb, although, to my relief, much of the

dress was noticeably less formal. The weather was due to improve slightly but the wind was in the wrong direction, so the whole event was to be moved to Wiltshire's Savernake Forest. A convoy of vehicles and trailers set off on what seemed like an interminable journey through the countryside to our new launch site.

…then the carcass is borne away, pursued by hundreds of thundering hooves.

Here, late that morning, we laid out Safia's balloon next to seven or eight others along the grass beside some trees. I remember being enchanted with the huge, colourful folds of fabric wafting around in the moderate breeze. I was incredulous that there were so many balloons in the country capable of being assembled in one place at the same time.

These were the early days of modern ballooning and there were no sophisticated inflation fans to fill the balloons on the ground with cold air. I noticed that someone did have a home-made two-stroke contraption with plastic blades, which looked akin to something Heath Robinson might have designed. Eventually, after an inordinate amount of effort had been expended trying to get it started, it spluttered into life, creating a gale of wind – only for the blades to shatter when a small stone flew through the mesh on the front. All the other balloon teams went through the long, laborious process of flapping air into their vast nylon envelopes. Each then selected an unwilling volunteer called 'Cremation Charlie'. This was the name given to an important member of the team who would, nevertheless, become redundant over the next couple of years as balloon technology developed. The unfortunate man had to stand in the mouth of the balloon and hold up an opening in the fabric to create a space for the powerful burners to be fired into it. Cremation Charlie's position was a careful compromise. The pilot had to place him close enough to the burners to allow an effective opening but far enough away to avoid setting fire to the poor fellow.

Needless to say, I was politely but firmly asked if I would do the job of Cremation Charlie with *Jammy*, and while I was apprehensive about this, it seemed a fair trade-off for my first balloon flight. I ended up with singed hair and eyebrows, which I was told was very much par for the course.

Once the balloon had crept upright Safia held the burner valves open for several minutes while I donned my black and white crash helmet. The seventy-foot-high, teardrop-shaped flying machine swayed in the wind in lazy anticipation of lift-off. Several minutes later we were lighter than air and I clambered aboard. A bearded gentleman appeared and presented Safia and me with a boiled sweet each. I assumed this was to prevent my ears popping after departure but I later discovered it was no more than a friendly gesture from a fellow enthusiast. When there was enough heat in the envelope my pilot signalled to our ground helpers, who were holding the balloon down, to let go of the basket. With much waving we were airborne among a gaggle of similar craft floating alongside us. After heaving ourselves over the trees immediately ahead we climbed effortlessly. We traversed the edge of the forest and continued noisily up to a height of 2000 feet above our launch area, where everything suddenly went silent. 'This is amazing,' I understated absurdly.

We flew along for just over an hour in the murky, dank air, but it did not matter one iota that the view was partially impaired by mist and cloud. I was wholly in awe of a magnificent and dreamlike experience. Yet at the same time the unnatural situation in which I found myself left me wondering how the balloon would ever be brought down to earth again.

After an hour of wafting along in the air, conversing about little besides this superlative experience, we started to go down for the landing. 'Don't be frightened,' I was told, which meant that immediately I was. The descent appeared to be fast and I could feel the air rushing up to meet us. I wondered momentarily if we were out of control until the balloon suddenly levelled off above a field at Bampton, Oxfordshire, as we passed over it at around fifteen miles an hour. Then we went crashing through a barbed-wire fence and across a small road. As we finally made landfall we were dragged along unforgivingly on our stomachs at the bottom of the basket. When we came to a crunching standstill entwined in each other's bodies we were in heavy rain on the perimeter of the airfield at Brize Norton.

I had barely landed and extricated myself from this chaotic finale than I started wondering how I could pursue this mad pastime. The insanity of something so graceful and calm and yet so unpredictably physical appealed immensely to my heightened sense of the ridiculous. It was all so wonderfully crazy. There was no means of steering, there were almost no controls and there appeared to be no instruments. In fact it seemed to me that there was barely any means of determining anything.

Sponsored ballooning existed only in the most basic form in 1975. It depended on occasional subsidies given to one or two jovial and eccentric characters in the sport. Although the deal required the pilots to attach company names and motifs to their balloons, they would more often than not fly them when and where it suited them, at weekends and far from the madding crowd, so that the sponsors' names were seldom seen. What was needed, I concluded, was a professionally managed service designed to bring a worthwhile advertising return to sponsors. As I had spent the past few years working for advertising agencies I thought I might have a chance of persuading a company to take a risk. I mentioned the thought to Safia and she said she would like to help. As well as possessing aristocratic charm, she was a lady of considerable enterprise, and it occurred to me that she might just be interested in making an investment in such a venture. I decided to keep the thought to myself at least for the time being. The next day we returned to London, and Safia stored her balloon in the small garage attached to my flat as it was conveniently on her way back into town.

As we were travelling home in the driving rain earlier that day, Safia's Renault ran out of petrol, forcing us to pull on to the hard shoulder of the M4. Sharon de Beauregard was in the car with us. We were giving her a lift because her husband had had to set off for a meeting in another direction. In a clear and typical demonstration of Safia's independence and drive she insisted that a woman had a far better chance of getting a lift to the nearest petrol station. She disappeared into the darkness, leaving Sharon and me to sit and chat away about life in a French château for what seemed likely to be many hours. Less than thirty minutes later our princess was back, can of petrol in hand. She had got a lift to the service station, found a man with a retrieval truck, travelled back beside him and bribed him to do a U-turn across the central reservation to reunite her with her car.

Just a few weeks later Amelia went to Victoria Station to wave her mother off on the night train to Paris. Safia disappeared to France to visit friends. A few days later I was sitting in my flat munching a grabbed piece of toast by way of breakfast. I heard the awful news on the radio of a horrific hot-air balloon accident in France in which two people had been killed. I knew immediately who one of them was.

The irony of the tragedy which was to befall this remarkable woman was that she had had no intention of flying on the day she died. She had merely taken up a last-minute invitation to step aboard another pilot's balloon. She was accompanied by a girlfriend of Sharon de Beauregard who had never flown in a balloon. While Safia was reluctant to fly with another pilot in command she was persuaded on the spur of the moment to accompany Sharon's friend. Disaster struck when defective hose connections between the gas tank and the burners fractured after a particularly hard landing. These released a cloud of propane vapour from pressurized tanks, which immediately ignited, starting an uncontrollable fire. The pilot instinctively jumped out, leaving his two passengers on board. The resultant loss of weight catapulted the two women back into the sky, now trapped within the raging furnace. While the pilot escaped with minor injuries his two passengers were horrifically burned to death.

Safia was just thirty-nine years old.

The idea of a ballooning business temporarily died with my friend, and I felt numb. Apart from the fact that I was dreadfully sad about poor Safia, it had never really occurred to me that ballooning might be dangerous.

But somehow the experience kept nagging at me. Then sometime in early May I was lying in bed with a bout of flu (another fateful coincidence because I am rarely ill). Without much interest I was watching Hughie Green presenting *Opportunity Knocks* on television. A man called Robin Batchelor appeared on the show to introduce an act that I cannot remember. What interested me was that Robin claimed to be a

Robin Batchelor introducing a band he had never met to Hughie Green on *Opportunity Knocks*.

balloonist and he was very funny. It immediately occurred to me that a character like this would make a good front man for the ballooning venture that was now forming in my mind. I contacted the television station and asked for his telephone number. It was against the rules to give it out, but I was promised that my interest would be passed on to Robin Batchelor. Soon afterwards he called me and we arranged to meet in the Water Rat pub in the King's Road one evening the following week. We introduced ourselves and it turned out that Robin was the same man who had given me a boiled sweet just

Opposite Robin doing what comes naturally. **This page, main picture** The Birdman flying tourists over the Masai Mara, Kenya, February 2000. **Insets** A Birdman gallery. From top: learning to bend spoons (he can play them too); obeying the letter of the law (see notice); up a ladder in another mess; hobnobbing with royalty.

Daily Express

LONDON TO PARIS

Above I even helped the Birdman to model some of his extensive wardrobe.

Opposite top The Birdman inflating a balloon on the lawn in front of Castle Howard, North Yorkshire. I am lifting the side of the envelope as George Howard looks on.

before lift-off of my first flight in January that year. After I'd given him a brief outline of my ideas he was more than happy to cooperate on the understanding that he would be paid if we could find a sponsor. Robin was on the team.

For reasons I cannot recall – neither can he – Robin soon became known as the Birdman. The name stuck and he is now called the Birdman by all his close friends at FlyingPictures. When I met him he was as wild as a hawk. Although he has mellowed a little since those halcyon days, he has lost none of the jovial eccentricity that has always been his trademark. He was and remains a great friend and has never been surpassed as the greatest character in our sport.

As a first priority Robin agreed he would teach me to fly balloons as part of our new partnership deal. He was hopeless at the task. After I passed the flight test for my licence more than a year later the Civil Aviation Authority (CAA) examiner, Joe Philp, sent me a letter. He wrote that he had passed me because I was competent and safe, although it was clear that I had never been properly trained. He suggested I make some further flights with other professionals before I got overambitious with my new qualification.

Robin had been working for a small manufacturing company called Thunder Balloons and as part of a deal with Unigate his company had to arrange to fly a pretty balloon emblazoned with the St Ivel Prize Yoghurt 'Prize Guys' logo at a number of events in the summer. The Prize Guys had originated out of a successful television commercial featuring animated fruits contained in the yoghurt. Robin had volunteered to do this tour and it seemed to me that this would be an ideal opportunity to tag along to learn the ropes when I could get the time off. The problem was that no one, least of all Unigate, the owners of the balloon, could ever find the Birdman. Somehow he had always just been seen departing from somewhere without a word about where he was going next. He had the balloon in the back of an old orange Volkswagen camper van, where he brewed cups of tea on a built-in Primus stove and occasionally slept. In the heat of that very hot summer there was always a Camembert-ish kind of smell about the place. Because he was constantly on the move his laundry got ignored for long periods and the scent of the unwashed socks he left from time to time on the dashboard permeated the interior of the vehicle with nauseating thoroughness.

In spite of these shortcomings, the Birdman put on a great display everywhere he went. He was a terrific showman, outrageously funny, and when he gave television interviews he frequently had reporters doubled up with laughter. He was a complex, intelligent and kind person. With his big red beard and his high-decibel noisiness he was the very caricature of the balloonist. I spent most of the summer cajoling him into taking me for the occasional flight. Everywhere we went there was either a second-hand bookshop he knew (from where it was impossible to extricate him in less than several hours) or a girlfriend holed up alone in some cottage. He would slow down his spluttering van and ask me to look at the map. 'Have a look and see if Minchinhampton is anywhere near here.' If it was we would head straight for it and arrive on the doorstep unannounced, where he would be welcomed with open arms. I was impressed by his widespread popularity with women, although the novelty of playing gooseberry on the sofa for the night wore thin after a while.

My first flight with the Birdman was from the lawn in front of Castle Howard, North Yorkshire. We had a pretty girl called Clare on board and he was out to impress her. When we dipped into the beautiful lake in front of this ancient pile, skimming a soft wake as we went, she was indeed impressed. As we rose gradually a gentle cascade of water spilled from the four-sided wicker basket and I wondered whether Clare lived locally and where we would have to spend the night.

Back in London, after flooding the capital's advertising agencies with phone calls and letters, I soon got a call from an agency account executive. He wanted to feature a balloon in a colour advertisement for an agrochemical product marketed by Fisons. I quoted £825 and was told this was considered reasonable. To me it was a small fortune as I did not yet have any offices, employees or anything much else

to pay for. I got the job, which entailed the simple task of flying a balloon across a mature field of barley in Scotland. I sourced a suitable balloon owned privately by a wealthy insurance broker and rented a car to tow the trailer to Scotland. All it needed was the Birdman to fly it. Unfortunately, at the critical moment of winning our first

Below My first-ever commercial job.

piece of business (albeit just a one-day job), the Birdman was nowhere to be found and turned out to have been missing for almost two weeks. I tried ringing round some of his known haunts to little avail. And so with a hired balloon I drove through the night to Scotland, where Kevin Meehan, a pilot recommended by the Birdman's employer, Thunder Balloons, waited for me. At five o'clock in the morning we set off for the chosen field and there we flew the balloon six times throughout a hot summer's day before the client was satisfied he had got the shot he wanted. This had called for the arduous process of inflating the balloon, flying it across the field, landing, deflating it and packing it away to transport it in the trailer back to the take-off point. Doing this six times in succession is something that neither I nor Kevin has ever come close to doing in the twenty-three years since then. He wrote in my logbook: 'Don't ever mention barley again – or else…'

A ground-crew member drove the balloon south while I treated myself to a cabin on the train from Edinburgh to London, where I had to be back at my regular advertising job the following morning. I had

Give your yield a lift.
Get on top of wild oats in spring barley.

FISONS B25

Fisons B25

43

With Julian Nott, kitted out for the first crossing of the North Sea by balloon in 1978.

44

driven all the way through the previous night and then had a day of uninterrupted physical exercise. I was so exhausted I remember nothing of the journey at all.

But I can't forget the feeling of euphoria that swept over me as I climbed off the train at King's Cross. We would now have money in the bank and while we needed long-term contracts we had just earned enough working capital to keep writing proposals and making presentations for another few months.

Just a few days later, on a Saturday afternoon after meeting my friend Guy Bigland for a drink in a local pub, I dropped into a supermarket in Kensington High Street to buy some groceries. Across one of the aisles I recognized Julian Nott. I had seen his photograph in the ballooning magazine *Aerostat*. Julian was Chairman of the British Balloon and Airship Club and held the world altitude record for hot-air balloons, which he set in 1974 in India when he flew in a pressurized capsule to 45,000 feet. On the spur of the moment I decided to introduce myself and explain my plans. He invited me back for a drink in his rented flat off Kensington Church Street and listened patiently. He was sceptical: 'People have tried this before, you know.' Yet somehow I managed to persuade him that he might like to become non-executive chairman of the new company I planned to form. After all there was nothing to lose and if I succeeded we might be able to pay him a small director's fee and it might lead to other opportunities. I was pleased with my little coup. I had never met Julian before and I had no idea what sort of person he was, but I felt sure that having on board the chairman of the CAA-approved ruling body of ballooning, and a world record holder to boot, would give us great credibility. It would also boost my confidence. For I was particularly conscious of looking no more than my twenty-six years and I was sure that potential clients would be nervous about the idea of dealing with such a young managing director. With Julian's relative seniority in age and position I felt we could demonstrate an aura of experience. Now we were three.

On 8 November 1976 the Hot Air Balloon Company Limited was incorporated with £500 of paid-up equity capital, £299 subscribed by me, £100 by the Birdman, £100 by Julian and a £1 investment by my mother, who was determined to have a share and whom we made company secretary. The working capital would cover the initial and barest of essential expenses. I had no other money available and it was clear that no sensible bank manager was going to give such a romantically nonsensical fantasy any attention, let alone cash. I consoled myself that I was at least single and I still had a job, at least for the time being. On the other hand, most of my friends considered me nutty as a fruit bat. 'He's really flipped this time' and 'away with the fairies' were typical of the remarks that filtered back to me. While none of this helped my chronic insecurity about what I was doing it had, in retrospect, the advantage of making me even more determined to succeed. It had to be worth a whirl. More than that, it most definitely was going to succeed. My determination bordered on the compulsive.

I then set about talking to a selection of marketing executives and brand managers over a number of months but got nowhere. Christmas with the family came and went with the usual get-togethers and merriment.

When I got back to my desk in early January 1977, after the seemingly interminable festive break, I had a piece of luck. French Gold Abbott, from whom I had now moved on in mock disgust at their restructuring plans, had finally lost the Terry's chocolate business. David Russell, who was chairman of my earlier agency, CPV, had won it back and, prompted by Terry's, he immediately invited me to rejoin him. I was tempted if only because the irony of the situation hugely amused me. After all I had been turfed off the Terry's account precisely because of that restructuring at French Gold Abbott. More importantly and more seriously, it was the perfect opportunity to negotiate myself a way of having my cake and eating it. I told David I would be pleased to join him on the absolute proviso that I should work a four-day week. I could then have one weekday and every weekend off to try to develop my dream of starting my own business with balloons.

This was fine. David considered my day off a temporary aberration and my business plan a pipedream. I was told by a colleague that he had explained my new arrangement to the Terry's board and had stated confidently that I would be reverting to a five-day commitment before long.

Fortunately for me, it was not to be. As my appointments to make presentations about balloons started to build I was soon negotiating a reduction to three days a week. Although this made David uncomfortable, he was good enough to go along with it. I now had to accept a substantial drop in pay, which in turn meant a cutback in my lifestyle, but it gave me a unique opportunity to really go for what I wanted.

I spent several months not really getting anywhere. We needed critical mass. The business wasn't going to work unless it happened fast and effectively. I was soon reaching the point where for the first time I began to wonder if I might fail. Then one evening I met Barry Ricketts, the Marketing Director of Unigate. He mentioned to me that his brand managers did not consider the St Ivel Prize Yoghurt balloon promotion to have been a success. It was not going to be continued into the Queen's Jubilee year. The St Ivel marketing team liked the Birdman enormously as their flamboyant pilot, but he was seen as unmanageable and a loose cannon. After a brief discussion about this I asked if Unigate might reconsider, now that the Birdman and I were a team. I suggested I could bring a bit of order to my partner's flamboyance. The financial outlay had been very little up to now and the cost involved would necessarily have to increase. Nevertheless, I felt confident that I could sort it all out and manage the programme for the client

Tessa Tennant at the start of twenty-two years trying to keep us all in order. (She's still trying.)

professionally. Barry consulted his brand group and they subsequently agreed to commit to a small schedule for the summer season.

This was at least a start. It was soon followed by a job for Fisons Agrochemical Division, who agreed to create a promotional balloon programme based on the advertisement I had arranged for them the previous summer. We had at last broken my definition of the credibility barrier – two clients on board – but we still had barely enough money coming in to cover the overheads and eke out a sensible living for ourselves. However, I was able to finance the cash flow for the time being by asking our new clients to pay a deposit of fifty per cent of the manufacturing costs and then persuading the manufacturers themselves to accept just twenty-five per cent.

Tessa Tennant, whose talent had impressed me when she was a secretary at CPV, joined me as my secretary and administrator and we hired our first full-time pilot. Ian Ashpole was a former journalist from Essex who had got interested in the sport after interviewing a balloonist for the *Ilford Recorder*, and went on to spend several months flying balloons.

Over the next few months clients started arriving in droves. I have always found British managers a nervous, conservative lot who rarely like taking risks with something outlandish or unproven. However, as soon as I could point to companies like Fisons and Unigate as signed-up clients people listened to my presentations a little more attentively. The clients that followed included Ty-Phoo Tea, BAT Industries and Osram, makers of light bulbs. Even Terry's, on whose advertising business I had now worked from within three agencies, commissioned a balloon programme. Finally Richard Hall, my old boss at French Gold Abbott, was now Sales and Marketing Director of Corgi Toys and he awarded us a contract to promote his Busy Bodies brand of toy people. By the end of our first year we had eight balloons and I had now moved full time into my new business.

We had managed to get going with £500 in a shared office, and for the first six years in business we had no other shareholders and never had even the smallest overdraft. I simply financed the growth by continuing to persuade manufacturers to defer the deposits on order and by obtaining management fees from our clients in advance.

Suddenly the summer of 1977 was upon us and we had a full calendar of events to perform at. This was a new kind of business and we really had little idea what we were doing. I said to Tessa in a rising panic that we might have overstretched ourselves: 'How the hell are we going to manage all this?' She was very reassuring: 'Don't you worry about it. It will be fine.' Administration was always my weak point, but Tessa balanced me perfectly in this respect. Recruiting pilots and ground crew was not a problem. There was no shortage of qualified people who would be more than keen to go ballooning for the summer and get paid. 'And you call this working?' one of them was to say to me. To attract project managers I put an advertisement in *The Times*. The headline read: 'Low Pay. High Excitement.' Four extraordinarily qualified people applied and we hired all of them.

With the Birdman (still so proud of the sleeveless jersey knitted by his mum when he was thirteen) in our first office in London's West End.

Because we had to recruit in a hurry Michael Edwardes introduced me to psychometric testing, which he had used very effectively at Chloride, where he was Businessman of the Year, and later at British Leyland. One of the people we hired as a result of the advertisement was Sean Byrne, and we sent him off to be tested. A small, rather unlikely-looking Cambridge engineering graduate, he sang and played in a rock band which had not yet broken through. He needed to earn some money, however little. Michael had seen literally hundreds of reports on potential candidates for senior management positions and when I got Sean's report back I called Michael. Had he ever, I asked him, found anyone who came in the top one per cent of the executive population for all the three main IQ tests and all eighteen sub-IQ tests? He told me he had not and that he thought it would be virtually impossible for anyone to achieve because of the variations in the types of IQ tested. 'I've got him,' I said. Michael then uttered a word I had never heard him use before: 'Shit.'

Sean was joined by Brian Rapson, who was also a very bright engineer, and they both set about their task of seeing our equipment through the summer with enthusiasm and drive.

I finally got my pilot's licence on 15 July that year and immediately got to work with the others on the circuit. This meant trips to all the outside events of the season, from the Royal Show at Kenilworth to Henley Royal Regatta. I loved it and although a full-time job of flying balloons professionally would drive me nuts, the novelty of it all kept me going for those last three months of the summer.

By midsummer Tessa had organized such a well-oiled administration machine that there were up to seven balloon crews at various points around the country at the same time. The Birdman, Ian and I were so busy rushing to the next event on the schedule that we lost track of each other's whereabouts for weeks on end.

One day in late August Ian was at Chivenor, near Barnstaple in north Devon, with the Busy Bodies team. It was raining hard and the wind was far too strong to contemplate a flight. Unbeknown to Ian, the Birdman had arrived at another event with the St Ivel

The Birdman and I flew together throughout the long, hot summer of 1976. We invariably ended up in a hedge.

balloon at Westward Ho! on the other side of the Taw estuary. He had very easily come to the same conclusion as Ian that it was a day to stay firmly on the ground. When he explained to the organizers that he would be unable to put on a show, a large envelope was pressed into his hand. 'See what you can do,' said the anonymous official and the Birdman pressed what felt like a tidy sum into his back pocket.

At six o'clock in the evening Ian Ashpole took the microphone into the main arena of his event at Chivenor. Through the public-address system he gave a convincing and very proper description of why it was unsafe to fly a balloon in the prevailing conditions. As he spoke there was a rustling in the crowd, which turned to laughter, followed by applause and then enthusiastic cheers. Hands were pointing upwards. The bemused Ashpole glanced over his shoulder to see the St Ivel balloon heaving its way into the sky some three miles off. The Birdman was airborne.

Shamefaced and incredulous, Ian took out his hand-held aircraft band radio and called the pilot. 'What the hell are you doing, Birdman?' he asked. 'Well, it's a bit of a long story…' The Birdman briefly told Ian of his incentive. 'What else could I do?' he asked.

When the Birdman managed to get down after a long drag landing across a field of cows, and then through a hedge, he pulled out the contents of his back pocket in eager anticipation of the reward for risking his life. The total came to just £7.

The Birdman learned his lesson.

As far as our clients were concerned, advertising was a serious business and they needed to see that ballooning was a suitable medium. Apart from the corporate entertainment, which worked well, and the undoubted positive reaction of the crowds, it was impossible to quantify our success in cash terms. What we were able to do was evaluate the media coverage we obtained of our clients' balloons on the television and radio and in the press. For this reason we hired a PR girl to maximize our potential. At the end of the year we were able to demonstrate that all our clients had had far more than their money's worth and we had no trouble in getting everyone to renew their contracts for another year. We had made a modest profit in our first chaotic year of trading and we looked forward with glee to the one ahead.

Up until this point I had never really contemplated how long this business would last before the novelty wore off. However, I had always assumed it would not be too many years. I thought that the best I could hope for was that it would lead to new opportunities on the fringes of advertising, sponsorship and promotions. How wrong I was to be.

I sold the idea of balloons to Ty-Phoo by first appealing to its advertising agency, Geers Gross. This company was renowned for its creative animation work and it had come up with a funky gnu character to promote Cadbury's tea brand. We had had two balloons built, each featuring a huge gnu drinking a cup of tea. Cadbury Ty-Phoo had allocated a budget which was rather more than necessary to fly its two balloons at the conventional shows for the summer. I hit upon the idea that a special project could soak up the surplus money available. It was early summer and Julian Nott was still working very much on a part-time basis for the Hot Air Balloon Company. I asked him if he had any ideas for a good stunt we could organize.

Julian pondered the idea of making an attempt on the world distance record for hot-air balloons, which was then only around 360 miles. After he had done all his calculations he reckoned that the larger of the two Ty-Phoo balloons was not quite big enough to carry the amount of fuel required to try for the record. He then hit on the idea of developing a fuel system which substituted kerosene, or jet aviation fuel, for conventional propane gas.

Ballooning had been resurrected in recent years on the back of the discovery that propane gas carried in relatively lightweight aluminium bottles provided a safe, easily ignited and highly effective heat source. This, combined with balloon envelopes made of rip-stop nylon (which in the event of fire would simply melt locally rather than burn), made the sport significantly less hazardous than it was when man first took to the air in 1783. The early balloons designed by the Montgolfier brothers in France were made of paper and powered by burning straw. The two unfortunate pilots of the first flight by any aircraft in history, Jean-François Pilâtre de Rozier and the Marquis d'Arlandes, had to walk around the base of the envelope with wet sponges to damp down the flames of small fires before the whole balloon caught alight. It was therefore hardly surprising that, after a brief flurry of excitement, many accidents and a few deaths, early hot-air ballooning never really caught on. For most of the next couple of centuries the idea of man taking to the skies was pursued in the form of *gas* ballooning, which relied on hydrogen as a lighter-than-air gas. No fire was required to provide hot air for lift and the controls were restricted to a valve for gas to escape (to descend) and ballast which could be jettisoned to reduce weight (to climb).

Julian's idea of burning kerosene rather than propane would be taking the evolution of hot-air ballooning one stage further. While propane had to be stored as a gas under pressure in aluminium bottles, kerosene could be stored in liquid form in much lighter

Jean-François Pilâtre de Rozier and the Marquis d'Arlandes made the first manned flight in an aircraft, taking off from Annonay, France, on 21 November 1783. It lasted five minutes.

Lift off from the Paris suburbs in 1905. The Montgolfier hot-air balloon (made of paper) never really caught on. Within twenty years the seemingly safer hydrogen-filled balloon was the norm.

plastic bottles such as the large ones in which mineral water is sold. All the saved weight could be used to carry more fuel, and this would give our relatively small Ty-Phoo balloon more time in the air and therefore the opportunity to fly further. However, the idea had its complications. Kerosene is notoriously difficult to ignite. A lighted match thrown on to a pool of kerosene will burn happily without ever setting fire to the fuel. This meant that Julian had to develop a system to pump kerosene through pre-heated coils (using a smaller conventional propane burner) so that the fuel boiled and turned to gas. Only then could it be made to burn effectively.

We sold to Ty-Phoo the idea of attempting the world distance record using this new technology and with Julian and myself as pilots. At the same time as attempting to set a distance record we also planned to make the first crossing of the North Sea, from Scotland to Scandinavia. Extraordinarily, at this time no hot-air balloon had ever flown through a whole night, so all in all it was a highly ambitious project. Julian immediately joined the company on a full-time basis and, assisted by Sean Byrne and Brian Rapson, he set about developing the new burner system. For several months they based themselves in the garage of my Chiswick flat, where Julian would run noisy burner tests all day long. The local residents were understandably upset and every time they inundated the local police station with calls of complaint Julian seemed to have packed up and disappeared by the time the men in blue arrived to investigate. One afternoon the team caused even more havoc by setting fire to the oak tree in the small garden adjoining my flat and someone called the fire brigade. Not surprisingly, this was no small matter as far as the other flat owners in my building were concerned and I had to call a halt to the proceedings.

From then on our three scruffy scientists would turn up early each morning and load the trailer with tangled coils of charred steel and a number of drums of kerosene. They would then disappear for the day to a field in Berkshire to carry on their experiments. When the development was advanced enough to work consistently for an hour at a time it was mounted over a lightweight box made of composite materials which would act as our 'basket'. As with all home-made contraptions, there was constant tinkering. Finally, in mid-August, our Ty-Phoo Gnu balloon was inflated and the burner was tried underneath it. Julian spent a good thirty minutes peering upwards at the roaring flames while he made last-minute adjustments to his invention suspended above him. Without looking down he put out his hand to Brian Rapson, who was supposedly standing outside the carbon-fibre gondola. 'Can you pass me the monkey wrench, please, Brian?' he asked. When he got no answer he looked down and found he was 2000 feet above the ground and well on his way towards Oxford. He had been so absorbed with fiddling and adjusting that he had overheated the balloon and taken off without even noticing. In a panic he pushed the transmit button on the radio: 'What are you doing down there, Brian?' In the circumstances it was reasonable for Brian to ask what on earth Julian was doing *up there.*

Julian and I set about getting fit for our flight and took advice from the Institute of Aviation Medicine at Farnborough, Hampshire. Importantly, we were subjected to sea-survival training in case we had to ditch in the North Sea, and we were lent immersion suits, life jackets, life rafts and all the supplies we might need in the event of a long wait before rescuers arrived. I went off to Sibson Aerodrome, near Peterborough, to make two parachute jumps from a static line (whereby the parachute opens automatically as the parachutist leaves the aircraft). The novelty of my first jump only slightly compensated for the fact that I was terrified.

After a day of ground training I was fully conversant with the body's exit position and the need to shout aloud: 'One thousand, two thousand, three thousand, four thousand.' Only then was I allowed to relax, look up and check that there was an open canopy above me. When it came to the actual jump the aircraft engine was cut and I was ordered outside, I clambered out with my heart firmly wedged in my mouth. I glanced back at my instructor and remembered him saying that if I made even the slightest attempt to get back inside the plane at that critical point of no return I would be met by his boot coming the other way. 'Go,' he shouted above the roar of the wind, and I did. I arched my back. 'One thousand, two thousan… bloody f…' I could stand it no longer as my arms and legs swung everywhere in my desperation to see if there was a parachute anywhere in my vicinity. It was not quite ready for me but I caught glimpses of it flowering dramatically above. I drifted down safely to the airfield. I was asked if I enjoyed it. 'No,' I said.

The second jump was far more frightening simply because I had a fresh memory of the first one. However, at least I would have some idea what to do if an emergency arose and we had to bail out. At least I would never have to go parachuting again, I told myself.

At that time in the late seventies the BBC was running a peak-time evening current affairs programme called *Nationwide* presented by Sue Lawley. Ty-Phoo was more than pleased that the BBC's commitment to follow our project would now guarantee the company advertising exposure worth far more than it had to pay us to make it happen. On the first transmission about our preparations for the flight *Nationwide* showed terrifying pictures of the North Sea in the worst gales imaginable. We were painted as two Goliaths determined to take on the elements against all odds. Footage of Julian's world altitude record was shown. In contrast I was described as resembling a rather well turned-out young advertising executive, which up until a few months before was exactly what I was.

By the end of August we were all set and Bracknell Weather Centre gave us a good forecast for 2 September. We would have light westerly winds for the take-off, stronger currents in the same direction at altitude and calm winds for a landing in Denmark the following day. We flew by conventional aircraft to Scotland and drove to the Earl of Haddington's estate at Tyninghame, Lothian, where we had selected our take-off site. We had good shelter of high trees for the inflation of the balloon and a clear run to the coast. When everything was loaded into the gondola and we were installed in our tiny space we heated the air in the balloon from our single back-up propane burner. We planned to start the kerosene system once we were airborne.

With Tessa and Julian, preparing for a trial flight in the tiny lightweight box made of carbon-fibre that was the basket for the Ty-Phoo balloon. (Ian Ashpole is crouching in the foreground.)

Airborne with Julian.

As soon as we could feel that our laden craft was lighter than air the 'hands off' command was yelled out and we set off to cheers and whistles from the assembled masses. In spite of leaving the propane burner going full tilt we started to sink as soon as we were at the height of the sheltering trees and the balloon tried to catch up with the speed of the wind above them. We bumped back down to earth and then rose into the air again. We were still not climbing fast enough and although we had now gathered speed it was becoming apparent we should have put more heat into our very heavily laden balloon before release.

At last, after half a mile we started to rise very gently as a venerable Scottish oak, the sole obstacle before the open sea, loomed dead ahead on our flight path. I looked for something to throw overboard to give us an extra boost, but there was nothing obvious to hand. There was about fifteen seconds of total realization that we were at the point of no return. We knew we were not going to clear the tree and it was too late to land. There was nothing we could do but crash at fifteen miles an hour straight into the heart of the vast and ancient oak.

The branches cracked like pistol shots and the vast gnu drinking a cup of tea gift-wrapped the entire tree as the wind helped slice the balloon apart. We came to a heaving halt as the wind in the towering canopy planted us firmly into the bosom of the sprawling trunk. It made a comical, though sad, sight. We were so wedged in the foliage that we were completely stranded. People were running from everywhere and through the rustling leaves I could see vehicles hurtling over the bumps towards us.

It was an early and ignominious end to my first big ballooning adventure and of course the media lapped it up. The headline in the *Sunday Mirror* announced 'Ty-Flew' and the photograph showed the whole sorry mess, with the grinning gnu staring incongruously from the centre of the front page. Duncan Gibbins, who was directing the camera team for *Nationwide*, immediately diverted all his footage to the BBC in Edinburgh so that the story could be piped out nationally on the evening news. It was the first (but not the last) time I felt like a complete pillock in my new career and I wasn't sure I could face the press. 'Come on,' Duncan said, 'you're a hero.' I didn't think so. He told me he had never had so much fun in his life and he thought the whole thing was hilarious, and in retrospect it was. He was delighted with his story, which looked wonderfully, spectacularly disastrous. He had been very good to work with, always very encouraging while politely requesting the shots he needed but never expecting anything as good as this to turn up.

It was not until late at night, as we perched in the only tree among hundreds of acres of flat and grassy Scottish countryside, that the crane arrived to get Julian, me and the remnants of the balloon out of the tangled branches. The pitch-darkness was compensated for by a maze of crisscrossing car headlights. I had no home telephone numbers to warn Ty-Phoo executives of the embarrassing news that was about to break. Therefore it was with some trepidation that I called the marketing manager, Ken Mack,

Everything was just fine on the final test flight…

…but not on the day.

on the following Monday morning to apologize. To my astonishment Ken and his department were absolutely delighted. He just wanted to know if we were all right. No one was hurt, it was a good story, it would have amused millions and in the competitive market for tea bags it was just the sort of fun they wanted. It had never occurred to me that such an ignominious failure could paradoxically become such a communications success. Ty-Phoo was adamant that the media exposure was far higher than it would have been if we had succeeded in breaking the world record. Someone from the company's Birmingham offices even asked, 'Can you do it again?'

I was never to see Duncan Gibbins again. He moved to Los Angeles, where he became a successful writer and Hollywood director. Tragically, several years later his home caught fire during one of California's notorious sweeping brush fires and he was killed going back inside to rescue his cat.

Most of our clients were fun to work with and they in turn enjoyed their relationship with us. I always made a point of encouraging them to do so. Yes, of course their balloons were there for the serious business of advertising, but they should own them with pride and indulge in the fun and glamour they brought with them. After all what better way would they find to cheer up their customers and improve the morale of their staff?

The one exception to all this was Fisons, where we were dealing with particularly spiky clients, seemingly with little wit or imagination. Poor Tessa, with all her charm, could do nothing to make the company happy and its balloon business was taking up

TY-FLEW

for just 300 yards —then Biff!

UP, up and—CRUNCH! The magnificent men in their flying Tea Bag came down to earth the fast way.

Tea Bag, a hot-air balloon sponsored by the Ty-Phoo tea company, was setting off on a 300-mile flight from Scotland to Denmark.

But it had travelled just 300 yards at Dunbar, East Lothian, when disaster struck.

Tea Bag hit a tree and landed balloonists Julian Nott, 35, and Colin Prescot 27, in a proper stew.

They had been attempting a new distance record for balloons. Tea Bag was fitted with sophisticated equipment, including radar.

Colin and Julian, who were unhurt, unhappily inspected the damage and then went off to calm their nerves—with a soothing cup of tea, of course.

In a stew—Tea Bag is badly torn as it makes an unhappy landing.

53

almost as much of her time as all the others put together. 'We will have to fire them,' I said to Tessa, Ian and the Birdman one day. Their faces were a study in horror. We couldn't possibly do that, they all argued; we couldn't afford it anyway. I didn't think we could afford not to. I reminded them that we were in this business for fun and that there was little point in having clients who didn't appreciate what we were doing. We were all working hard enough without such distractions. In any case the Fisons malaise might spread to other clients, I added flippantly. As I reaffirmed my philosophy my three colleagues realized with increasing alarm that I was serious.

I duly wrote a formal letter to the Marketing Director of Fisons Agrochemical Division, rather pompously informing him that we would not be seeking to renew our contract with the company the following year. I gave the reasons for parting and an assurance that we would of course do our very best to look after their interests for the unexpired period of our agreement. Thank you and goodbye. It took a single day to get a

By 1985 our client list had grown considerably. We were managing all these balloons for sponsors whose products ranged from cars to beer, from financial services to shipping, from gas to New Zealand apples and pears.

telephoned response. Could the marketing manager come and take me out for lunch? Certainly he could. I like lunch.

Ian Heath arrived and as we tucked into pasta at Topo Gigio on the corner of Brewer Street he assured me that we were most definitely appreciated. He wanted to know if there was anything he could do about the situation that would change my mind. He was quite charming. We took Fisons back with open arms and had a wonderful relationship with the company for several more years. I have always believed in going the extra mile to give clients good service. However, relationships in our kind of business can only work as a two-way partnership and it was gratifying to see that we had reached a very satisfactory, if unexpected, conclusion to our problem. I triumphantly told Tessa that I thought that from then on we should make a point of firing at least one client a year. A sort of public hanging to keep the others in order. She was absolutely appalled at my irresponsible attitude and she resolutely refused to ever allow me to do such a thing again.

CHAPTER FIVE

THE NINE FINGER CLUB

NINETEEN SEVENTY-EIGHT WAS A DEFINING YEAR for the Hot Air Balloon Company. It was also a very strange one. It was the year I learned the hard way about running a business and it was also the year when I found out that nothing is ever predictable and rarely logical.

Towards the end of the previous year I had taken the precaution of contacting Ian Bishop, the producer of Jimmy Savile's BBC television show *Jim'll Fix It*, to let him know that if anyone ever wrote in with a request to fly in a hot-air balloon, I was his man. Ian had kept my details on file, so when a letter from young James and Louise was selected from the thousands of hopeful missives that arrived on his desk every week, I was asked if I wanted to organize a flight for the two children. My colleagues at the office couldn't believe it had happened so quickly. One of them even suggested that I had planted the letter and that the eulogistic, naïve prose about an apparently lifelong dream to go up was nothing more than a scam. It was a nice idea, but I hadn't indulged in any such skulduggery.

Jim'll Fix It was then in the early days of a phenomenally successful run which was to last for many years. Because it was transmitted on Saturday evenings at peak time it had the potential to give an advertiser immensely valuable exposure. I decided to offer it to Richard Hall at Corgi Toys and he was certainly not about to say no. It was a children's show watched equally avidly by parents. The audience was exactly the right target market for Richard's Busy Bodies, which were enjoying substantial popularity while competing head to head with Play People from a rival manufacturer. Free advertising on the BBC is *verboten*. Even 'paid for' advertising is *verboten*. Any sponsored activity is also viewed with great suspicion and goes against the very spirit of the great institution's charter. Therefore any attempt to get a sponsor exposure on the BBC has to be handled with great subtlety and when the programme is recorded there is always a high risk that recognition of the sponsor will be eliminated at the snip of the editor's scissors. In this case we resolved to

Previous spread Hans Büker and his trusty 1952 six-cylinder, five-litre Mercedes-Benz fire engine with a double bed in the back.

simply pitch up and play the whole exercise in a low-key way. If we tried to ram Busy Bodies down the throat of the BBC it would fail. However, the great advantage of balloons in filming is that they are so large in comparison to their surroundings that they can hardly be missed visually, and thereby gain exposure without any effort to meddle with the filming.

On 27 February, a beautiful anticyclonic day with crisp, clear air, I duly 'fixed it' for James and Louise by flying them in the Busy Bodies balloon across a snowy landscape from Newbury to Hungerford Common. The great man was nowhere in sight, but we made the children's dream come true in front of several interfering film crews. The flight lasted an hour and after we landed we had to inflate the balloon all over again, throw it up in the air about thirty feet and simulate the landing for a second time as none of the cameramen had made it in time for the real thing.

A week later the Birdman, Tessa, a couple of girls from the office and I went to the BBC studios in Shepherd's Bush to meet Jimmy Savile. His team had come up with the idea of dropping me and the children in the basket through the ceiling and down on to the stage. This was set up to the sound of crashing glass while the audience clapped our arrival with mock excitement. Jimmy awaited our arrival below and after we had crash-landed beside him he shook our hands. He patted the children patronizingly on the head and asked them what it was like. 'Was it truly, wonderfully, utterly marvellously fantastic?' Fortunately the answer was a shy 'yes' from both of them. He then turned to me, 'Dr Balloon', and asked me in front of millions of potential viewers at home what the Busy Bodies were. I was so astonished I almost choked on my reply, which was that they were toys from the company that owned the balloon. It was a straightforward, correct and truthful answer but I wished I'd had notice of the question so that I could have given a reply that would not automatically be cut out of the programme. We were all entertained to a BBC party of warm white wine and biscuits before saying our goodbyes. By way of farewell Jimmy Savile insisted on kissing all the girls ostentatiously on the hand and as he was doing so the Birdman remarked that it was at moments like this that he wished he was a girl. Neither Jimmy nor his production team were quite sure how to respond to this and we were ushered brusquely out into the cold night air.

Amazingly, when the story was transmitted nationally on Saturday evening two weeks later Jimmy Savile's question about the Busy Bodies was not edited out. Combined with pretty shots of the balloon, the sequence made a hugely successful PR coup for the toy company. It was effectively a ten-minute commercial on a channel on which advertising could not be bought for any money. Arguably, it justified the entire three-year balloon budget from Corgi at one fell swoop. It was then that I really began to realize the potential of the medium we were promoting and the business opportunities that might be open to us.

We now started to concentrate on how we could maximize the value of television exposure for our clients. One way of doing it was by staging a stunt or event that news channels and regional programmes would be interested in covering. We hatched a plot to stage the first-ever Cross-Channel Balloon Race, which would be restricted (although this was not publicized) to our clients' balloons, flown exclusively by our pilots. Tom Donnelly, the managing director of the manufacturing company, Thunder Balloons, had a balloon in the colours of the Union Jack. We decided to use this as the 'hare' in a 'hare and hounds' race. The object was for all the 'hound' balloons to chase the hare to France. The winner would be the first balloonist to land his balloon, deflate it and then get to the hare. This had the advantage of keeping the pilots concentrating on finding winds to follow the hare rather than simply using altitude to latch on to faster winds to cross the

The pilots of the first-ever Cross-Channel Balloon Race, 1978: (from left to right) Julian Nott, Paul Keane, me, Philip Hutchins and the Birdman.

Channel first. In this way we would create more of a spectacle by getting most or all of the balloons in a cluster throughout the race. Again, as with all public-relations exercises, there were risks. One balloon might inadvertently hog all the coverage or we might not get any coverage at all on a busy news day. All in all, though, it seemed a good scheme.

We persuaded four clients to participate with their balloons – Osram, Fisons, J&B Whisky and Terry's. Julian Nott was to be in fancy dress as the hare and the other balloons were to be piloted by Paul Keane, the Birdman, Philip Hutchins and me. There was to be a trophy and a jeroboam of Moët & Chandon champagne for the winner. We made a big play in the press release about the fact that the pilots were a merchant banker, a computer programmer, a solicitor and an advertising executive. With the exception of Phil Hutchins, who was still a practising solicitor, these were all previous careers, but as far as I was concerned this was a mere detail.

On 18 March we got a weather forecast of moderate north-westerly winds, which would be ideal for a crossing on the short Dover to Cap Gris Nez route, and we all assembled in a field in Barham, a hamlet about nine miles inland from the Kent coast. A man from Customs and Excise came from Dover to stamp our passports. A band was playing, the press had turned up enthusiastically and we were seen off to the boom of a cannon and cheering. Nowadays we use much bigger balloons than we did in the early years. At that time we wanted to keep costs down to entice the clients into our stable, but it meant sacrificing weight in the form of fuel and passengers. Therefore we all flew solo. Julian, the hare, was the only one equipped with a radio to negotiate with air traffic control and we all agreed in advance that if there was any problem he would land before the coast and we would all follow suit.

Just before the white cliffs of Dover Julian landed. There were no air traffic problems – he was just nervous that the wind was a bit lighter than forecast and if it dropped any more there was a risk we would all be becalmed over the Channel. The balloons were deflated and so was I. We all returned home in low spirits. It was an expensive business being on standby for very specific weather, and the costs of the aborted event had mounted up considerably.

To my surprise the BBC evening news had an extensive piece about our antics, which

I see no ships.
Self-portrait halfway
across the Channel.

was transmitted in a gentle light-hearted way and with sympathy. I could hardly believe it. If news programmes were going to put out long pieces on complete non-events we were well and truly in business. I called all the clients and not for the first time I found myself enthusing to them about a failure turned media success. I suggested they just imagine how much coverage we would get when we succeeded.

We had to wait almost eight more weeks before the weather looked suitable again and we all drove down to Barham for a second attempt. This time we set off in a stiffening breeze. Julian crossed the coast and we were set fair for France. The news crews were ferried across the Channel by light plane and all went well. Phil Hutchins won. I came second but only because I could speak French and succeeded in commandeering an ancient Citroën 2CV belonging to a local farmer. Even though the bald-tyred vehicle looked little better than a rusty pram, it proved to be fast enough to thunder past an exasperated Birdman, who had flown a far better race than me but was now hobbling to the finishing line on foot. Having landed three miles from the hare, I would, but for my good fortune, have been last – the natural position for me in competitions.

We congratulated ourselves with French wine and returned to England by boat. All the news programmes came and went throughout the evening without so much as a mention of the first Cross-Channel Balloon Race. It was a Saturday and earlier in the day the Queen had run out on to a racecourse to help stop some runaway horses. There were no pictures but the story was clearly considered far more important than our photogenic triumph. Ho Hum.

A few days after the Channel race I set off for a balloon festival in Aranjuez, south of Madrid, which had been arranged by the only qualified Spanish balloon pilot, Jesús González Green. Toots Murphy, a gorgeous American girl who was my current girlfriend and had recently moved into my flat, accompanied me on the trip. My sister Caroline, who was working as PR manager for my company, also came along. The three of us arrived at the Spanish border late on the Thursday afternoon at about the same time as Phil Hutchins and his wife Marjorie, fresh from their victory in the Channel race. We went together to see the border police, who refused to let us through. Although we had been assured by the organizers of the balloon festival that everything was in order, the officials didn't like the paperwork. We argued politely for a while and asked if they could perhaps telephone our contacts in Madrid. They refused to do this and insisted on authorization from their superiors, which could not be arranged until their offices opened the following morning. We resigned ourselves reluctantly to the fact that we would have either to find a hotel or spend the night in our cars.

While we were debating what to do an old 1952 Swiss-registered fire engine pulled up beside us. I hadn't met Hans Büker before, although I was to see quite a bit of him in the following years. Hans was a well-known Swiss *gas* balloonist who had also been invited to the festival, due to start the following day. He was now a full-time professional *hot-air* balloonist who flew rich tourists from the Palace Hotel in Gstaad. A tall, proud, wild-looking man, he stood straight as a ramrod with his bearded chin tucked firmly into his chest. There was invariably the last ten per cent of an untipped cigarette wedged between his fingers and he rarely smiled. His vintage fire engine housed his balloon and equipment in the back, alongside a huge double bed, which was revealed every time the back doors creaked open. Like most Swiss Germans, he was impeccably courteous, although, perhaps untypically, he most definitely did not like convention. We introduced ourselves and as I clasped both his hands I could detect that something was not quite right. This was because he was a celebrated member of *Der Neunfingerklub* (the Nine Finger Club) and he has only three fingers and a thumb on his left hand. It is extraordinary how many balloonists (particularly early gas balloonists) have lost a finger as a result of getting digits snagged in ropes. Hans has many fellow members.

Our new friend sympathized that we did not have the right papers. He politely promised us that as soon as he reached Madrid he would get the organizers to make sure the problem was sorted out. He then marched up to the border police with his own documents only to have them rejected in the same way as ours. Hans was outraged and let fly a torrent of polite, low-decibel, yet threatening abuse. He was asking the equivalent of 'Do you know who you are talking to?' in German, which irritated the police even more. He said he would be reporting the official in the kiosk to his superiors and returned to the fire engine to find his camera.

When he got back to the window he snapped a full-frame picture of the bemused official and was about to take a second when his camera was confiscated. Phil and I suggested he calm down and we offered him a beer, which he accepted. After a brief discussion about what to do, Hans decided that the whole situation was so absurd that there was nothing for it but for us all to disregard our detention and drive on. Phil and I took one look at each other and promptly got the giggles. 'We can't possibly do that,' we countered. 'In that case,' said Hans firmly, 'I shall go on my own.'

Phil and I watched in absolute astonishment as he sauntered back to his fire engine, climbed aboard, slammed the door and set about the not inconsiderable task of attempting to start it. The engine turned over four or five times, refusing to catch. Eventually it coughed, spluttered and roared into life while huge plumes of black smoke billowed out of the back. As the vehicle approached the border post the engine died once more. Hans then had to go through the whole rigmarole all over again. By now the Spanish policemen were peering from behind their sliding windows, trying to work out what he would do next.

At last Hans got his infernal machine going, rammed it into gear and set off down the road for the freeway towards Madrid. His contraption kept lurching forward, away from us, backfiring as it went. The expression on the faces of the policemen was a picture as they suddenly realized that this farcical activity was in fact a quick getaway.

Standing there doubled up with laughter, we caught a last glimpse of Hans's serious yet expressionless face as the fire engine shuddered onwards in almost slow-motion absurdity, now engulfed in a vast cloud of diesel smoke. Slowly he disappeared into the near distance. The noise of the engine eventually faded away into the half darkness as the police rushed for their cars. A scene not dissimilar to an Inspector Clouseau escapade followed as police cars swerved to avoid each other, sirens screaming, headlights blazing and blue lights flashing. No fewer than eight or nine of them set off in pursuit. Within five minutes everything was quiet except for Phil and I as we continued to howl with laughter at what we had just witnessed.

A single uniformed policeman remained to watch the near-deserted border post.

An hour or so later we were inexplicably called over to the office and told that

HANS BÜKER
AÉROSTIER
Février 1994 Gehaz

A rare smile from Hans –
showing the three fingers
on his left hand – as
depicted by a local artist.

everything had been sorted out and we were now free to proceed. And so Toots, Caroline and I set off in convoy behind Phil and Marjorie towards Madrid. We were fifteen miles down the motorway when we saw the blue flashing light of a police car approaching on the other side. It was followed in single file by two more cars, also flashing blue. And then, sandwiched between yet another two police cars, was Hans. He swept past us sitting bolt upright in his cab and staring straight ahead as he was escorted back to the border.

We resigned ourselves to the fact that we would not be seeing him for quite some time, if at all. At lunch the following day everyone was talking about our somewhat incredible story of the runaway fire engine when Hans entered the room. There was a sudden lull in the conversation and although the sustained atmosphere had been of mild exuberance you could now hear a pin drop. And then everyone broke into spontaneous applause. Although still expressionless, Hans betrayed a gentle satisfaction at his notoriety. I will never know how he got out of that situation. I never asked – I thought he would consider it a trifling irrelevance.

When I got back from our invigorating sojourn in Spain Julian Nott and I sat down to talk about a second (hopefully less ignominious) attempt at the world distance record. We had had a good first year in business, we were still afloat and we had no overdraft. In spite of this satisfactory position all the profit had been eaten up by Julian's prolonged 'mad professor'-style experimentation with kerosene burners and lightweight gondolas, eventually fabricated from the latest bonded composite materials. He assured me that the development work was complete and there was no reason why we should not use the same gondola and burners as those that had visited the Scottish oak tree the previous September. All we needed was a new balloon envelope as the original had been destroyed.

I asked Ty-Phoo if the company would like to sponsor a second attempt. Several weeks went by and I got no response. And then out of the blue Wells O'Brien, the advertising agency of British Gas, offered to sponsor the project for a higher sum than I had been asking. I grabbed their arm off and said 'yes' straight away. This was discourteous and I should at least have informed Ty-Phoo that I had received an offer and then given them a short time to respond to it. I never really thought about it at the time but I got hauled over the coals by the executives at Ty-Phoo, who were, not unreasonably, upset. There was nothing I could do now because I had already signed a contract with British Gas. An apology seemed pretty feeble but I did the best I could. We continued to work with Ty-Phoo for several more years. We did not deserve to retain the contract and I learned a valuable lesson in business etiquette as a result. I would never behave in that way again.

In some ways my faux pas came back to haunt me. If we had waited longer before signing the sponsorship (whether it was with Ty-Phoo or British Gas) Julian would have had less time to go through yet more money in preparing for the flight. As it was, he was the typical prototype engineer, never quite happy with what he had developed. And so the work went on. As it did so the money leaked ever faster from the coffers.

A young Swedish entrepreneur had recently left his native country, where labour costs had become unaffordable, and started a balloon manufacturing facility in Ireland. Per Lindstrand was very hungry for business and offered us a good deal, so we agreed to let him manufacture our new big blue balloon for British Gas. In spite of this, it was not long before we were nursing a substantial loss from Julian's activities which could not be recovered, irrespective of the result of the forthcoming flight.

In the meantime I had a small problem to sort out. My faithful and trusted client Terry's of York, who had followed me around several companies for many years, had just been taken over by Colgate Palmolive. The idea of a toothpaste company buying a chocolate factory seemed rather disgusting to me, but of more immediate importance was the question of whether or not this would spell the death knell of the ballooning programme. John Plackett was the new Colgate Palmolive-appointed Marketing Director of Terry's and I put in a call to him. He assured me he had an open mind and he would like to see the balloon in action some time. We fixed the date of 12 July, when the balloon was due to appear at the Great Yorkshire Show. I made sure the Birdman was there and the night before the proposed flight I briefed him about the need to entertain our new client at dinner.

My professional relationship with Per Lindstrand spanned more than two decades.

The Birdman rose to the occasion beautifully. With conscientious zeal he launched himself into tales of derring-do and never let anyone get a word in edgeways throughout the starter and main course. John Plackett looked interested and was certainly amused. And then, inexplicably, over pudding the Birdman simply lost it. To my horror he leaned across the table and grabbed the executive's tie firmly by the hand and hauled him towards him. 'You're being ruddy quiet. What do you think about it all?' he said. I watched in desperation the astonished look on our new client's face as he gazed paralysed up at this madman with his spoon and fork stuck vertically in his hands. That's blown it, I thought.

The weather was kind the next day but it all seemed to no avail. John Plackett got his flight and I summoned as much enthusiasm as I could while apologizing for the Birdman's antics of the night before. He seemed unconcerned and I asked if he would like me to fly his family some time. He would. Maybe we were in with a chance after all. Toots and I were invited to John's house the next weekend and we took the balloon with us. John knew Toots's home town of Boston well and they got on like a house on fire. 'Did you ever eat at Jimmy's Harbourside?' was the start of the conversation and it went on from there. We had another great balloon flight and we went away much heartened.

I heard the following week that John had been telling everyone at Terry's what an amazing character the Birdman was and that they must try to secure his services as their pilot for as much of their balloon programme as possible. I also got the feedback that he was enchanted by Toots. There was no mention of me at all but the business was secure.

The Terry's All Gold balloon in Hyde Park, London. We continued to enjoy a strong client relationship with Terry's, even after it was bought by a toothpaste company.

One great dream that Julian and I had been fertilizing during this time was to become the first balloonists to cross the Atlantic. The feat had been attempted many times and the history of this great adventure was littered with stories of storms, ditchings, drownings and some pilots who had set off and simply never been heard of again. All the attempts had been made in gas-filled balloons flown at low level. Every pilot had anticipated a crossing time of about five to seven days. Julian's idea was that the way to make the flight was by avoiding all the bad weather systems altogether. This would be achieved by flying over the top of the weather in a pressurized capsule. This could be done in the jet-stream winds of the lower stratosphere in not much more than two days in a hot-air balloon. I was utterly persuaded by this argument, which made complete logical sense, and we agreed that after we had set a world distance record in a hot-air balloon we would set about raising sponsorship for this grand scheme.

In the meantime two more conventional gas attempts at the Atlantic were scheduled for the summer. One consisted of three American pilots – Ben Abruzzo, Maxie Anderson and Larry Newman. The other was made up of the British balloon manufacturer from Bristol, Don Cameron, and his co-pilot, Major Christopher Davey.

The first to go were Don and Chris, who set off on a fine day from St John's, Newfoundland, in July. Their attempt was sponsored by Zanussi, the Italian washing-machine manufacturer, whose adviser was Alan Noble. Alan was also to take on the role of flight director in the Control Centre in Bracknell. The two Britons had a very good run over several days and ended up becalmed just over 100 miles west of the French coast.

Julian, I and a few colleagues had taken an afternoon off and gone waterskiing. We had adopted a habit of closing the office on Monday afternoons as compensation for the fact that weekends were our busy time and I used them by going to a gravel pit near Marlow, Buckinghamshire, to indulge in my hobby. On a portable transistor radio we listened to the hourly radio reports of Zanussi's progress and resigned ourselves to the fact that they were about to make it. We were relieved when they fell short of their target and we felt that the goal would remain unattained at least until the following summer.

The American trio had been waiting patiently for the ideal weather window. They had been publicly wishing Don and Chris luck and had stated that if their rivals succeeded they still planned to make their flight anyway. Just like any chaser of a 'world first', they did not mean a word they said and they were hugely relieved that they still had a record to go for when they lifted off from Presque Isle, Maine, on 17 August.

By this time there was fever pitch among the international media and the photograph that was syndicated around the world showed *Double Eagle 2* shot from below, with the strange sight of a hang-glider suspended underneath. Abruzzo and Anderson were veterans who had failed in their previous attempt the year before. Newman had joined the team as an additional enthusiast and the plan was that when they crossed the Atlantic he would bail out in his hang-glider and set foot on earth in the machine with which he felt most at home. They were rich individuals and had no need of sponsorship.

Double Eagle 2's flight was long and slow and the world awaited the inevitable splashdown. However, after four days of a fine August with settled weather the three balloonists found themselves within striking distance of Ireland. A bad weather system was brewing and it was night. To their alarm, the Americans found that they were sinking uncontrollably through cloud near the Irish coast. They started to throw everything overboard, ultimately including – probably with great reluctance on Larry Newman's part – the hang-glider. Whatever happened, he would now have to land with the balloon. As dawn broke the following day they were back in control and the headline news all around the world was that the Atlantic had been conquered by balloon.

The trio flew on across southern Britain. Ben Abruzzo's dulcet tones were transmitted worldwide as he explained calmly how they were looking forward to some French wine. They somewhat arrogantly crossed the Channel for good measure and went on to make landfall in a cornfield in Misery, east of Amiens. They were happy to compensate the farmer for the fact that the local followers annihilated the entire crop as they trampled their way to the conquering heroes.

Julian and I were too late for this particular challenge. Timing is everything and we had been beaten to our dream before it had even got under way. In spite of this we had a job to do as hot-air balloonists and the small matter of an attempt at the world distance record for hot-air balloons still had to be made under our contract with British Gas.

On 31 August Julian and I returned to our launch site in East Lothian for a launch scheduled for the following evening. The forecast was ideal and it was coincidentally within a day of the anniversary of our first attempt. We spent the afternoon preparing the balloon and pouring 160 gallons of kerosene into plastic bottles, which would be suspended on thin Kevlar lines from our burner frame. Our forecast was different from the last time in that we had calmer winds for take-off and the upper air currents would take us out over the North Sea and then south-east towards Holland.

The launch was perfect and we got away cleanly soon after six o'clock. Julian had our kerosene burners going before we took off. We were both jammed together in our tiny box. There was so little room that even in our standing position it was impossible to avoid scraping our immersion suits against each other with every move. As I stretched my arm out to wave goodbye to the assembled masses on the ground, only my hand and wrist could be seen by them because of the vast cluster of plastic bottles of kerosene suspended beside and below the four-sided gondola. We flew at low level for the first two hours and burned off some fuel to gain height. Darkness fell and we headed east as forecast, crossing the invisible coastline below.

The first few hours were uneventful apart from the fact that it was becoming increasingly clear just how uncomfortable our flight was going to be. This was several years before the advent of GPS, the small global satellite navigation system, and every half-hour or so we had to spread out a large chart over the side of the gondola and go through the laborious process of plotting our position from three separate fixes from our Decca Navigator. This was a large, heavy, soldier-proof green box with dials on the top, which slowly took coordinates from three separate satellites to give us a reasonably accurate idea of our position. By around midnight we were both already feeling fatigued and it was proving harder and harder to stave off cramp from the awkward positions in which we were planted in the confined space. Julian kept adjusting the flow of kerosene to the burners to fly at the most advantageous height while I had the job of hauling the kerosene bottles up over the side to refill the on-board supply.

65

At about 2 am we received a call over the aircraft band radio. It was Peter Morgan, a British Airways pilot who was also a balloonist, whom we knew well. He had been listening to our conversations with air traffic control with increasing suspicion as to the identity of the balloon flying south while he took his airliner to deliver the morning papers in the other direction. This was great for our morale even though our ordeal was turning into an endurance test, given the impossible space in which we were trying to operate.

Just after 3 am we were at 8000 feet over the waves of the North Sea, some way off the Lincolnshire coast. The burners slowed suddenly, subsiding into nothing. It was pitch-black and we could not understand what had happened. We ignited the noisier, though easier to ignite and control, propane burner system to throw some light on the situation as well as keep the balloon airborne. We had at best forty-five minutes of flying time with propane. This would not take us to daylight, let alone anywhere near land. I had to climb with great difficulty up into the rigging with my feet on the top of our gondola so that Julian would have more space to search around for the cause of our shutdown. Apart from underclothing and heavy outer military immersion suits, we both wore parachutes strapped to our backs. On our heads we wore canvas helmets with an intercom system built in and, on top of that, huge military helmets to cover all the paraphernalia underneath. Combined with the awkwardness of wires trailing from the backs of our helmets to the intercom junction box inside the gondola, this garb made any shift in position a major exercise.

Before climbing up on to the side I disconnected myself from the communication sockets in order not to get in a real muddle. I did this with some reluctance because to have no contact with each other during an emergency, however temporary, is unnerving, to say the least. After coming down I grabbed the rigging wires with one hand and plugged my untangled cables back into the intercom, so that I could talk to Julian again.

'What do you think it is?' I asked hopefully. 'I don't know,' was the unpromising reply. We rehearsed the bail-out procedure verbally. This entailed clipping our one-man life raft pack in two places on our harness, disconnecting the power leads, jumping clear and pulling the ripcord. None of this would be carried out except as a last resort, but even just talking about it sent shivers down the spine. Julian checked the plumbing for a leak by following the system with a small pencil torch. As he bent over to trace the pipework to the floor of the gondola the outward pressure of his parachute pressed against my shoes and almost tipped me overboard. 'Hang on, stay where you are,' I shouted down my microphone as I shifted uneasily by edging my trainers along the thin rim.

Our problem turned out to be ridiculously simple. The switch which allowed the pump to push the fuel through the pipes to the burner coils had been inadvertently nudged off as Julian had fidgeted in discomfort. Having established this, I immediately operated the back-up propane burners (which had been installed for just such an emergency) to keep afloat, while at the same time leaning over Julian to keep a careful eye on the altimeter. Meanwhile Julian went through the process of restarting the kerosene system.

As the steel burner coils were reheated to a red-hot glow the kerosene was eased gently through the system to start the boiling process. To my horror, I watched flaming liquid squirting out of the burner jets and falling on to Julian and into the space I had vacated in the gondola. I smothered the small flames as they licked at my partner and managed to keep the situation under control while the burners were primed further. At last they roared back into life and we thought we were finally back in command of the system.

As I eased myself back inside the relative security of the gondola I noticed that the floor had caught fire. Spread across the base was a foam mat, placed there in the belief that anything that alleviated the hardness of the floor would help our well-being. However, this had acted as a wick when the flaming kerosene drips had fallen on to the floor. The occasional flame reaching its destination had now set the whole mat alight. 'Fire on the floor,' I shouted. We stamped furiously at the flames as the only immediate way of dealing with the situation. In our constricted state we were probably unsure exactly which side the fire extinguisher was hanging, besides which there was too much equipment, as well as us, on the mat to have any chance of throwing it overboard.

It was a furious scramble to contain the spread of the fire and prevent our immersion suits catching alight, but we eventually managed. With my heart pounding against the pressure of my harness I heaved a huge sigh of relief and went back to the task of hauling up the full kerosene bottles one by one from below. My gloved hands were becoming numb from the heavy weight on the end of the Kevlar lines, which were as thin as piano wire. I began to wonder how much more I could lift before my hands gave out completely and the muscles in my fingers started to spasm.

At 6 am on 2 September we had covered almost 300 miles since our departure from Scotland some twelve hours earlier. The light was coming up, which gave a huge boost to our morale. We had veered back inland and were flying at 11,000 feet through one of Heathrow's approach airways with the permission of a helpful air traffic controller. We asked if he could check the radar trace from our transponder (a radar tracking device) to give us our speed over the ground. 'Seventy knots,' came back the reply. We looked at each other in disbelief. This was far faster than the forecast. We weren't certain whether he had said seventy knots or seventeen, so we asked if it could be checked again and confirmed. 'Confirm seven-zero knots,' said the controller. This was very good news as at this rate we would not have many hours before the world record would be in the bag.

One thing that had been nagging at me was the sheer rate at which I had been having to refill the kerosene system. Before long I had to report that we had only three full bottles left down below. However, we were lightly laden now and the sun was up, and both these factors would make a significant difference to the duration of our flight. Less weight meant less heat was required in the balloon envelope and the sun's effect on the dark-coloured fabric added several degrees to the internal temperature. The remaining fuel would certainly last much longer than it would have done earlier. Even so, we quickly worked out that, of the thirty-two bottles containing 160 gallons of fuel, we had planned on having far more than just three bottles plus the on-board supply (twenty gallons) left at this stage of the flight.

We were heading quickly now towards the Essex coast for the start of the North Sea crossing to Holland. We peered up into the balloon and could see nothing untoward. Nevertheless, the depletion of our fuel suggested that the parachute valve at the top of the balloon, which can be regulated to allow hot air to escape for a descent (or to slow a climb), was not fitting properly. This meant that hot air was leaking constantly. The only other possibility was that Julian had got his sums wrong, although this seemed unlikely considering the care with which he had worked out his calculations over several months. It was now touch-and-go as to whether or not we would be able to make it to dry land if we crossed the coast again.

Eventually we concluded that although the world record would be beaten halfway across the sea, the balance of probability was that we would ditch in the water just before the Dutch coast after the fuel ran dry. Julian got on the radio and had a number of conversations with the coastguard, who confirmed that we would naturally be rescued in

67

A cheesy press photograph as Julian and I prepare for another attempt at the world distance record.

the event of an emergency ditching. At the same time it was clear that a ditching that could be foreseen before we crossed the coast would not be popular with the rescue services. It would also be bad PR for British Gas.

We agreed to throw in the towel and started a fast descent to ensure we touched down before land ran out. The wind eased, we swept gently over a housing estate and came down in a light breeze in the penultimate field before the open sea near Colchester.

We had flown for over 300 miles, which was the longest balloon flight within the British Isles, a record which still stands today twenty-one years later. But this was an accident as the flight was never intended to be within the British Isles in the first place. It was also the first hot-air (as opposed to gas) balloon in history to fly through the night from one day to another. This was something we didn't realize we had done until about a week later. We had broken new ground, yet we had failed in our objective. It had certainly been an adventure, but not one that either of us would want to repeat.

We sat for several hours with extreme fatigue in the corner of the field until our retrieval crew arrived. They had driven through the night from Scotland, but at least we two were not far from home. Julian was hard on himself. He looked profoundly depressed at our second failure. As for me, my relief at having survived the experience at all was equally profound.

A month later I went up to Rugby to take part in the nine-day British Balloon Championships. On the face of it, it was an absurd idea. Although I understood some of the theory I had no experience of precision competition flying and was unlikely to be very successful. However, John Plackett at Terry's had agreed to sponsor me and it would be fun. My two ground crew (crucial elements in a competition series) were my girlfriend, Toots, and Ian Smith, a good friend from my advertising agency days at French Gold Abbott. The first day was taken up with a tedious briefing, lasting many hours, about the rules and procedures. Pilots and crew had to attend. Any chance I might have had of scoring well during the week was sharply reduced when my two crew simply abandoned the briefing early through boredom.

Competition ballooning is all about understanding the winds and using their varying direction and strength to reach a target. As it happened, I wasn't very good at it and didn't do very well. In fact it may well be true to say that I am the only contestant in the history of the British Balloon Championships to end up with negative points at the end of the week. This infamous record was attained by breaking the rule of 'low flying' in one of the competition tasks, which automatically relegated me to last place. The Air Navigation Order – an instrument of law laid down by the Department of Transport through the CAA – decrees that no aircraft may fly within 500 feet of any vessel, vehicle or object, and one of the prime rules of the competition was that no laws could be broken. The charge by the championship committee was that I had flown at lorry height across an 'A' road on one of the competition tasks. By this time I was second to last anyway and I thought there was nothing to lose by taking advantage of the rules of appeal, which I duly did. It was not a clever move. BBC television news that night showed very clearly that I had done exactly what I was charged with, as it depicted the golden balloon crossing the road with two characters waving frantically at the TV cameras from the basket.

I was fined the maximum number of penalty points and sank below zero overall. The real consolation was that I had attracted far more television coverage than any other balloon pilot and I was totally unconcerned with the ignominy of my situation, which some considered funny while others did not.

I was never to enter any serious championship again. I didn't enjoy this side of ballooning. It was too serious, run by people who reminded me of the most pedantic schoolmasters from my Eton days. The successful competitors were awash with compasses, set squares, rulers and calculators. It was also far too subject to the vagaries of unpredictable winds. It is no accident that the good competition balloonists do consistently well in championships, but it is a very different discipline from the raw, eccentric, get-up-and-fly style of ballooning that had attracted me to the sport.

It had been quite a year. The only disappointment was that yet again the modest profit we had made on all our promotional ballooning activities had been eaten up by the costs of our record attempt, which had gone way over budget. Everyone had worked very hard and had a great time but morale was low that so much money had disappeared into the black hole of engineering development. For a couple of months Julian Nott and Per Lindstrand blamed each other for our leaking balloon and our failure to break the world distance record.

I took an inordinate amount of time to come to the conclusion that we should give up record attempts which cost more than we could anticipate. The Atlantic Ocean had been conquered, and in any case I couldn't really see what big newsworthy event could be dreamed up in its aftermath. I realized with increasing clarity that we had to concentrate on the business, which was profitable and with which our clients were delighted. The reason I took so long to reach this inevitable conclusion was that I dreaded having to tell Julian that there was really nothing left for him to do in the company. He was a balloon pilot but he had nailed his personal colours firmly to the mast of engineering design and he did not fit in with the rest of the business; nor did he really get on with anyone except me.

One morning I finally plucked up the courage to suggest we go out for lunch. In a very ham-fisted way I told Julian it simply wasn't going to work. I think he must have experienced a sense of betrayal and I felt terrible about it. He had given every waking hour to the business for two years and we had become good friends. He cleared his desk immediately and disappeared with few words.

October 1978

Aerostat

JOURNAL OF THE BRITISH BALLOON AND AIRSHIP CLUB

Waving to the launch crew as I set off with Julian in 1978 on the longest balloon flight within the British Isles. This was also the first hot-air balloon in the world to fly through a whole night from one day to the next. The first record still stands, the second can never be taken away.

69

CHAPTER SIX

AMAZING HUMPING NOISES

WITH THE DEPARTURE OF OUR FIGUREHEAD, the world altitude record holder and Chairman of the British Balloon and Airship Club, our plans for 1979 were less overtly ambitious. I wanted to grow the promotional business, which, with Tessa's very able support, had really proved itself. We already had a client list that would have made many advertising agencies jealous.

We were thinking about recruiting another full-time pilot. By chance Joe Philp, the CAA examiner who had checked me out for my licence, popped in to say hello. Joe was a small, wiry and very fit man. He was a true British gentleman who displayed the utmost courtesy. Although he was a substantial landowner from Cornwall he was not ambitious and he had recently been languishing as a quality control inspector in an electronics firm in west London. It suited him because he could amuse himself running a daily book on horse racing while management turned a blind eye. Most of Joe's body had been subjected to a horrendous list of accidents, mainly during his years as a National Hunt jockey. The poor man creaked with joint problems and he was constantly stretching a limb or some other part of his body. His arm was the most obviously damaged part, although this injury was incurred as a result of ballooning. Flying in a strong thermal a couple of years earlier, he thought he had landed in good, calm conditions when the wind suddenly got up. He was hurled into a concrete post and his arm was lacerated and broken in many places.

I took a chance by asking Joe if he would be interested in doing some flying for us. 'Do you know, there is nothing I would like more,' he said, to my surprise. He was quite a few years older than all of us and made the ideal replacement for Julian in terms of experience. Joe worked flat out all summer, with his wife Heather as crew assistant, and stayed with the company right up to his retirement in 1995. They both became very good friends of mine.

Previous spread
Mustafa bin Crazy.
Heavily made-up and
disguised for a television
commercial for Lipton
Tea, shot in California for
the Middle Eastern
market.
Above Mild exuberation
augmented by an infusion
of champagne. Joe Philp
(right) with the Birdman
and me after another safe
crossing of the Channel.

While I was now pleased that the Hot Air Balloon Company was on an even keel, I was mindful of the fact that the bubble could always burst. On top of that the business was very seasonal and most people now employed in it had little to occupy them in the winter months. I was therefore always on the lookout for any other entrepreneurial ideas that might pay some bills and provide us with a safety valve. One day someone in the office produced a joke white cotton glove with red fingernails on it. Somehow we came up with the idea that if we attached a plastic diamond ring to the third finger and ten green woolly pompoms to the palm and beneath the fingers it would make a rather good duster. I showed the idea to my old J. Walter Thompson friend Philip Gunn, who had by now been my flatmate for some seven years and who was in the gift business. He was wildly enthusiastic but that was simply his character and I thought little more of it.

A week later Philip returned from a business trip to Ireland and left a piece of paper beside the living-room telephone for my attention. It was an order from the Dublin department store Brown Thomas for seventy-two-dozen pieces of this ridiculous duster. I could not believe it. I asked if he had shown it to anyone else. Sure. Everyone thought it was terrific. This is going to be a real winner, he predicted. As it happened, I had set up a separate company two years earlier called Happy Anniversary Limited. The reason was that under an absurd law, which was later changed, it was illegal to put any markings on an aircraft (including balloons) unless it was the name of a company or a registered trademark. During the Queen's Jubilee Year of 1977 we had therefore been unable to convey our clients' good wishes on their balloons without setting up a company to do so. Now, two years later, through Happy Anniversary Limited, we were in the gift business.

We ordered a container of half a million green woolly pompoms from a bemused gentleman in Hong Kong called Wilfred Lo. We then set about manufacturing the Glove Moppit, whose headcard on the box proclaimed it the 'handy' way to dust. To our astonishment it sold like wildfire. Joe and Heather Philp were keen to run a stand at the gift fairs, which conveniently took place outside the balloon season.

During the Christmas of 1978 the Birdman agreed to join Philip Gunn in performing demonstrations in Harrods and Harvey Nichols in Knightsbridge. They were dressed in overalls with 'World Dusting Champion' emblazoned on them in bright red. To this day I declare that Philip and Robin remain the two funniest people I have ever known and in their new roles they were devastatingly effective. 'Can I introduce you to the Glove Moppit, Madam? The handy way to dust. You can bring glamour to the housework, chuckle over your Chippendale or simply tickle your fancy.' Sometimes, when they had amassed large crowds, who were mesmerized by the performance, Robin would turn over his Moppitted hand, pick a pretty girl and, with his wide smile and easy charm, he would come out with an outrageous invitation: 'Would you like to feel my balls, Madam?' The fact that he was never thrown out of the store is explained by the speed at which the product was being sold.

The final confirmation that the world had gone irretrievably mad came at the Spring Gift Fair at the National Exhibition Centre in Birmingham, where it was announced that the Glove Moppit had won the runner-up prize in the Gift of the Year Award.

Keen to expand our new-found success, I came up with a few other products to

'Would you like to feel my balls, Madam?' The Birdman and Philip Gunn at Harrods.

extend our range over the next couple of years. The glamorous gloves became rubber for washing up (Dishy Hands) and sponge for the bath (Foam Sweet Foam). In addition we had boxes of tissues printed as £5 notes from the Bank of Hanky Panky (worth their weight in cold) and produced our biggest-selling line of all, a rope ladder for spiders to climb out of the bath. I had such trouble explaining to Wilfred Lo what the ladder was for that we had the cards on which they were mounted printed with the words: 'Hand made by mystified craftsmen in China'.

By 1984 we were marketing a range of plastic animals with light bulbs inside. They were being bought as kitsch fashion accessories for the tables and floors of living rooms. One was a particularly attractive woolly sheep. Since the Wool Secretariat were spending large sums of money on promoting pure new wool I thought it would make an ideal promotional item for them and would boost our now flagging sales. I could get no sense out of their head office in London and no one would take my call, so I simply sent one of our sheep round by hand to their reception. Hanging round its neck was an envelope addressed to Dr Hardesty, the marketing director. Inside was a letter from the sheep itself. It read:

> *Dear Doc,*
> *I hope ewe are wool.*
> *I tried counting humans last night but I couldn't sleep through the excitement of thinking of an idea to light up your life. I am sure you are lamb-basted with ideas but this is a natural. I congratulate you on those nice little TV ads with my glamorous cousins strutting around, looking shampooed and fluffy. It was also clever of ewe to introduce the 'ping' into Pachelbel's classic piece of music. Very jolly. Anyhow, how about gambolling a small part of your huge advertising budget on a few replicas of me? I have no idea how ewe'll use them but I presume your title of Doctor is because ewe are a PhD rather than some quack medicine man, in which case ewe clearly have the intelligence to work it out for yourself.*

By the way, please tell your secretary she's a miserable old boot with no sense of humour and she nearly lost ewe the chance to obtain this gorgeous product at a special giveaway price.

When you are ready give Colin Prescot a ring at this number. He's OK for a human and he's waiting for your call.

Baa baa for now.

Love from Sheila the Sheep.

Sadly there was no response to this masterpiece of literary nonsense and we never saw the sheep again. I expect it got as far as the secretary, who nicked it for herself. However, by this time the public's appetite for useless upmarket tat was on the wane. I finally sold the company for next to nothing to another friend in the gift business as an easy exit.

Back in the real world of 1979 the Hot Air Balloon Company was going international. On 25 February I was in the departure lounge of Terminal Three at Heathrow at exactly the same time as the Birdman. It was a big day for us. We were suddenly an international business. I was on my way to Los Angeles – the first time I had ever been to America – to fly a balloon for a Middle Eastern commercial for Lipton Tea. The Birdman was leaving for Kuala Lumpur for the first phase of an international tour of the balloons that we were operating for BAT Industries, advertising the State Express 555 cigarette brand. We wished each other luck and went to our respective departure gates.

Tony Beerbohm had been Creative Director of CPV in my advertising days and it was he who now gave me my first, brief taste of the film business. Each day for three days I was made up with full black beard and dressed in virgin-white Arab clothes. I then flew the balloon for a number of different camera angles.

During the last weekend of May the Milton Keynes Development Corporation ran a balloon festival to promote inward investment into the city. I asked why Milton Keynes qualified as a city as there was no cathedral. There are three ways in which a town can qualify as a city, I was told. You either have to have a cathedral or you have to have a royal charter (like Southampton). The third way, as in Milton Keynes's case, was simply to have a hell of a lot of cheek.

The significance of the weekend as far as I was concerned was my own personal achievement. The weather was terrible and the thirty assembled balloons spent all Friday and Saturday grounded. Conditions were not much better on the Sunday, when there were freshening winds and the threat of rain. It was marginal as to whether or not pilots should be allowed to fly. The committee appointed to run the event decided to leave it up to individual balloonists to make up their own minds.

In the end, only five balloons took off. Ian Ashpole led the way with his usual consummate professionalism, followed by Joe Philp and me. On board the other three balloons were the Birdman and two of our other company pilots. It was a Hot Air

My footwear is a bit of a giveaway as I tow my balloon back to the film crew during filming of the Lipton Tea commercial.

74

Balloon Company full house, with no one else unpacking their balloons from their bags. Up to six flights had been scheduled as a spectacle for the public between Friday morning and Sunday night. Competitions had been organized and the pilot with the best overall record was due to receive a huge cup as the champion of the first annual Milton Keynes festival. The present flight was now the sole event and only five balloons were in it. The competition was to use piloting skills to find the right wind directions at various levels in order to arrive at a predetermined target, marked by a red cross in the middle of a field. I ignored the competition itself and resolved to concentrate on having a safe flight in very mediocre weather.

After about three-quarters of an hour flying along at no particular level and without making any attempt to reach any particular point I noticed the large red cross in the field I was approaching. I scrabbled around in my bag in the hope that I might have brought along the streamer with a sand weight in a pouch which had to be thrown from the balloon as a marker. I was in luck. I pulled the line which released the parachute valve and swooped down over the cross, planting my marker some fifty feet from the target. As I climbed again I looked around the sky to see that all my friends were quite a long way off.

I was the champion.

As I received my trophy I was hailed mockingly as a hero by my colleagues. It had been a complete fluke: they all knew it, but no one cared. There never was another Milton Keynes Balloon Festival and I still have the silver cup in my downstairs loo. It is the only championship I have ever won in the sport of ballooning.

While I was away being a champion in Milton Keynes someone from a film production company, James Garrett and Partners, had left a message for me. The company was the largest of its kind producing television commercials in Britain. One of its production managers was making a general enquiry about having a balloon made for a series of films for Fanta, a brand of fizzy orange drink owned by the Coca-Cola Corporation and distributed internationally. This sounded too interesting to ignore and I asked for a copy of the script and explained that we could coordinate everything with a one-stop service. James Garrett had a roster of big-name film directors on his books. Anything produced by his company was likely to have a big budget. I persisted in selling my wares but was dismayed to hear that the producer already had a balloon pilot in mind to fly the balloon but the company would not disclose who he was.

Because there was still interest in having the Hot Air Balloon Company manufacture the balloon (I didn't dare tell them that it would have to be entirely subcontracted) I got an appointment to see James Garrett's senior producer, David Fanthorpe. David was producing a series of thirty-second films directed by Richard Loncraine, a young and hot director who had been making some very successful commercials. Loncraine would go on to make the famous British Airways award-winning advertisement featuring the whole of Manhattan flying to London in a scene resembling *Close Encounters of the Third Kind*. He later made a number of movies, including *Richard III*.

David Fanthorpe is one of life's unrepeatables. When I first met him I could see immediately that he was extremely jolly, very funny with a powerful personality. He wore elegant tweed jackets, plain shirts and brightly spotted bow ties. He had a wonderfully colourful vocabulary and mouthed equally colourful expressions. He also had an acid wit. More than once I heard him describe people he did not consider to be up to standard as 'impenetrably dim' – with a strong emphasis on the word 'impenetrably'. If he liked someone he would more than likely address him as 'my dear fellow'. He ruled his crews with a rod of iron. He spoke plainly and was completely unflappable when one of

Right Shuna Harwood, who was nominated for an Oscar, with David Fanthorpe, who wasn't. **Opposite** Moments before my ordeal in the British Gas 'Mr Wonderfuel' balloon. Château de Balleroy, Normandy, 1979.

76

those huge production disasters reared up in front of him, threatening any chance of his film coming in on budget.

David was a unique kind of producer in that he could pull in business on the strength of his character. Normally clients would come to producers because they wanted the services of their directors. However, David was universally popular with advertising agencies and was known as someone to trust with complex big-budget productions.

He was also a *bon viveur* who loved lunch. It was only because he was such a good producer that he could shrug off the well-known fact that if you wanted to do business with him it had to be done in the morning. If you did occasionally get hold of him in the afternoon the claret would interfere with any meaningful discussion and the detail of it would have been forgotten or even denied by the next day. One legendary story is that when his chairman asked him if he might perhaps curb his expenses a little, he asked what sort of allowance his boss had in mind. When the figure was suggested David clearly considered it derisory for a man of his position and seniority and replied tartly, 'My dear fellow, I *drink* that much.'

During our first meeting I made up my mind that David was most definitely a character worth working with in the mornings. I warmed to him enormously and he made me laugh out loud all the time. I enthused about his project and pleaded with 'love to do' enthusiasm about being his balloon pilot for the series. 'Can you act, dear?' he asked in his mildly affected way. 'Yes, I think so,' I lied.

Somehow I managed to win him over.

The commercials were for screening internationally and would be shot over a two-week period in Brittany. Per Lindstrand built the orange balloon in a hurry and I was measured up for an orange and white-striped blazer, white trousers and straw boater by David's lovely long-time lover Shuna Harwood, who was in charge of costumes. I would be Mr Fanta and I would fly a number of small children on fantasy-style travels around the French countryside.

While pre-production was in progress David wanted me to come to France with him to seek out the locations for flying the balloon. We took the ferry from Portsmouth to St

Malo overnight. His production assistant had booked us a four-berth cabin, which we would probably have to share with two other unknown passengers. As we arrived at our sleeping berths David asked me if I knew the form. Without having a clue what he was talking about I simply said no. 'Right,' he said, 'what we have to do is this. Up until the time the boat leaves, whenever we hear anyone coming down the stairs, we must make amazing humping noises. That way we won't be disturbed and we'll have the cabin to ourselves.' He was the boss, so I duly obliged as we grunted hysterically every time someone was hovering outside the door. It worked perfectly, since whoever was booked in with us had clearly gone to the purser to insist on another cabin. We had an undisturbed night.

We spent three days being flown around in a small plane by a pilot who adored garlic. We selected our spots, which were chosen as much for their proximity to somewhere David had found in his Michelin guide as for their suitability for flying a balloon.

Mission completed, we took the plane back across the Channel. It was the first days of Margaret Thatcher's new Conservative government and when I phoned the office from the airport I was delighted to hear that Michael Edwardes had been knighted in the new Prime Minister's first Queen's Birthday Honours list.

For the weekend of 16 June I was invited by Malcolm Forbes, the American multimillionaire publisher of *Forbes Magazine*, to his incredible Château de Balleroy in Normandy. Forbes was a flamboyant figure who indulged in any toys that took his fancy. He had a large jet called *Capitalist Tool*, with the name inscribed in large letters along the side. He also had a mind-boggling collection of Harley-Davidson motorcycles and an equally large number of homes spread around the globe. Most well-known about Forbes's lavish lifestyle was his love of ballooning and his extravagance in having large balloons built in the shape of symbols of the countries he would visit. Each year he would spend a weekend at Balleroy with members of his family and friends. He would then invite business contacts from around the world, to create the ultimate weekend of corporate entertaining. This included an extravaganza of food and wines, marching bands, fun fairs and the most spectacular fireworks display synchronized to the *1812 Overture*.

The final piece of Forbes's weekend jigsaw was the invitation to a handful of international balloonists to come and create an aerial spectacle throughout the festivities. Balloonists were only ever asked once to this event, and were selected individually for having made a significant contribution to the sport or for having achieved some specific feat or other. There was no reason for my invitation other than the fact that I had started a commercial enterprise and now had some special-shape balloons, although these represented products rather than the national symbols which were our host's speciality. This was a relatively new challenge and I was left in no doubt that the balloon I should bring should not be of the standard shape.

The invitation I received from Washington was for me and two crew and included detailed instructions. Toots had some weeks before abandoned any plans to return home to Boston and was now a fairly permanent feature in my life. She came along and we invited Guy Bigland to make up the Prescot party. 'Biggles' had long been one of my greatest friends and now worked for the advertising agency McCann Erickson.

The weekend was every bit as special as it was cracked up to be. The three American transatlantic balloonists were there, along with a plethora of captains of industry and politicians from various countries. The only blot on the weekend was that I experienced one of the two moments in my life when I thought I might be about to die. I had brought our new balloon for British Gas. This was a tall, thin, flame-shaped balloon with arms and eyes to represent Mr Wonderfuel, the company's animated advertising character. I was not used to the shape, and because it was a windy morning and I had to inflate in a confined space, I heated the balloon much more than normal in order to clear the trees in front of me. When everyone finally let go I went up like a rocket and had no trouble clearing the wood. However, as soon as I was above the fir trees a violent wind hit the balloon, partially collapsing it, and I found myself looking out from my basket at a sea of fabric blown sideways.

From the ground it looked like a catastrophe about to happen. There was absolutely nothing I could do except squat down in the basket and pray that the balloon somehow sorted itself out. One of the design faults in the balloon (which was corrected on my return) was that there was no parachute valve at the top to spill the hot air. All I had by way of control was a rip panel, and the effect of pulling it open was so drastic that it could only be used as a final deflation on landing. With a terrifying roar and ear-splitting cracks the fabric flapped as the surge of hot air fought against the howling gusts of wind. Finally the balloon rearranged itself and continued upwards in a more acceptable swaying motion until all was calm again. That weekend I learned a valuable lesson: balloons of unusual shape must always be treated with special respect.

On 15 July I set off for France with two crew assistants to make the Fanta commercials. One was my highly gifted and trusty assistant Sean Byrne, the other Charlotte Billson, who had been working for my friend Ian Smith at Saatchi & Saatchi.

On the first evening we checked into the Hôtel Ibis in Quimper on the Brittany coast. David Fanthorpe had secured permission to use the adjoining football pitch as a landing pad for the helicopter which would be flying in from Britain with Albert Werry and Marc Wolff, the two-man team of aerial cameraman and helicopter pilot. At about six o'clock on a warm and balmy evening we all went to clear everyone off the field for the helicopter's imminent arrival. The sound of rotor blades got closer and closer until the angry machine came into sight, its single central headlight pointed directly at us. In what appeared to be sheer defiance of convention the pilot ignored the vast space that had been cleared for him and parked expertly and neatly in the tiny area behind the goalpost. Marc Wolff had arrived.

Captain Cool. Marc Wolff in familiar pose.

Would you give your business to this lot? From left: the Birdman (proud owner of the Bullnose Morris), Ian Ashpole, Joe Philp, Tessa Tennant, Marc Wolff and me.

Marc was the best-known and most sought-after film pilot in Europe. He was already a veteran of two James Bond films. Born in Chicago and raised in New Jersey, he had gone on to join the US Army for his national service. In 1968 he was posted to South Vietnam, where he spent a year of active service as a helicopter pilot with the rank of captain. Some of this time involved low-level, fast precision flying just above the tree tops of the dense jungle. He had learned his craft by swooping into clearings to collect the wounded before rushing out again for the same death-defying journey back to safety. When he had finished his commission he was posted to Germany for a while before coming to London. At the time there was an acute shortage of good helicopter pilots in Britain, and as he liked the country he got himself a work permit and soon found jobs flying for the likes of the Metropolitan Police and Ordnance Survey. Marc was to make England his home. His fascination with the film industry led him to start knocking on studio doors and after a couple of early breaks he was in. It was not long before the word spread that he was the best man in the business when it came to aerial filming or action.

Our director for the Fanta commercials was Richard Loncraine. He arrived with his family, by the more conventional means of a Winnebago mobile home, soon after the helicopter. The whole team then had a meeting to discuss the two weeks ahead. There was to be a lot of aerial filming from the helicopter of Mr Fanta and the three selected children, with loads of pretty backgrounds. We were to wave like mad all the time and look happy, which by and large we were. There were four or five preselected locations where ground sets were involved. For instance, I was to fly the balloon over a river while all the acting fishermen waved. There were to be cyclists on a road above some sand dunes and apple-pickers in an orchard. The French production team consisted of Antoine Compin and his American wife and colleague, Charis Horton. The two of them would fix the locations and follow behind me to compensate any landowners for any damage I might do. They had a contingency budget for this in view of the highly unusual nature of some of the locations.

The week began windy and I started with a hairy take-off from a river bank. Sean begged me to abandon this, but I persisted and the wind gusted so much that I burned a huge section out of the balloon. This proved something of a handicap as it could now be filmed from one side only. As the week improved we found some local seamstresses to repair my craft and all went well. We flew above cotton-wool clouds ('very Mary Poppins' the director remarked) and had a high old time. The catering was magnificent and personally selected by David. Every breakfast, lunch and dinner was a veritable feast concocted by 'Petit Louis' in his Peugeot van converted into a catering truck.

During periods of rest Sean was forever busying around preparing things for the next sequence, while Charlotte regaled us with stories of the island of Alderney, where she had spent all her childhood holidays.

One morning Richard Loncraine swam across a river in the briefest leopard-skin swimming trunks imaginable to get to the film location where we were waiting.

On the penultimate day of filming it was very windy again and I made the decision not to carry the children. For safety reasons I would fly solo. The helicopter followed as usual. It had to film from further away so that it could not be seen on film that the kids were missing. After half an hour the wind had turned into a strong breeze and I started to look for somewhere to land. All the fields for miles ahead were small and surrounded by power cables, a balloonist's worst nightmare scenario. After a further half-hour I was still flying and now in an even stronger breeze. Marc Wolff was scouting ahead for suitable landing areas but I was now approaching the coast, and I had to get down quickly.

I radioed Marc and told him I would have to make a hard landing in a field of mature maize immediately ahead. As I hauled on the red line to spill the air I plummeted into the tall crops and

Mr Fanta sets off on another 'jolly'.

81

ploughed a huge scar across the large field as I crouched in the foetal position at the bottom of the basket, hanging on for dear life. The wind was so strong now that I could not make an early halt and I snapped a barbed-wire fence before screaming across another field of maize with similarly devastating effect. I was then dragged across a small road and into a field of cows. I was still being pulled along by the wind at a terrifying speed as I spied the astonished expressions of several cows scampering out of the balloon's way. Finally, some 300 yards after landfall, there was a large bank of trees ahead and it was clear I was not going to stop before I hit them.

The end result was embarrassingly reminiscent of my crash into the Scottish oak some two years before. The only difference this time was that instead of being marooned halfway up I had been planted very firmly in a ditch at the bottom of the trees while the balloon hit the buffers in the form of hundreds of well-spread branches.

The crash had obviously looked far more dramatic from the air than it had from my perspective. Marc plummeted down to land beside me. Tony Bishop, the helicopter engineer, jumped out and ran at breakneck speed towards me. 'Are you *badly* hurt?' he yelled. He was amazed to see me crawl furtively out of my cocoon without as much as a scratch.

Soon the irrepressible David Fanthorpe was hurtling across the field to the scene of the accident, shouting instructions to his inseparable driver, Steve. I weakly mumbled an apology and resigned myself to the fact that the balloon had met its end. 'Never mind about the balloon,' he said. 'How about you?' It was typical of him to put all other considerations to the side if there was any issue of welfare involved. After I had assured him I was absolutely fine we started to contemplate how to get the balloon out of the trees. It didn't look as though it could be rescued without major damage, which effectively meant the shoot was at an end before we had achieved all the shots required. There was not much more to say until I suggested we wait until sunset, when the wind was due to drop. We could perhaps order a crane so that we could pull it out of the trees.

Marc had another idea which we thought was worth a whirl. I had found the eighty-foot crown rope (which is attached to the top of the balloon and is used to hold it down during inflation) dangling on the other side of the trees. We tied on a further 200 feet of cord and secured the other end to the cargo hook on the helicopter. With delicate and expert finesse Marc rose from the ground far enough away not to cause a massive wind interference and peeled the envelope out of the foliage. When we inspected it on the ground we found no more than minor tears which would not pose any safety threat. We would be ready to fly again the next day.

As it happened, the child actors had been given the following day off and anyway the morning was too windy. However, the forecast was for a calmer evening and Richard Loncraine thought that he and David might come for a ride. They would kneel in the basket and wear the children's caps. The helicopter would shoot long shots and the fact that the balloon would be occupied by adults wouldn't be apparent on celluloid.

I inflated the balloon beside a small bridge by a river and David climbed aboard. There was no sign of Richard. We waited half an hour as the sun sunk lower on the horizon. It was gusty enough to be difficult to keep the balloon inflated. Just as I said we would have to take off without our third passenger there was a cloud of dust as a Citroën 2CV sped round the corner and came to a sliding halt in front of the balloon. Out of the back seat poured our director carrying a bottle of Dom Pérignon and an enormous tray of oysters. We set off into the sky and my two passengers indulged in the ultimate decadence while enjoying their first flight in a balloon. At one stage during the journey Richard considered he had a bad oyster and spat it out over the side. As we were now in a descent the half-chewed oyster followed us down at the same rate a few arm's lengths away. I had to turn the burners on to allow the rather disagreeable sight to disappear downwards. When we viewed the film afterwards it was quite unusable. Silhouetted against the sunset the scene in the basket resembled octopus tentacles being wagged up and down rather than the small waving hands of children.

The fortnight in Brittany was one of the most enjoyable periods I have spent away. You could hardly call it working but I got paid handsomely by my standards and it provided more material to add credibility to our company presentation. There was another very significant bonus as well. Marc was self-employed and would leave his answering machine on for months on end at his home in Hampstead, north London, while he was on a movie location. I suggested to him that as we had a fully equipped office he could use us to field all his calls and chat up his customers when he was not available. It would ensure his customers were looked after and we would contact him from time to time to let him know what was going on. My motive for doing this was that it was a rather crude way of learning a little about the film business. Besides, I thought, it would cost us little more than a small part of someone's time and we might even get some business leads.

As soon as I got back to the office I called Per Lindstrand about an idea I had had. I had seen some old black and white prints of people balloon jumping. This entailed filling a balloon with hydrogen gas and attaching it to the jumper's harness. As soon as the point was reached where the balloon was almost lighter than air the gas would be turned off. The jumper was still on the ground but now all he had to do was to gently squat down and push off the ground hard with his legs. He would then ascend up to thirty or forty feet in the air before making a gentle descent back to earth. The early balloon jumpers had obviously enjoyed the sensation of seeing the countryside while bounding over roads, hedges and trees.

An example of the early-twentieth-century prints which gave me the idea for what was to become the Cloudhopper.

83

My plan was to use this idea with a hot-air balloon. I asked Per if he could design a backpack with a tank and as tiny a balloon as possible. It could be used for jumping but it could also sustain a person in flight for up to an hour. Once I agreed with Per that this could be done, I registered the name Cloudhopper as a trademark and set about seeking a sponsor. I would present it as the world's first aircraft to pack into a suitcase.

At the time Smirnoff Vodka had been running a cult advertising campaign which consisted of wacky situations under the headline 'Well, they said anything could happen.' I contacted Smirnoff's advertising agency, Young & Rubicam, and twisted the account director's arm to give me an introduction to the purveyors of the brand, International Distillers & Vintners at Harlow, in Essex. He said he would do it provided he was present. He offered to schedule it for a maximum of fifteen minutes at the end of a client meeting at their offices near Regent's Park.

Ian Hannah was the marketing director and I gave him my carefully rehearsed presentation, which lasted exactly fifteen minutes. I ended by immodestly suggesting that this was a big PR idea. I would have no trouble selling it to a sponsor, but it just had to be Smirnoff because it fitted so perfectly with the brand's advertising campaign. Ian listened patiently and asked a few very good questions. What guarantee could I give that the finished product would actually work? There was none. But Ian was a risk taker; he liked the idea and he bought it on the spot. I was elated.

After I gave Per the go-ahead we had the whole thing built in a matter of weeks. I took my new machine to a field in Fingest, the Buckinghamshire village where I was born twenty-nine years before. Clad in a thick and starchy parachute suit and full helmet, I prepared the tiny balloon for flight. As the balloon stood up I went through the most agonizing few minutes, wishing I had never started the project. In short I was terrified. This was unknown territory. Once airborne it would be an almost impossible manoeuvre to relight a failed pilot light because I could hardly get my harnessed arms to reach it. I

couldn't even get sight of it above my head. If the small flame blew out and I failed to relight it the result would almost certainly be broken legs at best. I took an inordinate amount of time to check everything. Before finally strapping myself into my harness I checked the quick-release connection between the propane supply hose and the burner. I snapped the connection to shut off the fuel, but instead a cloud of propane gas poured out. To my horror, I realized that I had to dive in and laboriously turn the tap off manually, as the slightest spark would have started an uncontrollable blaze.

That was enough for me. I wasn't flying anywhere. Instead I strapped myself in and checked the feel of the balloon by allowing it to rise no more than ten feet on a tether rope. My parents (whom I should never have brought along) hovered reluctantly close by with fire extinguishers at the ready. 'Really, darling, you must give this up immediately,' said Mum.

I took my Cloudhopper back to Per with suggested modifications. He agreed with masterly understatement that there was a design fault that needed correcting.

Opposite I boasted I could walk on water…
Above …and on air.

Balloning off to work? It's a lot of hot air

Above and opposite A new invention to beat the traffic and get to work on time. This bit of nonsense was covered by the media all over the world. The Cloudhopper also inspired Trog's cartoon in the *Observer* during the week that Geoffrey Howe, the new Conservative Chancellor, floated the pound.

Once this had been done and the balloon had been test flown, we were ready to launch the concept. In order to create a bank of press photographs I took the Cloudhopper to a disused gravel pit near Reading and hired a small boat for the photographer and, more importantly, to rescue me if I got stuck. Harnessed to the propane tank, I wore a wetsuit, flippers and a snorkel. I was towed out into the middle of the lake and let go. As I drifted along in the light breeze I was able to control the heat just enough to flap my way along the water. The caption was to be 'Walking on water'. A handful of mystified fishermen looked on.

We decided to have the press conference to launch the Cloudhopper at St Katharine's Dock, just east of the City of London. The idea was that I should wear a dark City suit and bowler hat, while carrying a rolled umbrella and a copy of the *Financial Times*. The Smirnoff Cloudhopper would be billed as the new way to beat the traffic to commute to work. It was completely daft, but of course that was the point. It fitted perfectly with the slogan 'Well, they said anything could happen.'

We prayed for good weather and I was concerned I had finally flipped and bitten off more than I could chew. There was a risk that the whole enterprise would turn into a total fiasco. We were lucky. The day was reasonably calm and there was an extraordinary turnout from Fleet Street. I had never seen so many notepads and cameras in my life. I confess I also felt a complete idiot (which I hadn't anticipated) when I finally donned the bowler hat, but the press loved it.

Almost all the national daily newspapers carried the story with a range of pictures the next day. The press conference was over by ten o'clock that morning and afterwards I rushed to Heathrow to catch a flight to New York, where I was to make a presentation the following day. When I arrived I was handed a copy of the *New York Times*. Inside was a large picture of an imbecile in a suit and bowler hat, dangling from a balloon.

CHAPTER SEVEN

MEXICAN MADNESS

T HE SMIRNOFF CLOUDHOPPER SET OFF on an amusing tour that was so daft
as to be absurd. But that was the point really. The Birdman and Ian Ashpole soon
took to this diddy little flying machine. It was a two-minute process to inflate it from a
heap on the ground and it took no more than that to pack it away again at the end of the
flight.

We set about having fun. We simply sent a ridiculous spoof press release all round the
regional television stations and waited for calls inviting us to come and give an
exhibition of our toy. In Ian Hannah's words, television coverage was the holy grail for
Smirnoff. There was an agreement between the spirits companies not to advertise on
television, yet his vodka brand was now getting television exposure in spades. It was
quite legitimate PR through the back door.

The stunts got crazier the more we brainstormed the Smirnoff slogan. The Birdman
spent November and December of 1979 going round dressed as Father Christmas, ho-
hoing to everyone in sight. He would then fly the Cloudhopper to the tops of houses and
anchor himself to a chimney. Once he had got a good enough hold he would make a
great play of trying to stuff the wrapped presents down it. It was hysterical. There was no
way any of the gifts would fit, so he would throw them in all directions and they ended
up scattered all over the garden. Then the burners would go on and he would fly off,
supposedly to the next lucky household.

The nadir of ludicrousness took me to Loch Ness. After a very pleasant night at the
famous Drumnadrochit Hotel I inflated the Cloudhopper on the lawn and set off at low
level across the loch, dragging a bottle of vodka as bait for the monster. I never tempted
Nessie to the surface but I hooked a ten-minute film report on Scottish Television instead.

In February 1980 Per Lindstrand and I got lured into spending ten days in
Grindelwald in Switzerland. The Cloudhopper craze was catching on and a
documentary maker, Julian Grant, wanted to feature two of them in a mountain-sport
spectacular. As well as enjoying some good skiing on several days off, we flew a
Cloudhopper each over the mountains dressed in several different costumes to suit the
scenario. In addition we got tempted into a hairy stunt with a much bigger balloon.
Julian had the idea that perhaps two parachutists could freefall from the top of the

balloon rather than from the basket, which had been done many times before. We saw no reason why not.

The two jumpers were equipped with helmet cameras and we took an additional cameraman in the basket. At 15,000 feet we shouted up to our two wayward passengers that we were ready for them to jump. From inside the basket we watched their shadows and indents in the fabric as they slid down the envelope and into thin air. Their bodies turned over past the basket and they whooped with delight at their adrenaline rush as they disappeared down to the snows below. When we landed they had already looked at the video from one of the parachutists' cameras and it was spectacular. The video showed the balloon from the jumper's point of view and the whole scene was turned upside down in the picture as he somersaulted past. The look of stunned astonishment could clearly be seen on my face as they dropped past me. Then came the inevitable result of such success. Could we do it just one more time?

Only one more time, we agreed, to dispel any doubt. The two parachutists attached themselves to the crown ring at the top of the balloon. It was Per's turn to inflate the balloon this time, but in his enthusiasm he may have heated it a little too quickly. The envelope rushed up from the ground with the two jumpers attached to the top. The suddenness of this caused the two men to collide with each other and something sharp dug into the fabric, causing a lengthy tear. As we stood in the basket, still attached to the ground, we looked up and saw two men dangling *inside* the balloon. They were huddled together, hanging on for all they were worth, as they peered nervously down at us some eighty feet below.

No, we could *not* do it just one more time, we told the director. He would have to make do with what he had got.

On my return from Switzerland I met up with Marc Wolff. We had been getting a lot of calls about his availability and he was pleased that Tessa Tennant and her team had been praised for their friendliness and efficiency by several of his clients. A package had recently arrived for Marc. It was a draft script for a film called *Green Ice*, based on the novel by Gerald Browne. An all-action caper set in Colombia, it had the winning ingredients of sex, drugs, revolution and greed. Marc had worked with the film's producer, Jack Wiener, on his last film, *Escape to Athena*. Jack was a seasoned Hollywood movie-maker who had spent some years in partnership with David Niven Junior. His new associate director for *Green Ice* was Colin Brewer, who was organizing the team for the film and Colin wanted Marc to advise on the aerial sequences. By coincidence I had recently read the novel on which the film was based and I remembered that the robbery took place in the top storey of a skyscraper, where emeralds were stored in vaults. The robbers, clad in black, had descended by parachutes to the top of the building from an overflying plane. Marc checked through the script and confirmed that the scene was pretty much the same in the film.

Previous spread The Citibank building in the heart of Mexico City – the scene of a heist which involved three of us landing on the roof by balloons at night.
Above The Birdman as St Nicholas. Or was it the other way round?

'Parachutes are old hat,' I said precociously. 'What this film needs is Cloudhoppers.' Marc laughed heartily. He didn't hold out much hope but he said he would mention it to Jack Wiener. I made sure he did so very quickly by accompanying him to Elstree Studios, armed with a raft of photographs. Jack was intrigued but at this stage he had neither a director nor a lead actor for the movie. He had more important things to consider. Anthony Simmons was eventually hired to direct the film and Jack disappeared to Los Angeles to try to hire Steve McQueen for the lead role. I was getting concerned. I had great belief in my idea and I knew that the longer the parachutists stayed in the script and the more Colin Brewer talked to experts about it the less likely it would be that the sequence would ever be changed. At the same time I knew that Colin would get irritated if I pestered him any more.

Several weeks went by and Jack Wiener was still in Los Angeles trying to get to see Steve McQueen's agent. He was apparently doing little other than trying to secure his star. I decided it was time for action. I called Colin Brewer and told him a complete lie. I said that I had to go to LA on business and did he think it would be worth me giving Jack a call while I was there? He agreed it might be worthwhile if I was going to be there anyway and supplied me with Jack's hotel phone number.

I flew to Los Angeles and checked into the Hyatt on Sunset: it was where we had stayed for the Lipton commercial and the only hotel I knew. As soon as I was settled in I pulled out the scrappy piece of paper with Jack's number on it – a futile gesture as I knew it by heart already. Jack answered immediately. 'When did you get in?' 'Just now.' 'When do you want to meet?' 'I can see you at any time that suits you,' I said. 'OK, I'll give you a day to rest up and how about meeting me for lunch at the Beverley Wilshire Hotel on Wednesday? Let's say 12.30 in the lobby.'

Wow. I had an appointment. I had had a dread of Jack saying he hadn't got any time and I would have gone back to London feeling a complete idiot. I hadn't dared suggest an earlier rendezvous although I had absolutely nothing else to do in the interim except

Another theatrical Cloudhopper stunt for television, filmed in Grindelwald, Switzerland.

91

The poster for the film.
From left: me, the
Birdman and Ian aloft.

to find out where the Beverley Wilshire was. I spent the following day at the pool on the roof of the hotel, rereading the script of *Green Ice*.

Although it was now three or four months after the event a double-page spread about me and the Cloudhopper was due to appear in *People* magazine on the day of my lunch. I bought a copy at the news-stand down the road and I was at the Beverley Wilshire on Rodeo Drive on the dot of 12.30. Jack was waiting. 'Hello, I'm just having a drink with some friends. Come and join us,' he said, leading me to the cocktail lounge. His friends were Michael Caine and his beautiful wife, Shakira. I was introduced to the film star. ''Allo, Colin,' he said, shaking me by the hand. Jack explained who I was and that I had this new device he was considering using in his new movie. 'Do you have a picture?' he asked. As I had brought my whole presentation in a case this was not difficult. They all looked suitably impressed and I produced my copy of *People* with a flourish. 'That's great. A lot of people read that,' said Jack. It was all going well and my nerves had already subsided when we said our goodbyes to the Caines. Jack took me in to lunch.

'So what are you doing in Hollywood?' he asked as we were handed huge menus. 'I've come to see *you*, Jack,' I replied. He didn't believe me but it didn't matter. I went through my proposal, which entailed flying three Cloudhoppers roped together. All the flying shots would be from a helicopter in open countryside where the ground could not be seen. The location of the take-off was up to him. I proposed that the landing on the skyscraper could be achieved by taking off from the skyscraper and reversing the film. It would have to be executed on a calm night. We would inflate three balloons on the roof and they would fly off linked by ropes. When the Cloudhoppers were far enough away we would simply be winched back in. Jack asked if we could do a number of things. I said 'yes' to all of them on the basis that I wanted this work and we would work out how to deliver on my promises when the contract was in the bag.

He liked it. He all but bought it. He needed his production designer, Roy Walker, to decide whether or not it would work. Roy and the first assistant director, Ricky Green, were currently in Mexico City scouting for a location. Would I be prepared to go straight there to see them? Jack would cover all the costs. I left for Mexico the following morning.

I was met at the airport and taken to the Presidente Hotel in the fashionable Zona Rosa, where I met Roy and Ricky. They were terrific and took me straight to the top of the Citibank building, which was under construction in the busy Reforma. From thirty-two storeys up the view looked daunting, but after a good snoop around I said it would be fine. It would be fine by them too. They started to quiz me about how we would organize everything. When I told them I thought we would need a good ten days of rehearsals to get used to a very complex piece of flying they were completely unfazed. In a way I think they were relieved that I acknowledged that this was no piece of cake. Ideally I wanted flat, open countryside away from the city, where there were calm early-morning conditions. They agreed that the rehearsals could be done far more quickly in the reliable weather of Mexico than in Britain. The Mexican location manager had an idea of a suitable spot and I was more than happy to be driven south for two hours to see what he had in mind.

After passing through Cuernavaca and following the Acapulco road we spotted a sign indicating that Hacienda Vista Hermosa, where we would be based, was a further twenty-two kilometres. We drove down a dusty track with chickens scattering in all directions in front of us. Simple peasant dwellings stood all around. And there, right ahead of us, like a mirage forming out of the cloud of dust, was the most stunning hacienda I had ever seen. It was like an oasis in a huge desert. As I looked out towards the horizon across the sand plains there was nothing to see except bits of tumbleweed and the occasional John Wayne type lolloping by on a horse.

Once we had checked in, my bags were heaved along a vast vaulted hall by a tiny, bare-footed Mexican dressed in white with a yellow sash around his waist. The hall was big enough to contain the bizarre spectacle of rows of pre-revolution carriages, all preserved in perfect condition. My room key was of centuries-old iron and at least six inches long. Its sheer weight must have ensured that no one ever took it away by mistake. As I turned it in the lock there was a huge clunk and the vast oak door creaked its way open. My window looked out over an extensive, modern and spotlessly clean swimming pool. The sight before me was a stunning blend of ancient and modern. The original

arched aqueduct went straight across the pool, which was punctuated by little islands decorated with old statues. The grounds consisted of beautiful gardens tended by an army of workers in sombreros and the only sound, apart from the water flapping its way across the aqueduct, was the occasional scraping of rakes on the paths and a chorus of exotic birdsong.

Outside the main gates there was a private field which we could use as a launch site for the balloons, along with outhouses for our equipment. There was a restaurant and bar beside the pool, while, for real gastronomes, nearby Cuernavaca offered the alternative of a first-class restaurant with peacocks strutting the lawns. To occupy our spare time there was tennis or waterskiing on Lake Tequesquitengo, just three kilometres away.

I was asked if I thought the location would suit our purposes. It was heaven. It was paradise. I said it would suit our purposes fine.

Then it was back to Mexico City and on to London. What a week. I felt triumphant. This was no wasted trip after all.

'We're in the movies, guys,' I announced to everyone in the office as I swept in. I wanted the Birdman and Ian Ashpole to be the other two stuntmen and they were more than a little curious about exactly what I had been plotting. I ran through the details and they were genuinely excited. When I came to describe our new home for the rehearsals Marc Wolff observed drily that he thought it was essential that the helicopter team should be there too. After all, the helicopter was very much part of the whole process. It wasn't long before he got Jack Wiener to agree. We would be quite a team.

Per Lindstrand manufactured six Cloudhopper envelopes – three for filming and three spares in case of damage. We redesigned the backpack, propane bottle and burner to look more sleek than the Smirnoff prototype and we set off to Elstree to give a demonstration.

Whenever a big day was imminent I would always get paranoid about the weather. In ballooning the weather decides between success and failure. Over the years I have generally been very lucky with the weather. Not on this occasion, though. The day was breezy without being dangerous. There was instability in the air, producing those nasty gusts which make balloons so difficult to control. To the uninitiated it was the kind of day that looked ideal – the sun was out and the air gently soothed the skin. The key people in the production team were all there to watch. I explained that the conditions were not ideal and we would require much stiller air to perform the stunt in Mexico. The reactions I got varied from expressions of concern to 'Here come the excuses'. After laying out the balloons we connected the harnesses attached to them in a long line leading to an anchor point on a truck. We inflated the balloons and the gusty conditions created a scene like a row of elevators going up and down with three lunatics in control. There was no synchronization and it looked a mess.

Everyone shuffled off to the production office while the balloon team packed the balloons away. I

Opposite I took my wife, Susie, back to Hacienda Vista Hermosa, our paradise retreat during the filming of *Green Ice*, some fifteen years later. **Below** *Tres amigos*. Flanked by Sean Byrne (left) and Ian Ashpole (right) before shooting a scene in the old bull ring at Hacienda Vista Hermosa.

95

I had to double for some guy in a cowboy hat for this scene.

went to see the production team to explain what the problem was. It was little more than a rerun of what I had said before. Colin Brewer spoke for everyone in the room when he said that they were very concerned about the safety. 'You are concerned about safety? You should be with me,' I replied pointedly. I went through my routine for a third time and simply suggested they trust me. They were not convinced and I left the room with Jack Wiener to help the others to lift the equipment back into our van. Jack wanted my assurance that he wasn't going to end up looking like a complete fucking idiot. I hoped not, but he had hired experts in a highly specialized business and he wouldn't want me to compromise safety, would he? He returned to the production office. When I arrived there half an hour later Jack had left, leaving Colin Brewer to pick up the pieces. 'What did you say to him?' he asked. 'He's apoplectic.' We had a rational conversation and I said I hoped we weren't going to be axed because of a lack of understanding about how these balloons could be used. Colin was supportive but he asked me sternly to choose my words carefully with his boss. 'He's excitable at the best of times and he has high blood pressure,' he said.

We were not fired and, as luck would have it, the production team had been given clear instructions to give us everything we needed to ensure the success of the pivotal scene in the movie. We left for Mexico in high spirits and very much looking forward to our sojourn in the desert hacienda. We were quite a party. Ian, the Birdman and I were to be the stunt pilots, Graham Elson (no relation to Andy Elson), one of our regular pilots in England, came along as a reserve in case of injury or illness. We had three further ground crew, including the indispensable Sean Byrne. On top of that were Marc Wolff and his helicopter engineer Steve North, Canadian aerial cameraman Ron Goodman and his girlfriend and assistant, Margaret Herron.

We settled in to our new home with the approbation of the entire party, who could scarcely believe we were afforded such luxury. From the first day we found that the winds tended to be a little breezy before dawn and then abated into calm after the sun came up. For this reason we adopted a routine of getting up at about three o'clock in the morning and flying off into the darkness to rehearse our routine. The rest of the day was a write-

Tense moments before a windy take-off scene at Hacienda Vista Hermosa. The Birdman is helping me with my pre-flight checks.

off, owing to thermic gusts producing aggressive turbulence. This was to be the pattern for the next weeks as we got used to synchronized flying, linked together by ropes. Marc and Ron shot trial footage, which was dispatched to Los Angeles for processing. Messages of congratulations were quick to come back. It looked fantastic. Extraordinary, even. It was highly likely that a considerable amount of our test footage would end up being used in the film.

After 7 am the rest of the day was free time. There was nothing useful that could be done from breakfast onwards. We played tennis, swam in the pool and some of us went waterskiing in the afternoons. English pounds and American dollars went a long way and it was easily affordable to block-book the tuition services of the previous Mexican waterskiing champion, Eduardo López, known to everyone as Molacho. We employed him every afternoon for the duration of our visit.

On the evening of the fourth day I was chatting to Marc by the pool about the deal concerning the helicopter which he had picked up from Texas and flown down the week before. We were beginning to form the idea of setting up in partnership. We enjoyed working together and it was apparent that we could form a network of people, equipment and expertise which we could supply as an alternative to Marc's own services when he was not available. It also came out in conversation that in this particular instance the helicopter company was going to make a great deal of money because their charges were based on a minimum of three hours' flying per day. We were only using up an hour.

What if we attached a line to the cargo hook and went waterskiing? I asked. It was an outrageous suggestion and Marc laughed. But slowly, the more he thought about it the more he came round to the idea. With all the unused helicopter hours it would not cost

Unconventional waterskiing with Marc on the Laguna de Tequesquitengo, southern Mexico.

97

The awesome sight of Citibank in Mexico City's Reforma. We were to take off from the roof and land back there in darkness.

the production a penny and it would be enormous fun. After breakfast the next day Marc asked Ron and Margaret if they could de-rig the vast gyrostabilized camera system from the helicopter. They were not waterskiers and they weren't amused. However, Marc insisted and got his way. And so we went waterskiing – with a difference.

Our two weeks in paradise passed like a dream and we were soon back in Mexico City for the big stunt. The day before filming I took the team to the top of Citibank. Everyone went quiet as they looked across the crowded city, crisscrossed with electric cables as far as the eye could see. If anything went wrong and the balloons broke their moorings a safe landing would be difficult if not virtually impossible. The space on top was tight, and looking straight down the side of that towering building was at best disconcerting. 'What exactly did you say we could do?' Ian wanted to be reminded.

We had two days off while other filming took place on the roof of Citibank. Most of the team rested or went sightseeing. Sean started flirting with an attractive Mexican girl called Dianna at the Holiday Inn. (He was later to marry her.) Marc and I were summoned to a heads of department meeting to discuss the next phase of filming. Most of the discussion revolved around actors. Someone had to play the helicopter pilot for the scene of the delivery of a shipment of emeralds to the roof of the building. Marc could play the part himself, someone suggested. Patrick Clayton, the new assistant director, agreed but insisted he would have to shave off his beard. A lively discussion ensued while Marc and I got an uncontrollable attack of the giggles. No one had even asked him if he was prepared to do it. 'Why should he shave his beard off?' asked Jack Wiener. 'Because helicopter pilots don't wear beards,' reasoned Patrick. 'What do you mean, helicopter pilots don't wear beards? He *is* a helicopter pilot.' Jack was now almost shouting in exasperation. I suggested that Marc had shaved off his beard for films before and I was sure that if there was any doubt he would be pleased to do so again. I got a very dirty look in return. After another round of ridiculous dialogue Marc had the part and so did his beard.

We next discussed a scene where a security guard would receive the emeralds, which were to be lowered from the helicopter before the robbery sequence. The guard would then transport them to the hatch in the roof. Marc seized his opportunity for revenge at me for having tried to have his beard outlawed. He insisted that whoever was cast for the part of the security guard must be familiar with helicopters and conversant with the procedures of being around them. Before anyone could comment he had recommended me. Jack asked if I had done any acting, but before I could get a word in edgeways Marc was in full flow. He regaled the meeting with tales of my Oscar-quality performance as Mr Fanta the year before. 'OK,' Jack agreed, 'he gets the part.' I was never even asked if I was prepared to do it.

When I went to make-up the following morning I didn't know that Marc had got up early to be there first. After I had been attended to, I looked in horror at how little of my fashionable long hair was left on my head. The wardrobe manager explained that she had been told I had to have a very short cut to fit under the tight cap I was to wear. I knew immediately who was behind this prank and the perpetrator practically died laughing when I emerged from the parlour, looking sad. He had lined up the whole team to witness his triumph.

The first scheduled night shoot arrived and it called for only one Cloudhopper. I volunteered to do the stunt on the basis that I could hardly ask anyone else to if I was not prepared to undertake it myself. I was winched into the darkness on a long line from the skyscraper. It was hairy enough in the moderate breeze for me to realize I would not be looking forward to the big scene with all three of us involved.

The next night it was blowing a gale, which was unusual for May in Mexico during the hours of darkness. It was clearly impossible to do anything. The following night the wind was still there and Jack Wiener's blood pressure started to rise again. He took me to one side and said that if the next two days were the same, budgetary pressures would force him to fake the whole scene with models. 'They're cheaper and they don't answer back,' he said pointedly. There was not much I could say.

The next day came and Ian Ashpole had gone down with a horrendous bout of Mexican tummy. Montezuma's revenge, they called it. There was no way he could fly, so Graham Elson took his place as the third pilot. He would be the first to be launched on the line from the building. We arrived as usual at twilight and I was relieved that Jack would not be present for this session. The wind had abated and although it was by no means calm I had the feeling that it was now or never. As is so often the case with tricky and dangerous stunts, the tension tended to make the film crew witnessing the event even more frightened than the participants. I went into a huddle with the Birdman and Graham and we agreed we would go for it. Marc and Ron arrived in the helicopter and held off from the building as we got ready to go. The balloons were inflated and one by one we were winched out on the yellow Kevlar line. The pilot light for the burner was so unreliable that we had to keep puffing short flames into the balloons to make sure there

99

On Citibank's roof. I'm the security guard nearest to camera on the terrace while Omar Sharif comes down the steps, hanging on to the banister for dear life.

'What was it you told them we could do?' The Birdman looks on as I prepare to launch off from the roof.

was a permanent flame going. If any one of the pilot lights were to go out it would spell disaster, not just for the human pilot with the problem but also for the other two, who would be dragged down with him.

We floated about 100 yards from the building and I kept signalling to stop the winch. We were quite far enough out, but my radio was not functioning. My right arm was constricted by a very tight harness. I was already getting cramp and I couldn't get the winchmen to understand, even though I was frantically waving my arms. The Birdman and Graham were behind me at gaps of fifty feet, although I couldn't see either of them. While the Birdman was under control, what I didn't realize was that Graham was most definitely not. Like me, his radio was malfunctioning. But much worse than this, the gusting wind was blowing the burner flame on to the lines which were holding him up. One by one each line was burning through, to break with a loud ping. It was a desperate situation – Graham had just a few minutes before he would drop thirty-two storeys to certain death. He yelled as loud as his lungs could manage and amid the roar of the burners the Birdman heard his cries. Turning his head, he immediately spotted the problem. 'Bring us in – *quick!*' he shouted into his radio. Immediately I felt a jolt and then the surge as we started our slow haul back to safety. As I got back to the rooftop everyone rushed to grab me. 'Get the others!' I screamed as I hauled on the line to deflate my balloon.

Graham just made it back with only a single cluster of lines holding him up from one side of the balloon. Everyone heaved a huge sigh of relief. It had been that close. I radioed Marc in the helicopter. 'Did you get any usable footage?' I asked nervously. 'Yeah. I think we got the lot,' he replied with his usual calm. We all prayed we would never have to do any part of the sequence again.

We got to bed at 3 am. I didn't sleep. The sheer closeness to disaster just rippled through my brain. I got up early and wandered down to the lobby. The Birdman and

Graham were both there already. 'Did you sleep at all?' I asked. 'Nope,' the Birdman volunteered. 'Only for a brief nightmare,' said Graham.

At breakfast Vic Armstrong, the movie's stunt coordinator, told me that Jack Wiener wanted to see me in his office. 'He's a happy man. Well done,' he said.

Just before we packed up and left Mexico Marc told me of a coincidence so extraordinary that I thought he was joking. James Garrett & Partners had called him up about a commercial they wanted to shoot for the housebuilders Barratt the following month in England. 'Do you think it would be possible to tow a waterskier behind a helicopter?' he had been asked. 'Not only is it possible,' he replied, 'but I've got just the man to do it for you.' I suddenly had a new career as a stunt waterskier. Almost as soon as we landed in London we went to a production meeting together and the deal was done.

For two days I was hauled around the lake at Standlake, Oxfordshire, to slide up high ramps and perform jumps off the top. Over the coming years I was to go on to do a number of waterskiing assignments as I had somehow got logged into the database of film production companies as 'stunt waterskier'.

'And they call this working,' I said to Marc. There can't be many people who get paid to indulge in *both* their favourite hobbies – especially when they are as different as waterskiing and ballooning.

Above The Birdman and me, with Ian below us, taking advantage of the pre-dawn breezes to rehearse our routines for *Green Ice*.

Below Tray peculiar. In this later stunt I was dressed as Manuel the waiter for an advertising packshot.

CHAPTER EIGHT

FROGS, BEARS AND BANDITS

B ALLOONS WERE BECOMING FASHIONABLE IN FILMS. Scripts with balloon sequences started to come thick and fast, and I was becoming a bit of an expert. At least that was the impression I seemed to be creating. I had a track record and film-makers hate taking chances with untried people in case it all goes wrong and very expensive sequences have to be repeated. In 1980 the film business was still a small industry in Britain and on the whole everyone talked to everyone else. We had had something of a triumph with *Green Ice* even though the movie was to bomb. I wasn't about to let anyone else in on what I was already regarding jealously as my patch.

While I was concentrating on movies, Tessa was doing a wonderful job of babysitting the mainstream promotional business. In fact she was so bloody good I decided to make her managing director. This had two advantages. It made her happy and it gave me an excuse to go and play. She was just twenty-seven and had joined as my secretary just three years before. The *Sunday Times* did a big feature on her and the clients were impressed.

In December 1980 I got a call from Coca-Cola in New York. They wanted Mr Fanta back to do some more commercials in Brazil and I would be receiving the scripts in the next few days. My face had been visible throughout the previous commercials for Fanta and I therefore was Mr Fanta. Consequently I reckoned they would have to use me again. This time, in place of David Fanthorpe as producer and Richard Loncraine as director, I was to meet two Americans by the names of Rosen and Isaacson. At the same time Jim Henson had penned in a balloon for the opening sequence of the sequel to his hugely successful Muppet movie. It was to be called *The Great Muppet Caper*.

As soon as I heard this news I was on the phone like lightning and legged it to Elstree Studios even faster. I met the production designer, who showed me his carefully crafted storyboards, which depicted Kermit the Frog, Fozzie Bear and Gonzo in a balloon. When I enquired what kind of animal Gonzo was I was firmly told by someone at the next drawing desk that he was officially a 'whatever'. The three animals (or whatevers) are

Previous spread A poster
for *The Great Muppet
Caper*, signed at the top
and sent to me by Jim
Henson as a thank you.
Right Gonzo, Fozzie Bear
and Kermit the Frog take
to the air.

flying along in the sky when all the opening credits come up beside them. Needless to say
they start making jokes about the names and titles as they come up. 'What does B.S.C.
stand for?' asks the bear as Oswald Morris, the director of photography's name, is
emblazoned across the sky. 'I dunno,' says the frog. 'No one reads those names anyway,
do they?' asks Fozzie. 'Sure. They all have families,' replies Kermit. In the meantime the
whatever, Gonzo, with his pop eyes and hooked nose, contents himself with speculating
on how long he could plummet before he blacked out. 'Don't even think about it,'
commands Kermit. 'We need you for the movie.'

The first thing I was asked was if my company could make a balloon to look like the one they had drawn up for the storyboards. It was to be a standard-shaped balloon in pretty colours. It had to be miniature to carry models of the puppets and capable of being pulled across the stage by thin wires which the camera would not see. This was a doddle and nothing was going to stop me making absolutely sure we got this high-profile work. In any case I relished the thought of amusing myself for a few days on set with a bunch of jolly puppeteers. I returned to the office to talk to Per Lindstrand on the phone. He was able to manufacture the balloon, together with a spare one, in the time I had promised. I then set about working out how to create the sequence for real rather than by the use of special effects. I believed we could actually fly this miniature hot-air balloon in the sky by remote control. We worked out that I would sit in the front seat of a following helicopter and switch the balloon's burners on and off by a radio signal. I relayed the message through the Muppets art department that we had come up with an idea which had never been done before.

I spent a nervous couple of days wondering if I should chase up my proposal to see how it was being received. I was paranoid that the word might get out to every balloonist in America and Britain, amateur and professional, who would soon be bombarding the studio with calls claiming to be the world authority on miniature hot-air balloons and promising the earth. The Muppets were big news and everyone would want to be associated with them. I finally got a call saying that Jim Henson and Frank Oz had seen my proposals and were asking when could I get my arse around there to see them.

'What happens if we're blown out to sea, Kermit?'

I assured the caller that my arse could be over there as soon as they wanted.

Jim Henson was a delightful, witty, intelligent man who was the voice of Kermit. He and his wife Jane had spent years since their student days together refining their act, which was to make them, and their partner Frank Oz, many millions of dollars.

I was immediately at ease with Jim and Frank, who clearly thought the idea of a real hot-air balloon to fly their babies would be enormous fun. We started to go through the mechanics and however serious I tried to be they were intent on showing that this was going to be a light-hearted project, and they cracked jokes incessantly. They did, after all, run a phenomenally successful laughter factory for kids and seriousness was the last thing anyone needed.

I was then introduced to a zany-looking bearded man seated at the end of the table, who was fidgeting coquettishly in his enthusiasm to be brought into the conversation. 'This is Faz Fazakas,' said Kermit in disguise, upright and also bearded at the end of the table. Every time Jim Henson spoke it was the New Mexico twang of American English, which *was* the voice of the frog. No one can be called Faz Fazakas, I thought. But he was. 'Faz is our robot expert,' Jim told me.

It surprised me to hear that there was normally only one hand puppet (plus occasionally a spare for the principal characters) for each of the Muppets. Consequently

Fozzie Bear, Frank Oz (the voice of the bear) and Jim Henson (the voice of the frog) rehearse their lines before getting airborne.

106

they were carefully guarded and looked after. Generally the puppeteers would be hidden under a table or behind a screen in the normal way while their hand, with puppet, protruded into the picture. From their hiding place they could watch their own action on a television monitor. Occasionally this method of puppeteering did not work.

This is where Faz came in. He had a number of metal skeleton structures with motorized joints and a radio control device. He would cover the structure with a puppet and use radio signals to operate its movements. In this way the mouth could be opened and shut for talking, and the head could be turned to left or right and made to nod up and down. Our three little heroes in their own tiny balloon would appear to be moving their heads and talking as they flew across the sky.

Things seemed to be moving a bit quickly. I now had to deal with three perfectly functioning robots. I pointed out that the balloon would go its own way with the wind and I thought it would be near impossible to radio-control the puppets from the distances it would inevitably be flying away from me as their controller. 'We've thought of that,' Jim said. 'We're all coming with you in the helicopter.' To which Frank added, 'You didn't think we were going to let you have all the fun, did you?'

They had made up their minds they were really going to enjoy this sequence. The entire movie, with the exception of this scene, had been shot on a large stage at Elstree, so this was to be the first time after months of filming that they would be allowing themselves out to get some fresh air. I pointed out a small difficulty. If there was to be a pilot, me and three of them on board the helicopter there was no room for a cameraman. 'Well, we'll have to have a second helicopter then,' was the quick and very obvious reply. 'Of course,' I said. I couldn't wait to get back to see Marc Wolff's face. He had roared with laughter when I had told him that I had actually got him work as the helicopter pilot in a film featuring the Muppets. Just wait until I tell him that there are now *two* helicopters, I thought.

My next question was, when and where did they want to shoot? My worst fear was quickly confirmed. The shoot dates clashed with my provisional Mr Fanta commercial. This was bad news – I would have to investigate whether the New York production company had confirmed or not. When I came to the question of where to film the Muppet balloon I suggested a piece of open countryside outside air-traffic-controlled airspace about seventy miles west of London. 'We want to shoot in Albuquerque, New Mexico,' said Jim.

I couldn't for the life of me see why on earth we had to go to New Mexico when practically the entire sequence was to be shot against blue sky. The only cutaway from this was when the balloon is seen crashing into a street, which had been built as a film set in the studio. However, I was certainly not about to argue. 'Fine,' I said.

After a few conversations with New York I managed to persuade the Fanta producer that the Birdman could take my place for the first three days of shooting until I could arrive in Brazil, fresh from shooting with the Muppets. Everything was set.

A small administrative problem arose about who would be paying for which part of my air tickets. I first had to go to Albuquerque and then on to Brazil for Fanta, but I would not be returning to England between the shoots. The Muppets were planning to

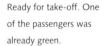
Ready for take-off. One of the passengers was already green.

send me first class – something I had never done before and have never done since. They saw the problem and simply agreed to pay the cost of a first-class return ticket to New Mexico. The New York production company then agreed to make a similar arrangement based on a business-class ticket from London to São Paulo and back. Even this was quite generous, as many production companies would send you as cargo if they thought they could get away with it. I worked out that I could fly first class to New Mexico and then first class to São Paulo. From there I would indulge in an ambition I never thought I would realize by flying Air France Concorde from Rio back to Paris before connecting to London. After all this I would still make a handsome profit on the money the two companies were paying for my air travel. It all seemed too good to be true.

I began my luxurious journey by arriving so late at Heathrow that when I had passed passport control and arrived breathless at the TWA plane the boarding door was already shut. 'Mr Prescot?' came the inevitable rhetorical question. I waved my first-class ticket pathetically at the airline official with the helpless gesture of someone playing his last card before going bust. Meanwhile inside the aircraft my colleague Jo Whiffen, a fabric engineer and designer, was resiliently pleading with the cabin staff with such gusto that anyone would have thought there was a man overboard. To my great relief the combination of these two factors seemed eventually to persuade the airline

'Wouldn't it be neat if we
were struck by lightning?'

representatives to relent. They finally reopened the door and slid me inside. But my
pleasant anticipation of the most decadent trip of my life had now been shattered. My
calm was then further undermined by spontaneous applause from the first-class
passengers as I shuffled along the plane, red-faced with embarrassment, to be greeted by
the chief stewardess's clearly audible question above the din: 'What happened to you?' Jo
also wanted to know and I was forced to make my cringing explanation as every
passenger craned their neck to see what excuse I was offering.

When we changed planes at Chicago it was a relief to be accompanied by anonymous
and uninterested fellow passengers who had no inkling of my ignominious arrival at
Heathrow some ten hours earlier.

Ian Ashpole joined us in Albuquerque to make up the three-man team for the aerial
caper. I was now romantically unattached, as Toots had recently returned to America. It
was therefore a pleasant surprise that there were some very attractive people working on
the shoot. I seem to remember that both Marc Wolff and I had a high old time during
our week on location. It started with two overzealous Midwestern brunettes in cowboy
hats, one of whom was attracted to Marc's 'come to bed' eyes and the other to my
English accent. They persuaded us to accompany them into town one evening, the two
of them in the front of the car, us in the back. As we stopped at some traffic lights Marc

and I realized at the same time that we'd perhaps bitten off more than we could chew. We looked at each other, then simultaneously swung the back doors open and disappeared into the traffic without as much as a goodbye to our new friends. After that our luck got much better. The only thing I can console myself with about that week is that Marc behaved rather worse than I did.

The morning after I arrived I entered the large aircraft hangar to which the two Muppet balloons had been brought from the cargo depot. In the middle of the concrete floor there was a big table on which the inanimate, crossed-legged puppet of Kermit the Frog was sitting alone. I went up to look at it and practically jumped out of my skin as its head swivelled towards me and its mouth opened and said, 'Hi, are you the balloon man?'

My new friend Faz Fazakas had got his first robot operational. He was under the table when he had seen me coming. Delighted with his little coup, he laughed with a satisfied staccato. Later Marc's cameraman, Albert Werry, joined us and we were all ready to start shooting the next day.

And so we took to the skies with a basketful of puppets. Ian was the launch chief on the ground. With his usual cool professionalism he inflated the balloon and helped prepare the intrepid furry travellers. When everything was ready he would flick a switch on the burners so that they were ready to receive my radio-controlled commands from the helicopter. Squashed in behind me as planned were Jim Henson, Frank Oz and Dave Goelz – Kermit, Fozzie and Gonzo respectively. While the helicopter sat with rotors running and ready to take off, I pushed my little button to give two puffs of flame to the balloon and it was airborne.

It soon became apparent that it wasn't going to be at all easy to fly it level. Normally when I am flying a balloon as pilot in the basket I have a horizon for reference. However, as the helicopter rose to follow the balloon the illusion was created that the balloon was level simply because the two aircraft were climbing together at the same rate. I talked to Marc on the intercom to get him to tell me what rates of climb or descent were indicated on his instruments and I started playing the equivalent of three-dimensional chess in the sky. In the meantime I was trying to ignore the ludicrous conversation going on behind me. Our three passengers had taken on the personas of the characters they were mimicking and as I looked at the balloon I could see the three puppets moving to their remote commands as they continued their hilarious chit-chat.

Fozzie: 'Gee, a lot of people worked on this movie.'
Kermit: 'This is nothing, wait till you see the end credits.'
Fozzie: 'Nice title.'
Fozzie (again): 'What happens if we're struck by lightning?'
Gonzo: 'That'd be neat.'

When we heard over the radio from Albert in the filming helicopter that he was reloading film it still did not stop the puppeteers from continuing their banter while they awaited the next call for action. They then began to speculate about what the catering truck was preparing for lunch. Gonzo fancied rice pudding, Fozzie whitebait (off the bone) while Kermit was anticipating a snog with Miss Piggy, who would be pleased to see him back safe and sound.

Suddenly, owing to a momentary lapse of concentration, we were climbing faster than we should have been. I had overheated the balloon. The top of the envelope melted at about 2000 feet and a large tongue of fabric flapped out of the top. 'Oh my God,' I exclaimed. The chatter in the back seat came to an abrupt halt. From the gravity in my voice Frank thought we were about to crash – something he reminded me about for several days afterwards. Fortunately it was only their make-believe counterparts who were about to crash. The balloon went into a sharp descent, burners blasting in an attempt to slow the speed downwards, pursued by us in the helicopter. I relayed the message to the ground that we had a problem and I could soon see the pickup truck haring across the scrub-covered desert, stirring vast clouds of dust as it sped towards the likely crash site. Just before impact I switched off the burners and watched as the stricken craft piled into the sand.

We jumped out of the helicopter and joined Ian and Jo, who had already inspected the damage. The envelope was, temporarily at least, a write-off, so we were glad that we had asked Per to build a second one. The more serious situation concerned Fozzie. 'You've burned my bear,' said Frank painfully. Indeed I had. 'I am really sorry. Do you have another one?' I asked weakly.

'Do I have another one? Do I have another one?' he repeated unnecessarily. 'This *is* the bear. This *is* Fozzie.' The sad, poorly puppet was immediately rushed to hospital, in the form of the sewing room, for repair. It took almost a whole day to complete the painstaking task of grafting on new fur without detracting from the character of Fozzie, who had survived both movies and countless television shows. Then we were ready to go again, but it was clear I would have to retain the utmost concentration to complete the filming without further disasters.

The apparently nice, easy jobs I have taken on over the years have rarely turned out to be so. This was a classic example of how a simple task can bite you the moment you get complacent.

Quite apart from the generous first-class travel we had been allocated we had by now also been given an equally generous per diem, or eating and laundry allowance, for nine days. Marc, Ian, Jo and I had managed to save most of it and on the penultimate evening we all resolved to go with a few other friends to the plushest place in town for dinner. We had been told about this by some local dignitaries who had come to see the filming. They advised us it was a forty-minute taxi ride away. As we entered the restaurant we saw Jim Henson at a table on the far side. I waved at him and he waved back. We then tucked into an extravagant meal washed down by fine champagne and wine. By the time we had finished our meal Jim and his party had already left. I asked for our bill but the head waiter said it had already been settled by the gentleman from the table on the other side of the room.

I have never forgotten that gesture. Jim was a wonderful, generous and hugely witty man. We had enormous fun on that film both at Elstree and in the New Mexican desert. It was therefore with great sadness that I heard, a few years later, that he had suddenly taken ill and died. He was just fifty-two. Frank Oz went on to become a successful film director in his own right, while Dave Goelz and his girlfriend were to visit us when they were in England, and they even got a real balloon flight over the Hertfordshire countryside. The following year I was invited to see the puppet masters in action again – this time on the film set of their next, more macabre movie, *The Dark Crystal*. Afterwards we had a splendid reunion lunch.

Anyway, to continue my story, armed with my first-class ticket for the next leg of my journey I hurried off to São Paulo via Los Angeles. A limousine met me and transferred me straight to the stifling heat of the Fanta location near Parati, which is on the coast midway between São Paulo and Rio de Janeiro. The Birdman was there with Sean Byrne and they looked tired and hot. Robin immediately regaled me with the story of how he had landed in a hornets' nest and proceeded to show me the most horrendous array of red-raw stings. Nevertheless, he seemed undaunted by the experience. More than that, the producers were very happy with Robin, who had done an excellent job as well as making them all laugh. And as they no longer cared that he didn't look like the original Mr Fanta, there was really no need for me to stay.

There was just about time to get to Rio that evening to catch Concorde to Paris, an experience I had been looking forward to. I had been in the taxi that was taking me to the airport for two hours when we bumped to a halt in a cloud of smoke on the hard shoulder of the highway. It was approaching dusk, and after my driver's head had disappeared for a few minutes under the bonnet, spluttering unintelligible expletives in Portuguese, it emerged shaking in resigned perplexity. After casting his eye around the area and trying to make me understand what I never did understand, the man simply said goodbye. The last I saw of him was his silhouetted shape clambering over a hedge some two fields away as he dissolved into the fading horizon.

This was dangerous country and I knew it. On one side of the highway were shaded and forbidding tree-clad mountains where I imagined bandits lurked with guns, willing to kill for a few cruzeiros. And there was I in my pleated fawn trousers and tailored shirt accompanied by a large holdall and a somewhat new-looking briefcase. I would stick out like a sore thumb. It was getting dark, I was all alone and I was frightened. I found myself rehearsing what I would say to approaching foes. A long time ago I had seen a television programme about a white man confronted by cannibals. He came out with something like: 'Hello. I'm from the BBC.' Whether it did him any good or not, I couldn't remember. I tried to pull myself together, wishing I was in Chiswick.

As the dark darkened further I tried in vain to thumb a lift from the occasional passing headlights. As each car whooshed past and into the distance I would wait in the terrifying silence that followed for the faint sound of another approaching. I was starting to wonder where I could hide for the night when another car came past. This time it overshot me by fifty yards, stopped and reversed. The driver wound down his window to reveal two astonished unshaven men in the front two seats.

'Rio.' It was all I could think of to say. Without a word of Portuguese in my repertoire, it seemed futile to even try to mime how I came to be there. A great deal of consultation followed while I looked nervously around. '*Americano*?' the passenger asked. I wondered what I ought to be. '*Inglés*,' I said. I must have looked a caricature of Britishness anyway with a 'Bond Street lunch box' attached to my wrist. I was gestured into the back, an invitation I accepted nervously, having little choice in the matter.

My clammy hands and dry throat reminded me how apprehensive I felt about my rescuers. There was little conversation as we spluttered our way down the highway and I wondered where I would be taken. As we approached the outskirts of Rio and the first signs of civilization, I was becoming a little more relaxed. Then came the extraordinary question from the front: '*Aeroporto*?' '*Sí*,' I said, incredulous. And that is where we went. My saviours refused to take any money, but simply dropped me off at Departures. With a wave and a smile they were gone.

My huge relief must have shown when I arrived at the check-in counter. I had missed Concorde, which had left an hour ago, but I couldn't care less. I was pleased to be alive. There was a British Caledonian flight leaving for Gatwick a couple of hours later. 'Perfect,' I said, 'I'll take a first-class ticket,' flashing my credit card. The man apologized and explained that they could only take a certain amount on that credit card without checking with London, which was presently asleep. In the end I bought an ordinary ticket and travelled at the back of the aircraft, cramped but happy.

It had been a strange couple of weeks. As the plane thundered down the runway I reflected that no one would believe my tales of frogs, bears and bandits.

CHAPTER NINE

'HOW SWEET TO BE A CLOUD'

I N THE LATE SUMMER OF 1982 I was sitting in my office, musing about what to do next. 'I've got an idea,' I told my colleagues. This was always a signal for groans and a chorus of 'Oh no…'

There was a peak-time national TV show that went out on Saturday nights to a huge audience. It was called *Game for a Laugh*, which was an apt description of the participants, who engaged in a wide variety of nonsense. I contacted the producer and asked him if he would like a real-life re-enactment of a celebrated aviator bear. A. A. Milne's creation Winnie the Pooh, as depicted by the book's illustrator E. H. Shepard, had famously risen into the sky by balloon, holding on to the string with a single paw. His purpose was to collect the honey from the bees in the tree tops. Even though the producer of the television show was understandably sceptical, he agreed to see me. When I finished my presentation he loved the idea but said he couldn't possibly afford the cost. 'Leave it to me. I'll find a sponsor,' I told him.

It was not long before I got a follow-up call from the producer, promising that if I really could get a sponsor he would like to feature the stunt on their special show scheduled for the evening of Christmas Day. Armed with this great news, I persuaded the department store Debenhams that it would be a wonderful way to promote their post-Christmas sale. I was soon able to report back to the producer that I had secured funds to stage the stunt.

Winnie the Pooh came from the Ashdown Forest in East Sussex, where A. A. Milne was brought up. On the top of a hill near Colemans Hatch is Hundred Acre Wood, which is

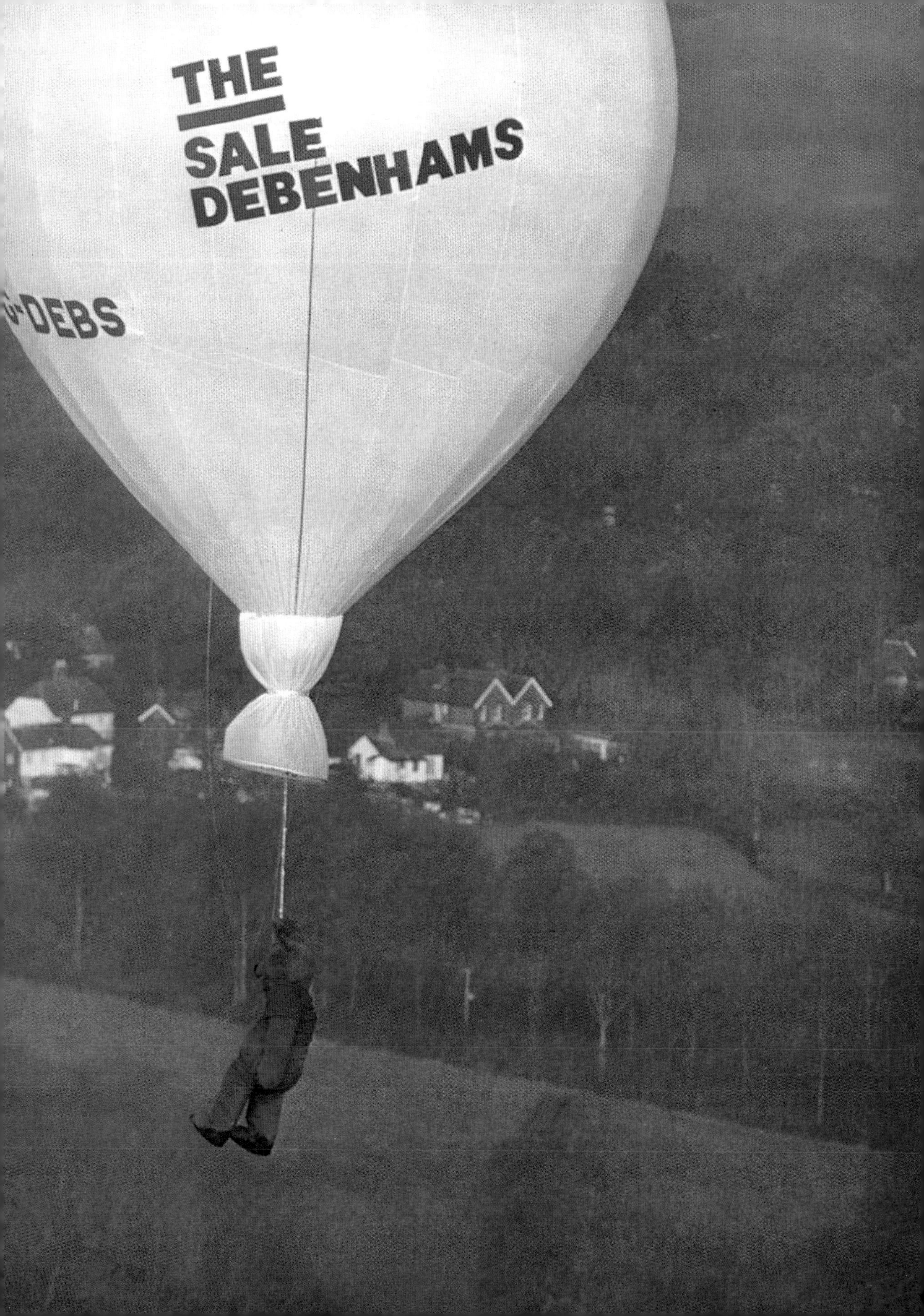
THE
SALE
DEBENHAMS
G-DEBS

Previous spread On prime-time television, Christmas Day 1982, my muddy feet betray an unscheduled intermediate landing in a bog.
Above left 'Hello, Pooh. What'yer going to do?'
Above right 'I must say, he's a pretty plucky little aviator bear.'

114

featured in the children's stories. Down a long, muddy track off the road to Hartfield is Pooh Sticks Bridge, still straddling a stream to this day. Beside it lies an open field which belonged to Gareth Johnson, who could normally be found propping up the bar in a nearby olde-worlde pub called The Hatch. His pewter pint mug was kept permanently on a hook above his favourite position at the bar. I was assured by a local farmer that I would find Mr Johnson there at lunchtime. Sure enough, he was. I introduced myself and explained my mission to this pig farmer, who peered at me with suspicious eyes. When he heard the word 'television' his ears pricked up as he started to smell money. He mumbled his exorbitant fee through a gulp of beer. I told him we could afford only ten per cent of that amount and he nearly grabbed my arm off.

Per Lindstrand built me a tiny gas balloon and a theatrical outfitter got to work on my bear suit, which had to be well padded in case I had to crash-land. It also had to be big enough to enclose a steel harness, within which there would be a false right arm leading to the rope hanging under the balloon. I would have two legs and one arm in the appropriate parts of the costume while my right arm would be kept inside the suit. Strapped around my waist would be a series of bags of sand. Whenever I wanted to climb I would grab handfuls of the stuff with my right hand and throw it out through an elasticated slit in Pooh's tummy. Higher up the bear's anatomy the nose was made of fine, black-painted mesh. This was at the same level as my eyes, so my vision was very limited.

I had two further problems to solve before I could re-create the story of the honey-gathering bear. First, I had to get the permission of Keith Bales, boss of the Disney Organization in Britain, which owned the rights to the character. I went to see him in his ridiculously oversized office in Soho Square. He gave the project his blessing as though it was some run-of-the-mill merchandising deal. I never saw him smile and as I left I wondered if he had really understood what I was going to do.

The other problem was more tricky. My pilot's licence was for hot-air balloons whereas this was a gas-filled balloon, to fly which the law said I required a separate qualification. I had never set foot in a gas balloon, let alone had any training as a pilot. The Civil Aviation Authority insisted that I must have the appropriate licence before I became Winnie the Pooh. I set off for its headquarters in London's Kingsway to argue my case. It seemed reasonable to imagine that the civil servants would take a dim view of such frivolity and even consider that I was simply wasting their time. However, the organization had always been ready to listen to the requests, however daft, of the Hot Air Balloon Company, provided we could convince them that our stunts could be done professionally and safely without endangering the public. Put more bluntly, their policy was that any pilot could go

and kill himself in any way he liked as far as they were concerned – as long as he did not endanger anyone else. The meeting started well and they saw the funny side of it all. Having argued my case, I was politely told that they could sanction only a gas-balloon pilot to fly the aircraft. They volunteered a list of two or three qualified candidates.

I was absolutely not going to allow anyone else to fly my bear. I pointed out that no gas pilot in the world had any experience of flying suspended in a harness and that my record as a test pilot of the Cloudhopper was far more appropriate. How I persuaded the men in suits to give me a special exemption from the rules of the Air Navigation Order I shall never know. Provided the country's only authorized gas-balloon examiner was present, I would be allowed to make a single solo flight. Wing Commander Gerry Turnbull (another member of the Nine Finger Club) was a tad crusty about my plans but to my great relief he eventually accepted my invitation to attend the launch of my idiotic stunt.

I went to Per Lindstrand's factory in Oswestry, Shropshire, to check over the balloon. The first thing I saw as I arrived was our Swiss friend Hans Büker's fire engine. He was clearly camping at the factory because an electricity cable and a water hose led from the premises into the back doors of the ancient vehicle. Hans was awaiting completion of his new balloon and the wait was going to be a few days. His presence was a stroke of luck. He was an experienced gas balloonist and he was more than happy to accept my invitation to try out my new toy. We rigged him a seat and harness and attached it to my tiny gas-filled balloon. Then we threw him into the sky. He disappeared over the horizon and we didn't see him again for seven hours. We assumed he had gone for a good long flight for the sheer fun of it. However, the valve had been far too small to let the helium escape from the balloon at anything like a fast enough rate. The result was that it had taken him many hours, and some fifty miles south-eastwards, to find a space big enough to stop the balloon and deflate it. I was profusely grateful to Hans for his pains and for discovering the problem before my big day. Two new huge valves were installed so that there would be no repetition of the flaw in the design.

In October we waited for a settled high-pressure system to move across southern England and then set off for the Ashdown Forest. We hauled the helium cylinders out of the disused pigsty where they had been stored. The balloon was soon spread out on a tarpaulin, to protect it from the frosty ground.

The television script was considered funny enough for London Weekend Television to send two of their presenters, Matthew Kelly and Sarah Kennedy. The pair arrived in a sparkling vintage Alvis saloon with lashings of ginger beer in the boot. A large contingent of cameramen and technicians trailed behind. Marc Wolff flew in by helicopter to provide the

Above left 'Let's follow him.' 'What a spiffing idea.'
Above right 'He's done it. Good old Pooh.'

115

air-to-air filming facility. As he looked over the inflated balloon and limp bear suit spread across the ground he gave me a studied look. 'Are you seriously going to fly this thing?' he asked. 'Of course,' I replied, whereupon he just started laughing uncontrollably. He had not quite appreciated the utter absurdity of it all until it was right in front of his eyes.

Wing Commander Turnbull was less amused. Someone remarked that he could perhaps play the part of Eeyore, which amused him even less. Gerry Turnbull didn't like what he saw and was looking gloomy. Without his permission I could not take off. I went to the side of the field with him and we had a serious discussion about what I wanted to do. He wasn't at all convinced. 'You have virtually no vision,' he complained. 'I can take the whole head off for the landing,' I countered. He called everyone together and addressed us from the top of a mound of earth. 'I will allow Mr Prescot to take off but he will have to fly at low level and immediately land on the other side of the trees. I cannot give permission for an extended flight. You will have to get your film done in the short time available.' The look on everyone's face said, 'This is a total waste of time...' I was immediately pulled to one side by the programme producer. It was easy to anticipate his complaints about fiascos and false pretences, but I could not have foreseen this problem. Nor was it in my control. However, I was sure that I would find it difficult or even impossible to land as quickly as the examiner wanted – after all I would only just be settled into flight. I winked at the producer and cheekily conveyed the message that once airborne *I* would be the one who would decide what was practical and safe, not Gerry Turnbull.

So off I went. I floated to the tops of the trees and ever upwards, followed by the helicopter. I kicked my legs and waved my free arm like mad to create the drama that I knew the director wanted. Anyone watching the film with a sharp eye might have noticed that I was holding a small radio at the end of my furred left paw. This was because I had to rely on Marc to tell me where I was going. I could hardly see a thing. I put the radio in front of the bear's nose and screamed like hell through the grille, 'Am I going up or down?' 'Rising slowly at 2000 feet,' came back the reply.

Wow. I had no idea I was so high. No bees up here, I thought, recalling Milne's poem:

> *How sweet to be a Cloud*
> *Floating in the Blue!*
> *Every little cloud*
> *Always sings aloud.*

> *How sweet to be a Cloud*
> *Floating in the Blue!*
> *It makes him very proud*
> *To be a little cloud.*

I groped around with my free arm to find the line which released the gas from the balloon. 'What's happening now?' I shouted. 'Descending,' said Marc with masterly understatement. My right fist tossed out handfuls of sand through Pooh's tummy and I stabilized. The one-hour flight, accompanied by the Walt Disney theme music and Sir Peter Ustinov's narration, would later provide some hilarious television.

As I descended for a gentle landing in a field beside some trees, little did I know that a beautiful girl called Susie lived in the farm at the top of the hill, which looked across the valley to Six Pines, immortalized in *Winnie the Pooh*. I was to fall in love with her five years later.

Hillside Farm looks across an East Sussex valley to Six Pines and Hundred Acre Wood. Little did I know that a beautiful girl lived there. I returned six years later to marry her.

However, there was to be a wedding before that. My first marriage was to Helen Buck on 16 April 1983, a few months after the Winnie the Pooh flight. Helen was a pretty blonde with a kind heart and a rather nervy disposition. She was known to all her friends by the unlikely name of Bucket. I had been introduced to her by Guy Bigland the previous summer and we got hitched at her parents' home in Essex. Three hundred guests had been invited and the reception consisted of wall-to-wall aunties in a vast marquee. Guy made what was universally described by those present as the best best man's speech ever. It was not flattering. My only talent, the guests were told, was persuading people to do things they had already made up their minds they didn't want to do. Marc Wolff's wedding present was to whisk Bucket and me away in a helicopter after putting on a death-defying James Bond-style show to the assembled guests.

Bucket had spent many years teaching people to cook at the Prue Leith and Cordon Bleu schools of cooking. My new life was therefore to include a daily diet of superb cuisine. We honeymooned in the Cayman Islands, where we dined divinely at the Grand Old House restaurant, waterskied and learned to scuba-dive.

As soon as I returned from the Caribbean paradise Marc was after me. He had a business opportunity that he thought we should invest in.

The Canadian aerial cameraman Ron Goodman, who had worked with Marc on several movies, including *Green Ice* , was falling out with the Swiss owners of the camera-stabilizing system he used. The equipment in question, known as an X-Mount, was remote-controlled, gyrostabilized and definitely state of the art. It was immensely complex but produced steadier helicopter shots – helicopters shake like hell in all three axes of movement (pitch, yaw and roll) – than any other system in the world. The X-Mount was derived from a system developed by the US military in the sixties which had since been declassified and sold off. A huge ball-shaped housing, to give protection against the environment, incorporated a platform which held the camera and its zoom lens plus a magazine of 1000 feet of 35mm film. The platform was stabilized within the ball by three massive spinning gyros and electronic sensors. Whenever anything moved – for example, the film within the magazine or the lens zooming in and out – a counterweight automatically compensated for the displacement by travelling in the opposite direction.

117

Helicopter and gyrostabilized camera system on location in Thailand for *Cutthroat Island*, directed by Renny Harlin.

The whole set-up was on offer for a quarter of a million pounds and there were enough spare parts to create the start of a second system if we wanted to build one up in the future. This was big money to us, and it was money we did not have. In any case the very notion of such an expenditure went against the rather conservative culture we had created of never having any money at risk at all. However, Marc had just been to a pre-production meeting for a new movie to be called *Supergirl*, which was a variation of the highly successful formula on which the *Superman* series was based. The director wanted to use the X-Mount, and this could involve three months' shooting and possibly more. At a rental rate of $10,000 a week, the return on the investment would be both rapid and impressive. If we wanted to acquire the system we would have to move quickly, before the president of the Zermatt-based company which owned the equipment discovered there was a very substantial contract in the offing.

I hastily put a very simple business plan together and went to see Geoff Spencer, our bank manager at Coutts. Geoff was a nice guy who had come chasing our business in the early days. Having never had an overdraft, we had never been any trouble to him. Geoff was a trendy young banker and he took great delight in our business, even if he did perhaps sometimes wonder if it was all too good to be true. He took us all out for lunch once a year. He had discovered that we all called him Geoff the Cash and whenever I phoned him he took the call with the words 'Geoff the Cash speaking. How can I help you?'

Marc and I scraped together £100,000 and we needed to borrow the £150,000 shortfall very quickly. Geoff promised to get back to me within twenty-four hours. He was true to his word but unfortunately he had to report that his bosses would not endorse his recommendation to lend us the money. I was exasperated. We had no finance director and I had always done the money side of the business myself, relying on little more than common sense. I simply couldn't understand how Coutts could be so stupid and so irritating as to turn me down. I called Darrell Nightingirl, my accountant, who had always been wonderful in his calm if rather disapproving way. Whenever I spoke to him on the phone I could picture him peering over his half-moon reading glasses and thinking to himself: What is he up to now? Darrell said he knew a senior man by the name of Richie Robertson at the Clydesdale Bank's head office in the City. He would be pleased to introduce me to him. 'It's going to have to happen fast, Darrell,' I said, 'or I am going to miss the deal.'

We trotted round to Lombard Street and presented my simple plan. Within a few days we had the money and I waved goodbye to Coutts for ever. We had enjoyed our time with Geoff the Cash and we had grown up with him in the period when we had been building the business from nothing with very little idea of what we were doing. Geoff understood my decision, but he was unable to get his instructions reversed, and he wished me luck for the future. By the time we signed the deal to purchase the system, on the day before the start of our contract with *Supergirl*, the gear had already been delivered to the freight forwarders for shipment to America.

My new wife got an immediate taste of how life was going to be with a ubiquitous

husband who would be constantly rushing from one project to another. I apologized that I had to leave immediately for Chicago to catch up with Marc and Ron and go over our plans for the new business. As soon as I arrived Marc told me they had finished the shooting schedule unexpectedly early and were moving on to a new location at Riverton, in western Wyoming, the next day. I could either return to London and talk with my colleagues later or go on to Wyoming with them. The fact that I could go with Marc in the helicopter decided it for me.

119

On 30 May I experienced one of the most unforgettable days of my life. I saw America in a day. We took off at dawn, flew across the Windy City and headed west. It was a long and fascinating nine hours. Just the two of us were in the front seats of a twin-engined luxury helicopter as we chased buffalo across the plains of North Dakota, watching the pounding hooves stirring up a trail of dust clouds in front of us. We tracked down the Mississippi, passing over paddle steamers. We witnessed nature so raw and beautiful it took our breath away, as the landscape unfolded beneath us. We flew over the Black Hills of South Dakota and hovered breathtakingly just twenty feet from the faces of the four presidents hewn out of the rock of Mount Rushmore. And finally, at little more than 100 feet, we swept over the awesome cowboy and Indian country of Wyoming, a state of rugged mountains that evoked a romantic, if violent, past. Looking at the map afterwards, it was clear that we had hardly flown in a straight line from Chicago to the new location, but *boy* did we have a good time.

Supergirl was not a successful movie, but as we were a supplier with fixed-price contracts it made no financial difference to us which films were smash hits and which ones were turkeys. We were only ever as good as our recent reputation and the last piece of work we had done within a film. We neither shared in successes at the box office nor wallowed in the failures. What *Supergirl* did do for us was to launch us firmly into the aerial camera business. We were becoming a one-stop service for aerial film production, and this move into a wider arena was to prove of critical importance to our commercial future.

Top Mount Rushmore as the sun goes down. Marc and I flew within twenty feet of a president's nose. **Above** Several hundred tons of pot roast roaming the plains of South Dakota. It didn't take much to get them moving.

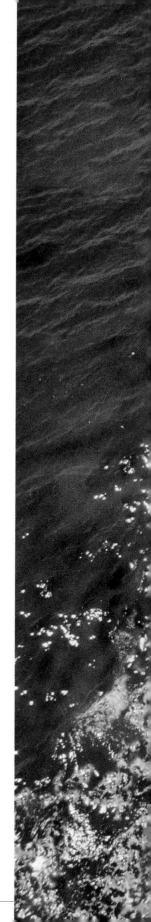

BEWARE OF SWEDISH PIANO TUNERS

I N THE SUMMER OF 1984 I WAS INVITED to spend a week on board a luxury ship, the *Welsh Falcon*, with her owner, Christopher Bailey. I had been introduced to Christopher by Michael Edwardes some years before and this was to be the third time I had been invited on one of Christopher's voyages. He was a wealthy Welshman and it was at his wife Sarah's house on the Cayman Islands that Bucket and I had spent our honeymoon the previous year.

I got on well with Christopher. He was as eccentric as hell, highly irreverent, and he loved to shock. I think he appreciated me because I laughed at his jokes, which I always thought funny but which some considered an acquired taste. He was a big, noisy, rumbustious man. He had very long hair and looked not unlike an outsize Jesus Christ as depicted in Victorian paintings. Equally striking was his choice of clothes, which included kaftans and any other garb which amused him. He was Chairman of C. H. Bailey PLC, a stock market-quoted company in the business of ship repairing, which also had game reserves and hotels in Tanzania.

Christopher was probably best known for taking on the Labour government over a period of five years in the mid-seventies, when he did more than anyone to get it to drop its plans to nationalize the shipbuilding industry. The *Welsh Falcon* was one of three boats that he chartered out for luxury cruises. Our cabin on board was more sumptuous than the best hotel I had ever stayed in. We had a huge four-poster bed on a thick-pile carpet and two *en suite* bathrooms. There were more crew than guests. In a cage in the deck bar was a small grey cockatiel called Turkey. It had been trained to say, 'Turkey's a pretty boy', to the constant annoyance of most of the crew and guests. Christopher and Sarah had two delightful children, Charlie and Georgia, who shared noisiness with their

father but were altogether more sane. They were nearer my age than Christopher's and they both became godparents to my children in later years.

On a previous occasion Christopher chartered the boat to some Americans, who invited him to join them on a voyage around the Aegean Sea. Christopher's friend Stephanos Manos, who was at the time Greece's trade minister, had suggested that Christopher look up the mayor of Paros when he visited the island. Christopher decided to pretend, for this occasion, that he was the Governor of the Falkland Islands for the simple reason that he had on board a costume of appropriate finery. The mayor invited him for dinner, saying it would be fine if he wished to bring along two or three friends. As he accepted the invitation Christopher announced that there was a small problem. In addition to his party he had five Argentinian prisoners on board. Could he bring them with him? They would, of course, have to sit at a separate table. Permission granted, he headed a procession through the streets with the crew carrying a piano on which one member was playing patriotic music. His 'prisoners', chained together, clothed in rags, daubed in tomato ketchup and with their skin darkened with make-up, followed behind as another crew member roused the astonished gathering crowds into booing the unfortunates as they shuffled their

Previous spread Airborne in *Mr Bailey's Balloon*, somewhere in the middle of the Mediterranean with no land in sight. My hairy knees can just be made out at the bottom of the picture. Christopher Bailey is walking towards me on the starboard side.
Above Christopher Bailey, 'Shipowner and Pirate'.
Right The Pirate meets a somewhat bemused 007.

way up to the mayoral residence. Unquestionably puzzled by the goings-on, the mayor nevertheless proved to be a diplomatic host and entertained the eccentric throng with a veritable feast.

Left The *Welsh Falcon*.
Below left Captain Turkey (RIP) on the bridge of the *Welsh Falcon*.
Below Christopher pretending to be the Governor of the Falkland Islands in ceremonial costume.

123

When we joined the boat at Monte Carlo for a Mediterranean cruise, Christopher was waiting with two glasses of chilled champagne as we came down the gangplank. I noticed he had a large briefcase with him and I asked him if he was going to be doing some work on the trip. 'Yes, yes,' he said, 'lots of work.' He opened up the leather case to reveal a small, specially made fruit machine nestling inside – typical of his love of gadgets and novelties. It was always impossible to repay his enormous generosity, so I just tried to come up with a present each year to amuse him. Hanging beside the cocktail bar was last year's gift – a big blue plaque I had had made, resembling those affixed to London houses to indicate that a famous person once lived there. This one simply stated: 'Christopher Bailey, Shipowner and Pirate, lives here.' It was inscribed with his date of birth with a blank for the date of death.

This year's present was much more spectacular, if considerably more dangerous. I gave Christopher one of the Cloudhoppers we used on *Green Ice*. I had had the name *Mr*

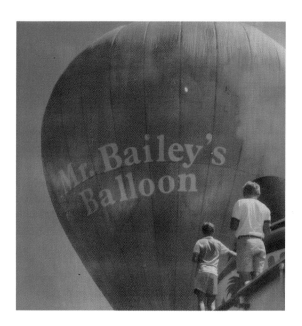

Just before lifting off from the *Welsh Falcon*.

Bailey's Balloon emblazoned in full colour on the side, together with his crest, which depicted a dragon holding a flag. He was very pleased with it and wanted to know how long it would take him to learn to fly. His pleasure turned to disappointment when I insisted it would not even lift him and it could not under any circumstances be flown by anyone except me for the occasional exhibition. I suggested foolishly that I might even try to inflate it during our voyage. We chugged out to sea for the first night aboard.

'Captain Nick, stop the boat,' shouted Christopher after breakfast the next day. 'We're going ballooning'.

'Oh no we're not,' I said pointedly. 'It's far too windy.' With a balloon flight ruled out, Christopher had all his other toys thrown overboard and his guests were made to go waterskiing, dinghy sailing and indulge in other aquatic tomfoolery. Abdul Shamji, a Ugandan Asian who had made a fortune from various businesses in the UK and was apparently interested in buying C. H. Bailey PLC, was given a sailboard to try. When he disappeared over the horizon, exhausted from repeatedly climbing on and falling off and failing to go anywhere other than in one direction, Christopher took the speedboat out to see him. 'Are you enjoying it, Abdul?' he asked. 'There is no question of enjoying it,' his guest replied, not seeing the funny side of it at all. Christopher's booming laughter was meant to cheer him up in his semi-drowned state. (Abdul Shamji's discomfort was to get far worse than this in later months when action was taken as a result of two television reports into his dubious business activities. He was to spend a short spell of time at Her Majesty's pleasure.)

The next day was glorious and hot, with a light breeze and a flat calm sea. We were in the middle of the Mediterranean with no sight of land in any direction. The sea was so clear that we could see porpoises skimming along beneath the surface, making the occasional sortie out of the water to see what we were up to. It was time to go ballooning. It was no easy task. We laid out the envelope as best we could on the lower deck with the single burner and harness unit on the deck above. Cold air was blown in as the mouth was held open by horrified guests using windsurfing poles. Nick Przybylski, the vessel's captain, was steering the boat with great skill at precisely the same speed and direction as the surface wind. This created calm for the inflation of the envelope. Somehow we got the balloon upright, and I struggled into my harness and launched myself into the sky.

As I disappeared into the distance I watched the pandemonium on board as the speedboat was lowered into the sea to give chase. In the calmer upper air I had the most glorious view of a vast, crystal-clear sea. The *Welsh Falcon* and its wake painted a tiny distraction in a vast seascape which spread to every horizon. Twenty minutes later the speedboat was 1000 feet below me and I descended to join it. As the wind picked up, Christopher increased speed and positioned the speedboat perfectly so that I could tiptoe on board for my landing. The balloon deflated into the sea and we hauled it out of the water before returning to a hero's welcome on board the parent ship.

Later in the year I was invited to the Baileys' New Year's Eve party at their house on Chiswick Mall. Needless to say, fancy dress was compulsory and this time the theme was

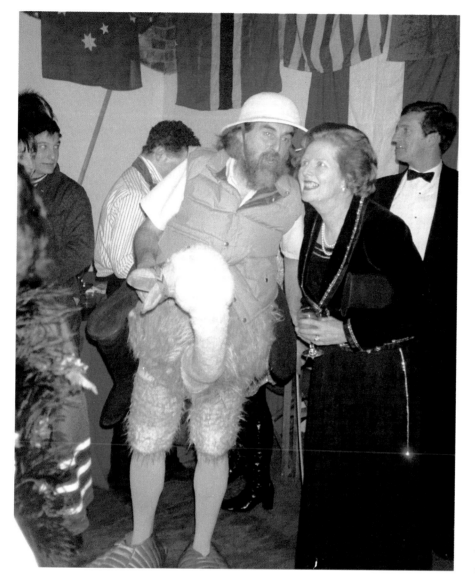

125

'Would you like to meet Winnie the Pooh?' Christopher Bailey on New Year's Eve 1984, as a big-game hunter riding an ostrich, with the Prime Minister as herself.

the circus. Christopher had found himself an absurd outfit which created the impression he was riding an ostrich. He was to wear grey tights and yellow webbed feet. The body of the ostrich was around his waist while from the sides of his midriff two false human legs protruded, with the feet planted in stirrups. The ostrich's long neck and head jutted out in front. This ludicrous illusion was completed by the use of reins, which Christopher held in his hands as the bird's neck and face swayed from side to side. I was asked if I would be prepared to inflate *Mr Bailey's Balloon* at midnight. Weather permitting, I would be delighted. I went as Winnie the Pooh in the same costume I had worn for *Game for a Laugh*. The party was for forty of Christopher and Sarah's closest friends, two of whom were Denis Thatcher and his wife Margaret, accompanied by their daughter Carol.

The Binswanger family from America were there and they were excited to be meeting such a celebrity as Margaret Thatcher. Before her arrival they set about digging up the road outside the house as a practical joke. The Prime Minister was well used to the Bailey family and she simply remarked that it was nice to see British workers hard at it on New Year's Eve without pay. We then all watched the incongruous sight of an ostrich galloping out of the house so that its rider could explain to an ashen-looking security man that the road workers were in fact 'with him'.

Mrs Thatcher had wisely decided to forego the fancy-dress element demanded for the festivities, choosing instead a long, black dress. When at last I was introduced to her I had a blurred vision of her through the grille in Pooh's nose. 'Who *are* you in there?' she kept asking as her face repeatedly swayed into view in front of me. When I inflated *Mr Bailey's Balloon* for 'Auld Lang Syne', Mrs T was invited on board. She declined, suggesting instead that Carol might like to go up while she watched from the first-floor window. When Carol also refused the invitation, the security man, who was now *au fait* with the situation and much more relaxed, volunteered instead. Everyone saluted as we rose on a long tethered rope. I don't think the Thatchers had ever had an evening quite like it. Nor, for that matter, had I.

Sadly, New Year's Eve was the last sighting of *Mr Bailey's Balloon*. It was put back on board the *Welsh Falcon*, which a few months later caught fire in the Bay of Biscay and sank. Although the crew were all saved, poor Turkey was never seen or heard of again.

On 30 April 1985 Bucket gave birth to a beautiful baby girl. I was crazy about her. We named her Angharad Larissa. Angharad is my mother's first name, although she never used it, and Larissa is a Russian name we just liked. When one friend heard what names we had decided on for our daughter he said, 'Good grief. It's a little girl, not a racehorse.' He needn't have worried. She very quickly became known as Lara and has kept the abbreviation ever since. Lara was just a few months old when she had her first flight in a balloon. We went for a little sortie across a field near Newbury. It lasted just thirty seconds, and her mother would have had a fit if she had gone on a long journey. However, it was enough to be able to award her a maiden-flight certificate, which she has kept on her bathroom wall to this day.

At this time Richard Lester had just started work on the pre-production planning of *Superman III*. He had already made a name for himself in big movie productions and I knew him because he had directed the commercials for Terry's All Gold in my advertising days. Marc Wolff had worked on both the previous *Superman* films and as a balloon sequence was being considered for the new one it seemed appropriate for us both to go along to the production offices to see what was up.

The sequence consisted of three balloons being unpacked from donkeys at the top of the Grand Canyon and being flown down to a cave at the bottom. Gas-filled balloons the size of my Winnie the Pooh craft seemed the obvious answer, but even this idea was not going to work for the director. He wanted much smaller, cartoon-style balloons with little metal seats underneath and propellers behind the riders to guide the balloons along. The best I could suggest was that we built them exactly as required and simply suspended them by wires from a helicopter. This was not going to be easy. The three balloons would have to be suspended from a frame, known as a spreader rig, in order to keep them the required distance apart. Richard Lester wanted the occupants to behave as though they were real, free-flying balloonists, so I suggested that my team of pilots would make the obvious stuntmen for the sequence. The movie's art department designed the seats and the propellers, which would be operated by battery-powered motors. We had the little grey-and-white-striped balloons made up by Per Lindstrand. As these couldn't be flown for real they would simply be pumped up with air.

The spreader rig beneath the helicopter was also designed by Per, who had carefully worked out the stresses to be coped with and he had it made collapsible so that it could be shipped to America. The old team swung into action again. The Birdman, Ian Ashpole and I were to be the stuntmen, while Marc would fly the helicopter carrying the whole rig and Ron Goodman, using our X-Mount camera system, would film it all from a second helicopter.

We talked to an Arizona helicopter company which was happy to supply the helicopters but doubted that the Federal Aviation Authority (FAA) would give permission for such a complex load to be flown. Normally any underslung load must be carried from a releasable hook operated by the pilot in case of emergency. I was absolutely not prepared to be carried under a helicopter in this way. Clearly, if the hook were released, we would simply drop to our deaths. We had ordered small, quick-opening parachutes which were to be hidden behind our backs in the sitting position, but any emergencies were most likely to occur at less than 1000 feet, in which case any parachute would be useless.

Al King was the chief helicopter engineer at the company we were using. He was an old-timer who knew all the tricks and he went to see the FAA. He returned with full permission for our stunt. 'How on earth did you pull that off, Al?' he was asked. 'Aw, I just told them we wanted to hang these three dummies on the end of wires and they said no problem.'

On 6 August 1985, just before we were due to depart for America, the Birdman took the Budweiser hot-air balloon to Lymington, Hampshire. It was Cowes Week, and there was considerable publicity to be had from floating over this annual yachting regatta and social event. The Birdman always enjoyed his crossing of the Solent and he was looking forward to it. His forecast was for a strong north-westerly wind which would slacken as the day went on. He would probably have to wait until late afternoon, when a flight from Lymington would take him straight to Cowes. However, around lunchtime he saw a lull in the wind strength and, to the chagrin of his ground crew, he decided to have a go at inflating the balloon. He got it upright and, as he did so, the wind returned to its evil ways. Instead of abandoning the flight he looked at his watch and reckoned that if he could depart there and then, he would still have time to make the last ferry back from the Isle of Wight, which would mean he didn't have to spend the night there. He heated the balloon more than usual so that he could make a fast ascent. 'Hands off,' he screamed to the two men holding on to his basket. He took off like a homesick angel.

Almost as soon as the Birdman left mother earth, a huge wind sheer hit the balloon, the parachute valve collapsed inwards at the top and he descended at great speed into a thick hedge at the end of the field. The impact was so great that he was catapulted straight out of the basket. To add injury to insult the balloon then ran him over, burying him deeper in the undergrowth. The loss of weight caused the unmanned balloon to take off again and it just cleared the house ahead before flying off towards Lymington. His eager ground crew ran over at great speed to see if he was all right.

'Don't worry about me,' he shouted, 'just go and get the balloon'.

The confused crew came to a grinding halt, turned on their heels and ran as fast as their legs could carry them back to the retrieval car. The engine turned over, there was a squeal of tyres spinning on tarmac and the car hurtled off roughly in the direction taken by the balloon. Back in the hedge the bearded pilot was pouring blood from a wound to his forehead and nursing a heavily cut and bruised leg. He struggled out of the brambles and hobbled back towards the road. After about half of an hour's awkward progress he staggered up the steps of a police station to report a runaway balloon. The boys in blue saw the funny side but insisted that they should take him to the casualty department of

127

the local hospital. 'No, no,' the Birdman insisted. 'I'm all right. We have got to find the balloon first.'

As the police put out an all-points bulletin for an escaped and pilotless balloon, the sergeant on duty went through the laborious process of taking down the details.

'Name?'

'Batchelor,' the Birdman replied. For good measure he added the same old line he had used a thousand times before: 'I come from a long line of them actually.'

'That doesn't surprise me, sir,' the sergeant quipped.

'No. Probably not.'

'First name?'

'Robin.'

'Description of missing object?'

'I think I would like to go to casualty now.'

As the Birdman stood up, a constable making a telephone call covered the mouthpiece and announced: 'They've found the balloon, sir. It's in the churchyard.'

'In the churchyard? Oh my God,' said the Birdman. 'There is some damage.'

The balloon that preferred to fly by itself.

'What? To the balloon?'

'No, sir. To the churchyard.'

They hurried to the patrol car and sped round to the church, where they found the deflated balloon draped over the wall at the far end of the graveyard. It had succeeded in carving a path through the tombstones, knocking most of them down on the way. Some had broken clean in half. Earth and debris were scattered everywhere.

'Oh Lord,' said the Birdman with a second inappropriate expletive. It made a bizarre sight to see a graveyard vandalized by a vast wafting advertisement for Budweiser at one end, while several uniformed policemen were spread out at intervals with their notebooks and pencils, trying to work out the identities of the unfortunate dead.

The balloon was packed away by the crew while the disconsolate Birdman was at last taken to Lymington Hospital. After registering with the nurse on duty he joined a long queue to wait for a doctor to stitch his head up. As he sat down he noticed that the woman beside him seemed to be in considerable pain. She was holding up two bandaged hands with blood seeping through from the palms.

'Are you all right?' It was a daft question.

'No. It bloody hurts.'

'What have you done?'

'Well,' she said, utterly deadpan, 'this big balloon came down in my garden and two blokes came running over, screaming at me to hold on to the rope.'

'No.'

'Yes.' She then related the details of her story, which had culminated in severe rope burns to both hands.

'Oh Lord. Are you going to be all right?'

The Birdman was momentarily lost for words. Should he tell her? Yes, he had to. 'I'm awfully sorry, but I'm the pilot of the balloon.'

'No, no,' she said, 'this balloon didn't have a pilot.'

'Ah. Well, no. Er…'

The Birdman was left to contemplate the mayhem he had caused in his vain attempt to get the last ferry home from the other side of the Solent. History fails to relate what happened to the unfortunate lady with rope burns. The Birdman was fine but our insurance company took longer to recover. Where possible, relatives were contacted and compensated for the desecrated gravestones of their loved ones. However, six years later we were still receiving letters from people who had been to visit a grave, only to end up complaining to the vicar that the tombstone had mysteriously disappeared.

His bodily wounds had healed but the Birdman was still nursing hurt pride when we left for Page, Arizona, and the stifling desert heat of late August 1985. For our sequence in *Superman III*, Glen Canyon, just below the dam on Lake Powell, was chosen for its dramatic scenery and its similarity to the much bigger Grand Canyon. It had been decided before the project started that the Grand Canyon's sheer scale would be too difficult to depict on film. For two weeks we stayed in Page's only hotel and ate in the only reasonable restaurant. There was little to eat except steak, which was consumed by the locals in such incredible quantities that I wondered how they managed it. I regularly ordered the child's portion and never once managed to finish even that.

The spreader rig was assembled by Per Lindstrand in the aircraft hangar of the nearby airport. As he was brought up in the north of Sweden he was much more used to the cold than the heat. Every few minutes we would see him disappear into the car outside. There would be a squeal of tyres as he revved the engine and sped up and down the taxiway to get the air conditioning to revive him. When he finally got his rig assembled it just didn't look right. Marc and I both expressed our doubts that it could possibly hold together with a weight of 150 kilograms hung from each corner. 'How do you know each of the tension wires is strong enough?' Marc asked. Per beckoned him over and asked him to put his ear right up to the wire. He then plucked the wire several times while he adjusted the tension with his spanner. The fine steel emitted varying twanging sounds. 'That's it. C sharp,' said Per. 'That means it's fine.' It was a good joke but it only momentarily disguised an impending crisis.

The spreader rig redesigned to carry three of us for *Superman III*.

We substituted barrels of water for the human load to test out Per's masterpiece of engineering. Then we signalled to Marc in the cockpit of the helicopter to lift gently. As the wires took the strain he very gently eased the barrels off the ground. He hovered at six feet for just two or three seconds before the entire contraption buckled and collapsed. Scaffolding poles and other bits of metal flew in all directions and the barrels of water exploded on impact with the tarmac taxiway.

Per exhibited his usual ice-cool façade as he pondered another monumental cock-up. He trotted out the familiar lines about the fact there can never be any guarantee that prototypes will work first time.

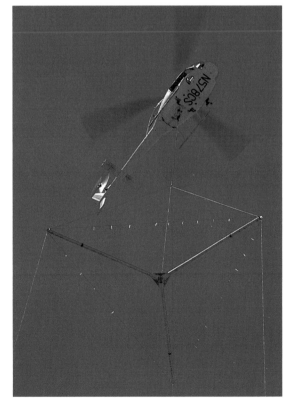

Right He makes a lovely girl. Ian Ashpole dressed up and ready to go. **Below** Ian descending into Glen Canyon, Arizona. **Opposite** Glen Canyon, which stood in for the Grand Canyon. Marc Wolff is flying the helicopter, with the Birdman, Ian and me hanging more than 300 feet underneath, suspended by 3mm thick wires.

Marc took the harsh view that if the rig hadn't been so dangerous, the absurdity of the total inadequacy of Per's work would have been quite funny. He told me in no uncertain manner that he and I would fall out after six great years working together if Per played any further part in *Superman III*. The Swedish engineer flew home.

With three days to go before shooting was due to begin we rushed into action. We found a local welding company to pen a design overnight. We had it analysed for stress the following morning and sent a truck to Phoenix to pick up the required materials. We were ready to go, with a day to spare. We ran through the same helicopter tests with some new barrels of water. The structure held fast. But what we had not contemplated was that each of the barrels on the ends of the three 300-foot-long wires would spin anticlockwise as the wires untwisted themselves. The second problem was that as soon as the ground crew grabbed the barrels to guide them gently to the ground, they received a fairly aggressive electric shock as the static in the dry air built up in the wires and discharged itself into the ground. We quickly ordered 1000 feet of special non-twist steel wire and invested in some long rubber strops to earth the metal seats when we landed.

As usual before a stunt of this magnitude, we had a full meeting about procedures on the eve of our first day of shooting. We were introduced to Ron Brott, the helicopter film pilot who would be flying Ron Goodman and the camera. He was a vast hulk of Arizonan male with size sixteen feet. Someone was to ask him how he managed to buy shoes, to which he replied, 'Oh, when I need a new pair I just kick a cow in the ass and trim off the excess.' Ron claimed to be a minister of some religious sect. He invited us all to his service on the following Sunday. When I asked what

the service consisted of, he explained, 'Oh, I just say a few words and then I hand round the collection plate. The whole thing lasts no more than five minutes.' It didn't sound quite my scene, so I declined. So did everyone else.

When the serious part of the discussion about the next day's activities was concluded it just remained to allocate the costumes. It was decided that the Birdman had the same physique as Richard Pryor and should double for him. Ian, who already knew his beard had to go, was closest to one of the actresses, leaving the job of looking like Pamela Stephenson to me.

Entirely predictably, Marc got to the make-up girls before I did and promised them a bottle of champagne if they really laid on the make-up thick. I was kitted out in a white jumpsuit, big boobs, white leather boots with high heels and tassels and a bubbly blonde wig. When I emerged from make-up, all my colleagues were ready with their cameras. I posed obligingly. There was little else I could do.

When it came to the stunt itself we all sat at intervals along the ground with the three-millimetre wires – if they were any thicker than this the camera would record them – stretched the whole distance to the now much beefier spreader rig. A much thicker cable then went from the rig up to a single bolt screwed into the bottom of the helicopter. Marc took off gingerly and

Opposite top Chaotic landing at the bottom of the canyon.
Opposite bottom No guesses needed who I had to double for – Pamela Stephenson.
Left The foolhardy four. What *did* we think we were doing?

gradually lifted us off the ground. We ascended to 1000 feet and were flown up and down Glen Canyon while Ron Goodman filmed it all from the second helicopter. The Birdman, Ian and I went through brief periods of sheer terror. When the helicopter was stationary it created a horrendous rush of wind – even where we were, some 300 feet below it. It made us shake uncontrollably and we felt desperately insecure. But when the aircraft was moving forward at just five knots the rotor wash dissipated behind us and all was well. We each had a radio and talked Marc up and down while he watched a fixed point on the horizon. Every time the sun came out from behind a cloud it would heat our air-filled balloons. The resultant expansion and pressure within the canopies above us caused a loud hissing noise as air escaped through the safety valves when the pressure became too high. This created a spooky atmosphere which at times undermined our outward professional calm. Day after day we flew, waving, acting and revving our little motors to turn the propellers until the director had everything he wanted.

In accomplishing the film sequence we also set a new world record. Never before had a human load been suspended at such a distance from an aircraft. Not bad, considering there were three of us hanging there at the same time. The Birdman kept the single bolt on which our lives had depended. He was a great storyteller and this was just the aid he wanted to add to his repertoire. For several years afterwards he kept it in his pocket and at an appropriate lull in conversation he would slap it on a table with a flourish which would surprise those present. 'You see this bolt? Well, this bolt…'

CHAPTER ELEVEN

UPSIDE DOWN WITH A HANGOVER

SOON AFTER WE GOT HOME FROM ARIZONA, Marc Wolff came up with a devastating double whammy. While he intended to continue with his career as a helicopter pilot, he had decided he also wanted to fly balloons. On top of this, he had fallen in love with a watermill in Cornwall and he was off to live there with a petite and gorgeous Texan called Lin, whom he had recently married. This was the good news. The bad news was that he had clearly gone mad. He was just thirty-seven and he appeared to be throwing away opportunities at the very pinnacle of his career. He had worked on many high-profile movies and he was the undisputed number one in his field. And anyway we were having a lot of fun. I tried to persuade him that he should stick to his knitting and remain within striking distance of both Heathrow Airport and Pinewood film studios.

Marc was a complex character who was never satisfied with what he was doing. He was forever contemplating trying something different. He had a supreme talent for boring the pants off film directors and producers if they didn't agree with his way of doing things. He did it to such devastating effect that he always got his way. The results were invariably very good. One producer once told me there was no top-class director in the world who was not impossible to work with. Marc was a bit like that too. He and I had now worked together for seven years and we had helped each other along, giving full respect to each other's contribution. He had spent a very high proportion of his time in hotels in foreign countries and, apart from the films we worked on together, we had conducted our partnership largely on the telephone. This was never cheap because Marc never knew

Previous spread On top of the world. Ian Ashpole with a little more death-defying theatre over Herefordshire.

when to stop talking. He now tried to convince me he could carry on as normal in Cornwall. 'Telephone lines don't even go that far,' I suggested. But he had made up his mind. I gave in and he set off for the West Country. As I write this, some fourteen years later, he's still there and I don't expect I'll ever get him out now.

By contrast, Bucket and I had been having problems of our own at home. With great reluctance we decided to separate in 1986, after less than three years of marriage. The union had never been a success. My itchy feet and impatience were always at odds with Bucket's desire to settle down to a quiet life. While she had been becoming more and more disillusioned, I had been finding it impossible to both fulfil my ambitions and spend more time at home. It was not a happy time and I was leaving Lara, whom I adored, when she was just one year old. As a result I found myself nursing a profound sense of guilt. The only way I could find to compensate for this was by finding enough money for Bucket to buy a lovely little house in Henley, in which she and Lara could live.

In September 1985 Tessa reported that she had had an enquiry from Hugh Band, who was the marketing director of the newly founded Virgin Atlantic Airways. Protracted negotiations took place right up to Christmas about managing hot-air balloons for the airline. At the end of the Christmas break Tessa went on a brief skiing holiday to Switzerland, where, by complete coincidence, she ran into Richard Branson on the slopes. 'We're looking forward to flying balloons for you,' she stated proudly. Richard knew nothing about it and when he returned to England he asked his marketing man what it was all about. The next thing we knew, Hugh was incensed that Tessa had blown his secret. As a result, he told her, the potential contract to promote the airline was now in jeopardy. There was really nothing we could say except that no one ever told us it was supposed to be a secret. In spite of this we did eventually agree terms and we were to go ahead with a balloon in the shape of a Virgin Jumbo flying through clouds which were painted on the main body of the balloon. There was also a second balloon, smaller and of normal shape, with a Virgin Upper Class seat suspended beneath it. A sort of modified Cloudhopper.

Hugh Band kept postponing the meeting arranged at his office to finalize the contract. We eventually got together during the week when the flying schedule was due to begin. I was not too concerned when I set off with Tessa to the airline's headquarters in Crawley because I thought everything was agreed. We were kept waiting for over an hour and when we were shown in, the ginger-bearded marketing man asked what we wanted to discuss first. I suggested that we had come to sign the contract, to which he replied, 'Why don't we do the amicable bits first?' My hackles had already been up for some time when we finally got around to the agreement document. I was stunned that discussion of almost every clause brought demands from Hugh Band that had never been mentioned before. I ended up by walking out of the meeting in muted apoplexy.

Tessa was concerned about my dramatic gesture after so many months of negotiation. As we drove back up the M23 towards London I asked her if she seriously wanted a client who behaved like that. It would be a nightmare. When we got back to our offices in Fulham, there was a telex waiting on our machine. It was from Hugh Band. He had graciously decided 'as a gesture of goodwill' to waive the demands I had considered so absurdly unreasonable. Tessa persuaded me to reconsider. We should go for it, she said. I weakened and we did. It was the start of something that would change the face of ballooning. The new face, of course, was to be that of Richard Branson.

I had a few things in common with Richard, although, sadly, mega-wealth was not one of them. We were both exactly the same age, we had both had a public-school education and I suppose you could say we both had a similar, rather childlike obsession with adventure. More specifically, we shared a passion for the eccentricity and theatre of adventure. This could be summed up as showing off. In other words, I suspect the two of us would agree that none of our capers would be nearly as much fun if no one was watching.

Continuing the parallels, we both have lovely blonde wives and beautiful children. My daughter Lara and both Richard's children, Sam and Holly, are at the same school in Oxford. Lara is in the same French class as Sam, and Holly was kind to her when I was making my attempt to fly around the world by showing her how to find her way around the internet site every day.

Ian Ashpole had now married Louise and as a result he had rediscovered himself. He had originally joined the Hot Air Balloon Company in its first full year in business, 1977, and he had flown for us throughout all the summer seasons since. During the winters he had disappeared to America, where he found occasional ballooning work but, more importantly, where he could indulge in his other passion of parachuting. Ian now started to put his new skills to use with daredevil stunts designed to attract substantial media coverage for our clients. The first of these was an attempt at the world's highest-ever trapeze act. (At the time the record stood at some 12,000 feet.) We agreed to stage this for the high-rating television programme *David Frost's Guinness Book of Records*. The plan was to perform the stunt underneath a hot-air balloon.

A younger-looking Ian (minus beard) preparing for his first trapeze act beneath a balloon in 1986.

On 16 May 1986 Ian and I set off in the Alka-Seltzer balloon – the brand's parent company, Miles Laboratories, was our sponsor – from the Cambridgeshire town of St Neots. It was a fine early morning. We took with us a trapeze, which we immediately lowered under the balloon after take-off, a supply of oxygen and a specially made circus-style cape for Ian, to disguise the fact that he would be wearing a parachute. We were pursued as usual by Marc Wolff with a lightweight camera operator in a twin-engined helicopter. It had all its doors off and all the non-vital equipment was removed, including all the unoccupied seats. Our target altitude for the stunt was 15,000 feet, which is very high for a helicopter. Because of the thinness of the air it would have to maintain maximum speed to maintain altitude. This meant flying fast circles around the balloon.

We went on past our target altitude and at 16,400 feet we were directly over Cambridge. I lowered a rope ladder from the basket to the trapeze. We took one long look at each other. Ian was nervous as hell. So was I. 'You don't have to do this if you don't want to,' I said feebly. We radioed Marc that we were ready and Ian climbed gingerly over the side. With a small canister of oxygen clamped to his arm he started breathing through a small, uncomfortable mask attached by elastic to his face. When he arrived on his perch fifteen feet below me he stood awkwardly with his feet firmly planted on the bar and his hands gripping the side ropes as though his life depended on it. He looked up and nodded that he was ready to proceed. I felt sorry for him, for I was sure that what he really wanted to do was scamper back up into the basket and call it a day.

138

I pulled the rope ladder back up to me, leaving the great trapeze artist isolated. With intense determination he very slowly got into a routine which, towards the end, looked like a credible circus act. He did one final twirl around the bar and by now it was obvious he had had enough. He just stared up at me blankly and I immediately realized something was wrong. I threw down the rope ladder, which he contemplated hard before putting a hand to it. Very, very slowly he started to make his way up. Halfway up he stopped. He didn't respond to my calls and I realized he was suffering from hypoxia. His oxygen supply was apparently malfunctioning and he was slipping out of consciousness. I couldn't reach him from the basket and I thought I was going to have to go down for him myself. This was the last thing I wanted to do. I had no parachute and I couldn't see how I was going to get an unconscious man, dangling precariously on suspended ropes, up a rope ladder into the basket. With one final heave, doubtless encouraged by my screams at him to keep going, he arrived just within reach of my outstretched hand. I leaned over the side, hooked my arm under his armpit and hauled him with all my strength to safety. As he lay collapsed on the floor I rammed the spare oxygen supply in his face and he gradually came to.

As we landed near Newmarket, Suffolk, there were suddenly scores of horses and riders filing past us as they embarked on their early gallop. 'Mornin'' seemed to be the only word we heard, a hundred times over. Little did they know that the man next to me had returned from a world record-breaking feat thousands of feet above while barely conscious.

The film looked terrifyingly impressive when it was televised two Saturdays later and it was Ian's first of many entries in *The Guinness Book of Records*.

On 6 June 1986 the Birdman had the honour of piloting the first flight of the balloon with the Virgin Upper Class seat suspended beneath. A jolly, blonde air hostess, clad in the airline's red uniform, had been selected to sit beside him for the flight from Leeds Castle in Kent. He purred his satisfaction and was grinning like a Cheshire cat as he took off. Most people would have looked ridiculous but somehow Robin looked magnificent in his immaculate captain's uniform, coiffed hair, neatly trimmed beard and cap.

The pair landed an hour later. It might have been earlier but the Birdman realized he had a captive prisoner to chat up and he made the most of it. When they did come down it was in a remote farm and I have no doubt it was a hard landing where bodies get entwined in the chaos of the bounce and drag and the pilot comes out saying, 'That was the most incredible forced landing I have ever made.' History does not relate if there was a convenient haystack to hand but it was a while before the Birdman was heard from again. He eventually presented himself at the door of a farmhouse and knocked. Somehow he was still looking splendid in his uniform and cap, so the farmer who opened the door was more than a little shocked at the sight that confronted him.

'Good morning, sir. I've just landed in your field.'

The farmer's jaw dropped as he steadied himself against the hall table. He had visions of a crashed jumbo on his land.

Richard Branson wasted little time in taking an interest in his new investment in ballooning, although I was not to meet him personally until 6 September 1986, a year after we had started discussions with his company. I flew his Virgin Jumbo balloon over a

Got any sisters? Captain Birdman and new friend.

140

The Birdman after a
standard landing in a
jumbo.

charity cricket match in Bristol in which Ian Botham was playing. Richard was at the wicket, dressed in medieval armour (surprise, surprise), preparing to face the ferocious bowling of the greatest all-round cricketer that Britain had ever seen. I saluted as I flew overhead dressed in the Virgin Atlantic captain's uniform and cap.

By the end of the year Richard had started talking to Per Lindstrand about adventures. Per's company, Thunder & Colt, had manufactured the balloons we were operating for Virgin Atlantic. Richard was interested in the possibility of a flight across the Atlantic. He believed it would create enormous publicity for him and his airline. I was sceptical about how big a story such an attempt would be. The fact that Richard was big news was not in doubt. However, the Atlantic had already been conquered eight years before. Per and Richard intended to fly by hot air rather than gas and this would be a first. Nevertheless, I thought the idea was a little flawed. I was to be proved wrong, of course. The master of illusion succeeded in somehow creating the impression to the media that no balloon of any sort had ever crossed the Atlantic. His costs were entirely recouped through sub-sponsors (whose payback in publicity was virtually non-existent) and he enjoyed a monumental news story a year later when he and Per chaotically abandoned their capsule – separately in two different landings – off Scotland's Western Isles. The survival of the Swedish piano tuner was not much short of miraculous. He had no sensible clothing as he swam undetected in the frozen waters for far longer than any normal mortal could expect to remain conscious.

As far as I was concerned, Richard Branson's new-found hobby was bad news. His employees at the airline set about coordinating their transatlantic record attempt without employing or even consulting us. Worse than that, they were calling our employees at home in an attempt to recruit them for their project. I was upset that the Birdman succumbed to the approach made to him. To me it felt like an act of treachery, although, to be fair to him, he didn't see it that way. What I was more concerned about was that our business could be systematically undermined by the tramp, tramp, tramp of the Branson machine advancing upon us.

The Birdman went to Spain and set about training Richard to a standard where he could obtain his private pilot's licence. Not surprisingly, the Virgin team took to the

Birdman, who entertained them the way that only he can. He has an enduring memory of keeping the Virgin balloon tethered through New Year's Eve while Richard supplied thirty-two bottles of champagne for the team of twelve, all of which were consumed. The Birdman bore an uncanny resemblance to his new boss with his red beard and open face. He was regularly being asked for an autograph by people who had mistaken him for the Virgin tycoon. It still happens today. He graciously obliges by writing an R, followed by an illegible scrawl, then B, followed by another illegible scrawl. The likeness of the two is uncanny, but the fact that they also share the same initials is ridiculous.

In October 1986 I went to Amsterdam to make the final flights of the Flying Sculptures tour. This display, which had been to all the big cities of Europe throughout the year and had enjoyed phenomenal success, took the form of a trio of surreal balloons designed by the Austrian artist André Heller. Without doubt it was the most bizarre public-relations exercise we had ever undertaken. The objective was simply to promote Vienna as an avant-garde city of art.

The following spring Michael Heycock, an old friend I had worked for in my advertising days, invited me to Wales for the Easter weekend. Michael had dropped out of the rat race to develop a beautiful old mill near Carmarthen. It was an escapist's retreat,

André Heller's fantasy shapes on a tour of America.

141

which we had used for several balloon gatherings. Michael's other guest for the weekend was Clare Francis, the novelist and round-the-world yachtswoman. All three of us had recently divorced, so we decided on a jolly divorcees outing on Easter Day. Over lunch of mussels and lobster Clare was to ask me if a flight around the world *in a balloon* might one day be undertaken. I told her it would be virtually impossible, because balloon technology, weather forecasting and navigation were not yet up to the challenge.

I was now resigned to at least a few years of bachelorhood. But then, out of the blue, came Susie Chitham. She had been going out with my friend and ex-flatmate Philip Gunn and when that fizzled out we started seeing each other. I was crazy about her, but the craziness was not reciprocated. She was as wild as a hawk, with lots of boyfriends, and it was not long before I realized I was on a hiding to nothing.

While I was in Australia in October that year I realized through increasing pain that I was developing a serious hiatus hernia. I headed home via Los Angeles for a one-night stopover. At 7 am one of the worst earthquakes to hit California this century shook my hotel. If I had not held on to both sides of the bed I would have been thrown straight out when the quake struck. When I arrived back in the UK the next day I found that I had locked my keys inside my house and went to stay with my parents for the night. The stock market had just crashed. Then, when I woke up in the morning, the hurricane had struck Britain overnight. There were so many fallen trees in the street that I couldn't even get my car out. I failed to get to my doctor's appointment on time but it did not delay the need for me to be admitted to hospital for surgery a few weeks later.

My mood lifted dramatically when Susie came to see me in hospital after my operation. I hadn't seen her for some time. She was wonderfully sympathetic and asked if I would like her to look after me when I was discharged. I couldn't believe my luck. While I was still recuperating in the West London Clinic, Susie moved her things into my recently acquired bachelor house in Fulham. She has never left me since.

Soon afterwards I got a call from Richard Branson, who invited me to join him for breakfast at his home in Oxford Gardens, North Kensington. This was a house I knew well because it had recently been sold to him by one of my greatest friends from my schooldays, Jeremy Cassel. When Tessa and I arrived I told Richard of the coincidence. I remarked that he hadn't changed the huge sweeping curtains which trailed on the floor of the living room. His response was that he thought he had paid too much for the house. Good for Jeremy, I thought.

Over breakfast Richard told us that he was keen to have his own ballooning business and wanted to know if we would sell the Hot Air Balloon Company to him. I replied that we were in the midst of doing a deal with a Scottish fund management group whereby we would receive a substantial cash injection to diversify into other areas. He didn't seem to be put off, so I arranged for a tripartite meeting between us all, which took place on Richard's famous houseboat at Maida Vale. Following that meeting we agreed to move forward by supplying Virgin with a full business plan.

There was no further contact after we had done this and within weeks Richard had decided to set up a business with our smaller rival, Lighter Than Air Limited, run by Mike Kendrick. The infamous Hugh Band, who thrived on confrontation in his role as marketing director of the airline, became joint managing director of the newly formed Virgin Airship and Balloon Company. Needless to say, the company's first act was to fire us and withdraw both the Virgin balloons into its own stable.

The Virgin balloon outfit became our bitter rival. More than that, it spoilt our near-monopolistic party. Even so, there is no doubt that the high-profile flights made by Richard over the ensuing years helped to raise interest in ballooning. In a curious way he

Opposite Two of André Heller's Flying Sculptures descending into the mist thrown up by Niagara Falls.

143

made the sport more respectable as a public-relations medium. Whatever we lost in the early days by welcoming a cuckoo into our nest has been more than made up for by the huge generic publicity that Richard drummed up for our business.

Above My future bride (lucky me)…
Above right …and on our wedding day at Hillside Farm in the Ashdown Forest.
Below With my children at home near Stockbridge, Hampshire, 1993.

The most memorable events of the ensuing three years were a marriage and a helicopter accident. Susie and I had finally decided to formalize our relationship. 'You're not everybody's cup of tea, Colin Prescot,' she told me, 'but you suit me.' She had been married before when she was twenty-one and it had lasted less than a year ('He was handsome *and* he had a fast car,' she told me). We didn't want a fuss, so we told nobody except immediate family that we were getting married. When we arrived at Crowborough Register Office on the edge of the Ashdown Forest on 16 December 1988, there was a large sign inviting us for contraceptive advice on the first floor (second door on the left). The marriage room was dark and dank and due for closure within weeks. Susie's sister, Nicky, was unimpressed, remarking that it was more like going to the vet than a wedding. Her younger brother, Rob, described the ceremony as mercifully quick. My colleagues Joe and Heather Philp had already invited themselves to our home for the night. When they arrived they couldn't believe we had been married four hours earlier and thought they should leave immediately. 'Why?' we said. The four of us went out for dinner.

A wedding present from my chief witness was a large, all-weather doormat to go outside our house, bearing the legend 'Beware of the wife'. It was a suitable tribute to Susie's personality. She didn't think it was funny but everyone else was somewhat embarrassed to find it quite hilarious. It disappeared mysteriously some weeks later.

The next day we had a fabulous party at my Uncle Donald's house in Hampshire. All the guests thought they had been invited to celebrate Susie's thirtieth birthday. The night ended with the quickest few thousand pounds I have ever blown – a glorious five-minute firework display synchronized to the music of the song that goes: 'If you knew Susie like I know Susie, oh, oh, oh what a girl…'

Meanwhile I had merged all my business interests. While still flying helicopters, Marc had become part of the family of balloonists. So had the helicopter pilots, engineers and cameramen. We had all been working under the same roof and there were more and more projects using the combined services of the Hot Air Balloon Company and our aerial filming business, the Helicopter Partnership. Tessa, Birdman, Ian, Joe Philp and I formed the majority in the balloon business, while Marc and I were shareholders of the other company. The new group was to be called Flying Pictures, and from now on we were all in the same boat.

On 17 January 1990 my son Archie was born. He gave his Mum a terrible time and I didn't sleep for thirty hours. He was worth it.

In July of that year Marc left for Greece and a film called *Hired to Kill*. He had had a busy few years notching up more and more impressive film credits for film sequences we coordinated, including several James Bond films, *Good Morning, Vietnam, Memphis Belle* and both *Indiana Jones* adventures. He had earned and kept his reputation by pushing film stunts to the limit. Unfortunately *Hired to Kill* was the film where it finally went wrong. Marc was flying in Corfu with four stuntmen, who were sitting inside the helicopter with their feet out on the skids. They were holding sinister-looking dummy rifles. The crew were making the last of many circuits of the film set when the helicopter skids hit the side of the mountain. The rotor blades shattered on impact and the helicopter crashed, cartwheeling several times down the slopes until it finally came to rest on a ledge above a deep ravine. Two of the stuntmen remained strapped in their seats. The other two decided to jump out. With merciless bad luck the helicopter toppled on to one of them. Marc leapt uninjured from his crippled aircraft and ran to his aid. He felt his pulse but there was none. Clint Carpenter had died instantly.

It had all happened so quickly that Marc will never be sure exactly what happened. He telephoned me after the event before being spirited away to a hiding place for several days. Under Greek law he could have been arrested and held for manslaughter at the scene of the accident. Only by him surrendering to the police several days after the event could we be sure that he would not be detained. Marc spent a lonely, reflective and depressing period of incarceration, which included the grisly task of telephoning the young stuntman's parents in America. This was the one blemish in Marc's otherwise glittering career.

The aftermath of the tragedy in Greece was not pleasant and it was bound to have a profound effect on Marc. He had always been on the edge of danger and everyone knew the risks. Because he understood the danger so well, he is the most safety-conscious person I have ever known. All the films for which he worked on our behalf were meticulously planned and if he ever detected that a producer wanted to cut corners on safety he insisted that we withdraw. In truth no professional film-maker ever compromises on safety. If it becomes too expensive the sequence will be cut or another

145

Still the same old team after twenty-two years. With Ian, Tessa and the Birdman, Northampton Balloon Festival, August 1999.

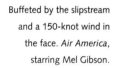

Buffeted by the slipstream and a 150-knot wind in the face. *Air America,* starring Mel Gibson.

way will be found to tell the same story. For it takes only a tiny mistake or lapse in concentration for everything to go horribly wrong. It is this fact that instils the safety discipline in all of us.

I was pleased that Hollywood took a sensible and mature view of Marc's misfortune, and within months he was offered the chance to direct the aerial unit of one of the biggest aerial-action movies ever. It was called *Air America* and starred Mel Gibson. The script called for some amazingly ambitious stunts. For one scene we built a special runway on the side of a mountain in Thailand and our pilot, Tom Danaher, succeeded in landing a small plane on the steep slope with its nose facing upwards. From touchdown to stop was an almost unbelievable seventeen yards. The movie was a triumph of heart-stopping stunts, all filmed with real action.

In September 1991 Susie produced Pollyanna, the third of my three children. The first thing I noticed about her as she arrived was her huge saucer eyes. Absolutely adorable.

Early the following year we won our biggest movie contract ever. It was another all-action film of the kind that was becoming our speciality. This was *Cliffhanger*, starring Sylvester Stallone. Again Marc led the aerial unit, which again got rave reviews for the terrifying action. One day the producer, Alan Marshall, took the trouble to come up the mountain to say to us: 'I saw the rushes of what you shot yesterday. I wanted to come and tell you it's bloody marvellous. In fact, if anything, it's too fucking good for this movie.' It was a rare accolade. All the climbing scenes were shot in the Italian Dolomites, but the most expensive stunt we have ever arranged was staged in Colorado. The movie's climax occurs when the FBI stake out an airport at which an airliner is due to arrive, stuffed full of stolen money. The gag is that all the money has been transferred to another jet, so that the target plane arrives empty.

Stallone was interested in the stunt being done for real. This meant that we had to find a way of getting a live person from one jet into another. It had never been done before and most suggestions of how to achieve it were extremely complex, if not downright suicidal. In the end we assembled four planes – a Douglas DC9, a Jet Star, a B25 bomber and a Lear jet. The B25 and Lear were the most suitable aircraft we could find to fly at high altitude, one carrying our large gyrostabilized camera system. Although it had never been done before we arranged for stress calculations to be carried out on a Douglas without a tail cone so that our stuntman could exit from the rear. Next we received permission from the Federal Aviation Authority to do this. We also got approval to fly the Jet Star with its forward port door removed. Finally we obtained the necessary paperwork to perform the stunt over the Colorado desert, the rationale being that if all three aircraft fell out of the sky no one on the ground would get hurt.

When the day came for filming we had a team of twenty-three people involved and the tension in the air could be cut with a knife. All four aircraft took off from Durango Airport and flew into the desert. At an altitude of 15,000 feet the DC9 pilot was briefed to simply fly straight and level as slowly as possible without stalling the plane. This meant cruising at no less than 150 knots if the big bird was not to spiral out of the sky. The result was that a deafening roar and a terrifying slipstream confronted Simon Crane, the stuntman, as he was eased out of the back on the end of a rope. Marc had decided to fly the Jet Star himself, and as soon as Simon was at the limit of his rope length they would fly up to the stuntman so that he could grab the door surround and pull himself inside. In the

Above On location in Italy for *Cliffhanger*. Using the rotor blades to shred the money…

Below left …and filming the human jet-to-jet transfer from a B25 bomber.

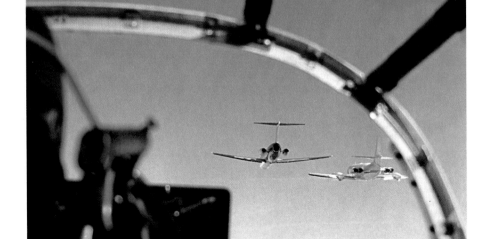

Above Simon Crane on his way out of the back of the Douglas DC9 on his way down to the open door of the Jet Star flying behind.
Opposite Marc Wolff depositing stuntmen on a pinnacle of rock in the Dolomites. There was only room for one skid.

meantime Adam Dale, our cameraman, had to make sure he captured it all on film from the B25, which was flying flat out alongside the action. No one had any intention of going back for a second time to do the stunt again.

As the Jet Star closed in with fingertip precision, Simon lunged at the door frame of the plane and grasped it. His foot was on the floor in the doorway. Just as he was about to haul himself through, sudden turbulence hit the aircraft and Simon was swung viciously right across the top of the fuselage and down the other side. The Jet Star instinctively backed off and Simon, sensibly, simply let go.

On board the DC9 were two freefall experts whose job was to jump out to rescue Simon in case of any mishap. Within a few seconds three figures were falling through the air to the desert below. All three parachutes popped open and the men landed safely. They were picked up, three tiny dots in the middle of nowhere, several hours later. The whole thing would, after all, have to be done again.

The following morning a full briefing on the rerun of the stunt was in session when the telephone rang. The film from the previous day had been processed and viewed. The director, Renny Harlin, had everything he wanted. He would use the close-up of the stuntman arriving in the doorway and then cut to a mock-up done in a studio. The message was: congratulations on one of the greatest aerial stunts of all time. 'It's a wrap, boys.'

A few months later we arranged for Ian Ashpole to make his second assault on *The Guinness Book of Records*. This time it was to be the world's highest bungee jump. The plan was that he would leap out of a balloon, bounce up and down on the elastic strapped to his ankles and then cut himself loose and parachute down. The rehearsal was staged early one morning over Ross-on-Wye, Herefordshire, as an exclusive for the Sunday newspaper the *People*. It worked fine except that there was a design fault in the bungee release mechanism. However much he struggled he couldn't get free. The previous night

Ian had washed down a take-away curry with an appalling quantity of lager, so his position upside down made him feel even more unwell than the damage already inflicted by the mother of all hangovers. He had no option but to scream up at the balloon pilot, Lenny Vaughan, that he would have to land with him still suspended from the balloon.

Lenny now had the task of touching down an aircraft that was over 100 feet in height. With little idea of how high above the ground his errant jumper was hanging, all he could do was listen very attentively to the shrieked instructions Ian was giving in talking him down. Fortunately the wind was very light and after a seemingly interminable twenty minutes they descended very gently into a valley of virtual calm. Still dangling upside down, Ian swung gently by a farmhouse. As he floated past the first-floor window, he was confronted by the indelible sight of the farmer and his wife sitting up in bed. 'Is it all right if I land here?' he asked, as the astonished farmer came to the window, craning his neck upwards to see what on earth Ian was hooked up to. With permission to land granted, Ian yelled up to Lenny, 'OK, bring us in.' Moments later he was in a heap on the ground. He managed to disconnect himself from the bungee before staggering a few paces to the hedge, where he threw up the entire contents of his misdemeanours of the night before.

Undaunted by the ordeal, Ian fixed the release mechanism and set off for the real thing some days later. Marc flew the camera helicopter in formation with the balloon as it climbed to 16,000 feet. Simon Ward, one of the world's greatest freefall cameramen, left the basket, upside down, a fraction of a second before Ian so that he could film with his helmet camera from beneath the bungee jumper. Spectacular shots were obtained from every angle, including the helicopter's view. A full sequence was cut to show the story and the result appeared on the national television news bulletins later that day.

In August 1993 Ian and I set off for Brazil to film some commercials for Maxwell House Coffee. I had managed to get the whole Flying Pictures team on this junket. Marc was to be the film pilot and Adam Dale, our cameraman, who had recently won the UK's Advertising Cameraman of the Year Award, was to do the aerial filming. I had had several meetings with the director, Michael Seresin, and his producer, Angie Mickleburgh. It was fairly banal stuff and it looked a doddle. The scripts called for a balloon in the shape of a coffee jar, which would be seen floating serenely over mountains and past waterfalls. This

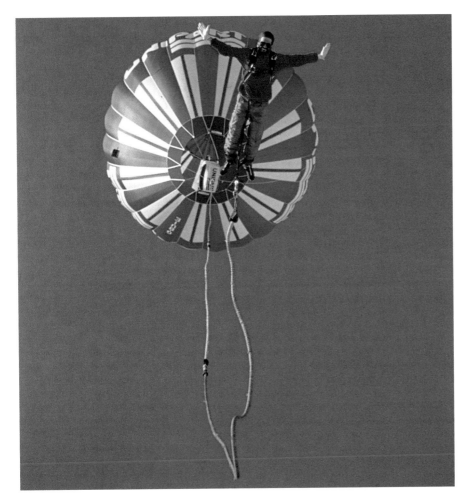

151

coffee was apparently 'mountain fresh'. It was all to be topped off with Mark Knopfler's music from the film *Local Hero*. I had already identified a couple of waterfalls through pictures supplied by a location company in Brazil. These I had approved because they had flat land beneath them which was clear of obstacles.

When I met up with Angie at Heathrow to fly out to Brazil, she calmly announced that there had been a change of plan. Michael wanted to go to the Iguaçu Falls. Over 200 feet high, taller than Niagara Falls, these are among the most fearsome cascades in the world. This panorama, situated where Brazil, Argentina and Paraguay meet, is one of the most stunning sights on the planet and was used as the location for the film *The Mission*. The job was not going to be a doddle after all and I was quick to point out that we couldn't guarantee that we could fly over the site. It was true that the Falls had been overflown by a balloon but only at a height above them that would be of little use for film photography, and even then the pilot had been on standby for six weeks before suitable weather arrived. I smelled a fiasco in the making. I was no longer looking forward to this project as I imagined a stand-off with a strong-minded director who would not want to know what our problems were. We all flew straight up to the location from Rio de Janeiro and took in the whole awesome vista from a helicopter.

There was a tiny beach just underneath the main cascade and it occurred to me that we might just be able to fly the balloon up the Falls from there. Permission was sought and granted. The next problem was that on the other side of the Falls was a narrow road. Beyond lay seventy-five miles of thick, unbroken thorn forest, and every tree was home to several active hornets' nests. We knew all about these because the Birdman had disturbed one during the shooting of the Fanta commercials several years earlier. He had been stung all over and rushed to hospital with his passenger, who had fractured a vertebra in the panic of getting out of the balloon and away from the swarm. In spite of all this Ian volunteered to have a go at flying the balloon if the weather was right. Good idea, I thought. Not me, thanks.

Astonishingly, the first morning after we arrived was flat calm. The balloon was airlifted down to the beach by helicopter. We inflated it and floated Ian off under the Falls. Small eddies of wind wafted him up and down and around the river. As the morning wind developed he was carried back to the middle of the Falls. He rose majestically over the top and made a perfect landing in the single-track road at the top.

Apart from the obvious skill on Ian's part, it was the most extraordinary piece of luck I have seen in twenty years of filming. The director wondered what all the fuss had been about. We left for the mountains, where Ian and I flew in the rainforests and down windy ravines to provide some of the prettiest balloon footage there has ever been. The only pity, perhaps, was that it was all for a brand of coffee that was ailing in the UK.

Opposite Mountain-fresh coffee. How else do you communicate that?
Below Ian sets off from beneath the Falls at Iguaçu.

As soon as we returned from Brazil we were organizing another little stunt for our resident daredevil. This time Ian was to make a tightrope walk between two balloons tied together and flown to a height of 16,000 feet. If he succeeded, it would be the highest-ever tightrope walk, the record at that time being held by a man who had traversed a canyon high up in the Andes. The attempt had to be cheated a little because a rope between two baskets would simply pull the balloons towards each other when Ian stepped on it. We therefore constructed a steel bar. Ian would disguise a parachute under his overalls. We persuaded our sponsors, Citroën and Champagne Mercier, to sponsor the event with their respective balloons and we called the stunt 'The French Connection'.

It was a resounding success. The spectacle looked so absurdly death-defying in the shots taken by Marc and Adam in the helicopter that they were broadcast on television news bulletins all over the world.

In the spring of 1994 we were sent the scripts for the new British Airways commercials, written by Saatchi & Saatchi. The airline wanted Hugh Hudson to direct them. Hugh was an Old Etonian who had won the Best Film Oscar for *Chariots of Fire*. He was one of very few Britons ever to win the coveted award. He had been a very regular and loyal customer of ours for many years. Whenever he was offered commercials requiring aerial work he would insist that he was only interested if Marc Wolff or David Paris (also one of our pilots) were available to fly the helicopter. Hugh had already made a number of British Airways films as well as some other big movies, including more recently *My Life So Far* and *I Dreamed of Africa*, all of which we worked on.

The scripts seemed to indicate that the commercials were to be an extravaganza of special effects as some islands are covered in red, white and blue fabric to create the new theme of 'We cover the world'. Hugh, a very well-read, intelligent and articulate man, was

Ian at it again. This time it's the world's highest tightrope walk.

Opposite top The easy life. Just string a hammock between two balloons at 10,000 feet, lie back with a newspaper and a gin and tonic and dream the world away. It's easy really. You just need to be called Ian Ashpole.

Opposite below Dawn surprise designed to amaze. The UFO reports flooded in for our promotion of the launch of the *Independence Day* video throughout Europe.

Overleaf Helicopters towing a sheet larger than Wembley Stadium for British Airways' 'We cover the world' campaign.

also a great creative talent and lateral thinker. His question was whether or not it would be possible to tow a massive piece of red fabric behind three helicopters. (The blue and white sections were to be filmed on the ground.) It was a hell of a question and Marc and I went into a huddle. We couldn't see why not in principle. It would certainly need to be tested out before going to the chosen location in Australia.

I researched some fabrics. Apart from the aesthetic considerations, the weight was a major factor as the piece of cloth was to be bigger than Wembley Stadium. Eventually I found a lightweight nylon with an open weave, which slightly aerated the material. I figured that this would make it waft in the wind rather than flap uncontrollably.

We talked to the man at the CAA, who displayed his usual quizzical grin and posed the inevitable question: 'What are you planning *this time?*' We got our permission. We found a huge set-aside field close to my home near Stockbridge, Hampshire. Here we laid out the vast sheet, which had taken several seamstresses two weeks to stitch together. The vast sea of scarlet was a surreal sight as it covered half the entire field. At one point we saw a petrified hare sitting on its haunches right in the middle. It seemed unable to comprehend where it was and when twenty-five people lined one side to pull the whole sheet down the field the poor creature just sat there and came along for the ride. The stunt test took a considerable amount of coordination, but it worked.

'It's *very, very* beautiful,' said Hugh Hudson. One of his affectations is to always repeat the word 'very' twice. 'Make arrangements to come to Australia.' And he sped off back to London.

We spent two weeks on the Great Barrier Reef, off the north-east coast of Australia. It was one of those situations which happen frequently when film crews choose locations for their guaranteed weather. The guaranteed weather laughs in your face and does the opposite to what is expected of it. When it did improve, Marc and the helicopters were required for other shots. There was nothing for me to do except go scuba-diving, write a few proposals for future projects and read books. All on full pay.

'It's Colin's big day tomorrow,' said Hugh finally. I organized the three pulling helicopters, the single filming helicopter and all the strops and shackles. The take-off went smoothly and the helicopters disappeared from view up a ravine. On the way back one of

155

the pilots got a little out of position and felt the huge expanse of fabric tugging at him. He was on the point of losing control and ejected his towing line. 'Cut,' he shouted over the radio, and the other pilots shed their load simultaneously. The vast sheet dropped down into a canyon, from which it would take a day to retrieve. I had brought a whole spare sheet from England in case of such an eventuality. There was no need, though. Hugh had the shots he wanted. I had come halfway round the world and waited for two weeks for fifteen minutes' work. That's show business.

CHAPTER TWELVE

TWO THOUSAND ALCOHOLICS CLINGING TO A ROCK

ALDERNEY IS THE THIRD BIGGEST OF THE CHANNEL ISLANDS, after Jersey and Guernsey. It is just three miles long and nowhere much more than a mile wide. Having been occupied by the Germans in the Second World War, it is dotted with forts and defences left behind by a grisly regime that ran a prisoner-of-war camp for Russians and Eastern Europeans on the southern side. Lying nine miles from the Normandy coast of France, the island is now a rugged place with a small town, sandy beaches, lots of wartime bunkers to explore, a popular harbour and a nine-hole golf course.

A small railway runs a service once or twice a week, although more frequently in the holiday season, from the inner harbour up to the quarry on the east side. It consists of two ancient carriages from the Bakerloo line of London's Underground railway. The island is just big enough to need a car to get around and almost all the cars are rejects from the mainland which have failed their MOT test. Victoria Street, in the small capital town, St Anne, is the main shopping area. Most shops have kept up with the times, but there are still some to be found where a notice in the window defines daily opening times as ten to four-ish. And in Alderney 'ish' means 'ish'.

'Two thousand alcoholics clinging to a rock' is an apt description of this minuscule outpost of the bailiwick of Guernsey Certainly there is a disproportionate number of pubs and never any shortage of booze, which is consumed in terrifying quantities by

Previous spread
The Channel Island of
Alderney, a tiny haven for
bons viveurs.
Above top Lara looking
out over Braye harbour.
Above Pollyanna, Susie
and Archie on the beach
at Braye.
Opposite A young Archie
teaching his even younger
sister the principles of
flight, Alderney, 1993.

some of the inhabitants and visitors. The island became well known to cricket lovers as John Arlott used to drone on about it on the radio in his familiar gravelly tones whenever there was not much happening in a test match. He once brought over Ian Botham, who fell in love with the place, bought a house and comes every summer with his extended family. Another famous regular visitor is Duncan Goodhew, the gregarious swimming gold medallist at the 1980 Moscow Olympics, whose mother was Miss Alderney in 1949 and still lives in Newtown on the north side. German industrialist Rolf Vogelsang has made a fantastic conversion out of a large old fort and plans to retire there. Sir Edward du Cann, who was Chairman of the 1922 Committee that steered Margaret Thatcher to the leadership of the Conservative Party, lives in another of the forts with spectacular views that are dotted around the coastline. He addresses me simply as 'Prescot'.

In the summer Alderney is busy with holidaymakers who come back year after year – a charming way for their children to make lifelong friends of the young companions they see during their school holidays.

I visited the island every year after meeting Susie back in 1987. As one of the Chitham girls, she had been coming to the family's holiday home in the cluster of houses called Newtown for almost thirty years. Her father, who had sadly died in 1994, had bought a bungalow there after he was seriously burned while serving with the Canadian Air Force, before Susie was born. The island was home to a small, friendly community. Its intimacy allowed him to be universally known and recognized while saving him the embarrassment of having his rebuilt face stared at whenever he went out.

In 1995 I bought a half share of a twenty-two-foot ex-Ministry of Defence rigid inflatable boat with an inboard diesel engine. My annual blast was to pound my way from Lymington through all weathers to reach Alderney some ninety miles and five hours later. I would always be drenched and my eyes were red for three days from the salt water driving over the bow, but the crossing always cleared the cobwebs from my psyche and I loved it.

One of my regular partners on the golf course is Chris Jones, a *bon viveur* not many years older than me who retired some years ago. He now moves between England, Switzerland, Barbados and Alderney according to the season. We are often joined by an amusing bunch for an eight o'clock tee-off which rarely sees a round of nine holes completed. Occasional participants include Ian Botham (who, not surprisingly, trounces everyone), his father-in-law, Jerry, and Colin Ensor, who owns the house alongside the seventh fairway overlooking the harbour.

Whenever someone doesn't turn up when expected there is an automatic assumption that a monumental hangover is the reason. One participant, Robbie Robbins, arrived one day and informed us that another player, Simon Strong, wouldn't be coming because his wife Charlotte was unwell. Colin Ensor looked mildly concerned. 'Oh dear. Drink?' he asked, to which Robbie replied, 'No thanks. It's a bit early for me.' That's Alderney.

Even before breakfast there is Pimms set out on the wall of Colin and Gill Ensor's house on the seventh hole and this means that the game is usually abandoned at that

My balloon laid out on the Butes on Cavalcade Day.

point. Coincidentally, in 1999, when I lifted off from La Envia Golf Club in Almería, Spain, in *Cable & Wireless* to fly around the world, it was also from the seventh fairway. After Andy and I ditched in the Pacific some eighteen days later Simon Strong wrote to say that he and his compatriots had decided to award me 'the freedom of the seventh'. I was assured this was an honour indeed as it was the first time it had been awarded. It probably also means I shall never again finish a game in an uninebriated state.

Another interesting feature about Alderney is that it boasts one of the strongest tides in the world. The Alderney Race rushes down the gap between the island and the mainland of France at up to twelve knots in a spring tide. I worked out with Duncan Goodhew that if we chucked him in at the right point with a pair of flippers and he swam like hell with the tide he could perhaps become the first man in history to swim a four-minute mile. Eat your heart out, Sir Roger Bannister. Duncan was amused by the idea but his American wife, Annie, was not. I knew that I could find a sponsor for a wheeze like this and that the media would go mad for it. So we enlisted the support of Steve Shaw, coxswain of the island's lifeboat, and David Macallister, who had been fishing the waters around Alderney since he was a boy. After more research we concluded that it was not all going to be as easy as we first thought. Much to the relief of Duncan's family, who thought me a bad influence, we abandoned the caper, although I am sure we will find a way of resurrecting it one day.

To the islanders of Alderney I was the 'balloon man who Susie married'. This led to the obvious enquiry each year: 'Have you brought your balloon with you?' Although the question was always posed in jest, I began to ask myself: Why not transport one over by boat and fly home? It had never been done before and it would entail a flight over water of up to 120 miles. Yet it would be much shorter than the 330 miles I had flown some fifteen years before, although that had almost all been over land. I had also crossed the Channel on the short Dover–Calais route three times, so I felt qualified to have a go. And anyway there had never been a balloon in Alderney, it would be the longest-ever sea crossing within the British Isles and it would be fun.

Ray Parkin was the coordinator-in-chief of Alderney Week, an eight-day festival which takes place every August. He jumped at the idea and saw it as a great swansong to his last year in charge of arrangements. 'Don't worry, I've got the music organized, we'll arrange weeping women and you can wear plus fours and goggles,' he told me. Happily, these ideas dissipated in the mists of time as he began to realize the complications of arranging the flight itself.

I thought my plans would make a good story and Channel Islands Television was keen to cover it in some depth. Finding a sponsor would therefore be relatively easy, and we would use one of the forty-five balloons managed by my company. Unfortunately we discovered that the selected balloon would have to shipped out to the island on one of the infrequent freight boats of Channel Seaways. This would mean that that balloon would be unavailable for use at events elsewhere for up to three weeks. None of our sponsors felt able to lose that amount of exposure time from their schedule during the traditionally busy high season in England and Europe.

I told Ray that the only solution was to use our own brand-new unsponsored balloon. Every two or three years we invest in a balloon for use in films, television commercials, high days, weddings and the like where the customer does not want advertising emblazoned on it. The new balloon had no commitments. I was happy to supply all the equipment but there would be some substantial expenses, not least the insurance – the brokers had taken two months to persuade underwriters to take it on at all. Apparently they felt very uncomfortable about the risks involved. Ray set about raising some cash and I had to thank a local sponsor, Bucktrout & Co, as well as the States of Alderney, for their financial assistance.

I called Ray Plant, the manager of air traffic at Guernsey, to ask if he would support my plan. He seemed a little apprehensive at first but when I explained that I would be carrying radio communication equipment and a transponder to track radar signals he was reassured, enthusiastic even. There are, not unnaturally, strict rules which absolutely prohibit the kind of foolhardiness I was proposing, so I would have to apply in writing to Jersey Airport for a special exemption to fly in the Channel Islands Control Zone, attaching full details of my experience as a balloonist. Several letters later I had my permission, together with good wishes from the authorities in Jersey and Guernsey.

'Right,' said Ray Parkin, 'you're going to fly just after the Red Devils have landed at 2.30 on Cavalcade Day.' Oh dear, he clearly didn't know what my limitations were. However, I agreed we would aim for that slot, but if it was unsuitable I really would have to choose my own time and date (if at all) for simple reasons of safety.

Jovial Jock in the control tower of Alderney's little airport was wonderfully supportive and kept poring over the weather charts at the same time as considering the duty roster. He was secretly hoping he would be in the tower when the event came round. 'This is a bit of a novelty for us, you see,' he said in his marvellous Scottish accent, 'rather like a fly-past by Concorde.' I was flattered by the comparison. Jock had worked out exactly where my take-off site was in relation to the control tower and thought he might set up his video camera pointing in that direction.

When Cavalcade Day arrived the wind was too strong and blowing in a direction that meant I would fly straight up the Channel into the North Sea with no chance of reaching land at all, let alone by nightfall. I telephoned Ray: 'I am sorry, it is not going to happen

Talking to the control tower by radio shortly before my take-off from Alderney.

163

Away at last, bound for England.

today.' He was understanding, though clearly disappointed. He wanted me to come anyway and have a go in case the weather changed. The event needed some drama. Fair enough. We provided a bit of drama as we blew cold air into the balloon. It tugged the Land Rover (with handbrake on) to which it was tethered for thirty yards and the flapping of the fabric rang out like rifle shots as the strong gusts of wind attacked it ferociously. We succeeded in frightening a few people as well. Unfortunately one of them was Susie, who couldn't sleep that night and admitted that, in spite of all her support and enthusiasm to date, she would actually prefer I did not fly at all. I reassured her that I had no intention of going if I didn't feel confident of a safe crossing.

There was a good forecast for Wednesday. When the day arrived it looked manageable for a take-off – good wind direction, particularly at altitude, and fine weather over southern England. The only alarming news, which I didn't tell Susie, was that moderate to severe thermic activity was forecast for the landing. This can be very dangerous for balloons in that heat pockets at ground level can, in a matter of seconds, produce gusts of wind of gale force out of flat calm. This knocks the balloon for six, forcing out the air, and can send it plummeting out of control. Naturally, we don't normally fly in these conditions but I felt this was an occasion when I would just have to take my chance. I was aware of the danger and resolved to give my landing razor-sharp concentration.

Ray rushed round the town with his loudspeaker system to announce a 10.30 am departure from the Butes, a flat piece of land high up the hill above the harbour. I set off for the airport to file my flight plan, a mandatory requirement for any flight over water. This caused some amusement as I was unable to state my destination. Nevertheless, it was graciously accepted and faxed to Guernsey.

The set-up went to plan. Lucius Peart, our operations director at Flying Pictures, had sent over an immersion suit, life jacket and flares in case of ditching and Marc Wolff had insisted that my gear should include a four-man life raft. Susie pointed to a huge black cloud behind us to the south. In retrospect it seems odd that I didn't take more notice of it. However, I had an up-to-date forecast and I had made up my mind to go.

I was lucky to have Susie's brother Rob to assist as launch master. Having spent a year at Flying Pictures, he was more than qualified. The balloon was inflated and ready to go. I radioed Sally Wilkinson in Alderney Airport's control tower: Golf Bravo was ready to depart. 'Golf Bravo, depart at your discretion. Not above 2000 feet. Squawk 1241. Wind south-east one-zero knots. QNH 1014.' This was my first test. A pilot has to repeat back his instructions. What no one knew was that although I hold a lifetime Radio Telephony licence I hadn't actually made a VHF transmission for several years. Flying balloons for films, commercials and display events is invariably outside controlled airspace and needs no communication with air traffic control. Although my 330-mile flight in 1978 had passed through several airways I had at that time a partner on board who handled all the communication and navigation while I flew the balloon. On previous cross-Channel flights I had been in the company of other balloons and one pilot had communicated on behalf of all of us. This time I had to do it all on my own. In addition, I had never in my life operated a transponder, which gives the air traffic controllers a blip on their radar screen so that they know where you are.

I read back my instructions and was relieved to get the reply 'Feedback is correct.' My two small children were suddenly produced from the crowd to say goodbye. I remember thinking how sad it was that Susie's father couldn't be there to witness the event. Bob Chitham would have loved it.

I pulled the quick-release mechanism which attached me to terra firma and I was away. I had the most fantastic send-off from a cheering crowd, and I shan't forget it for the rest of my life. From 200 feet the Butes looked astonishing perched up on the island and with all those waving hands. I waved back before returning to my radio to confirm that Golf Bravo was airborne.

I glanced back and realized that I was in full view of the tower, where the controller must have been observing from her vantage point behind all that sloping glass. I was asked to transfer to Guernsey Control, who had already been alerted, and I was wished a safe crossing. Guernsey repeated the instruction not to exceed 2000 feet. This was tedious because I wanted to go much higher to catch the stronger winds veering round from the west. I considered asking for a special clearance but they sounded so busy that I decided

My departure as seen from Victoria Street, St Anne.

to settle for 2000 feet. It would get me to England anyway. I was soon asked to change frequencies to keep in touch with Jersey Control for the rest of my flight in the Channel Islands Zone.

I turned on my GPS satellite navigation system, but I couldn't make it work. 'No satellites,' it kept telling me. I switched it on and off several times without success. I could not work out why it was malfunctioning as it had worked perfectly the day before when I ran up and down the beach at Longis in order to get a reading. It had told me with great precision that I was running at six knots on a track of 343 degrees from Alderney Airport. Jersey called me on the radio and suggested I contact them again when I was exiting their zone, which is on an imaginary line at fifty degrees north. I was forced to confess that my navigation system was down and I asked if they could keep an eye on me on the radar screen. I expect they thought they had some crazy balloonist on their patch with no idea of what he was doing. They would certainly be keeping an eye on me. However, in a matter of minutes I sorted out why my computer was playing up and reprogrammed it accordingly. Suddenly I had all the information I needed. I was 8.2 miles from Alderney Airport on a track of 350 degrees and travelling at nineteen knots. It was a relief to be updated with information every two seconds. Jersey called again to say they were having difficulty tracking me on radar and I was able to confirm the happy news that I could now tell them my position. At that moment they got their signal back and all was well. I would contact them again in about an hour when I exited the zone. So far so good.

Alderney had now completely disappeared from view and several hours would follow with no land in sight. There was now also full cloud cover, which I was not expecting, so I had no view of the sun in the south. Without a compass, as I peered out over the sea to every horizon I had no idea whether I was facing England, France or America. I had to fly entirely on my altimeter, which I kept tapping to make sure I had not induced too much of an ascent or descent.

I heard on the radio an aircraft being cleared into the Jersey Zone. After receiving his instructions, the pilot asked, 'Is there any news of the hot-air balloon that took off from Alderney this morning?' I'm famous, I thought.

The reply came back from the controller that I was twelve miles to his south-east on the same level. 'Oh great,' he enthused, although he couldn't see me. A few minutes later he reported back that he 'had me visual', adding the words 'at least the poor fellow's still going towards England'.

Then I settled down to Susie's lunch, which consisted of a bacon and cheese sandwich. I cast the bits of rind overboard and watched their interminable descent to the waves below. The second course was fromage frais eaten with a plastic spoon chewed up by my two-year-old daughter Pollyanna.

I was now approaching my exit point from the Channel Islands Zone when Jersey called to say that I would soon be in the navy firing areas but that they had contacted Portland, Devon, and there would be no problem flying through. I replied that I rather hoped to fly over the top of the naval danger areas. Jersey suggested I talk to Portland direct, so I thanked them for all their help and switched frequencies.

The controller at Portland Radar was well prepared for my arrival. 'You are cleared to fly through at your current level of 2000 feet,' he informed me. I asked if I could go higher. 'How high do you want to go?' the man asked. I replied that it depended on the winds, but that I would like to climb initially to 6000 feet. 'Cleared to 6000 feet,' he said, sounding a little surprised. He then took the trouble to research the winds at that altitude and reported back that I could expect about twenty-five knots on a track of fifteen degrees. When I reached that level I confirmed his prognosis as accurate.

166

The sky was clagging up and it was starting to rain. All around me I could see threatening, almost cartoon-like columns of water pouring down to the sea. No one told me anything about this, I thought to myself. I started to feel some gusts of wind, and rain spattered my face. This was unusual because the balloon normally acts as a huge umbrella. I looked up and was reassured that the balloon seemed to be behaving very well in these unexpected conditions. I could make out the ghostly outline of several ships and tankers over a mile below me, but little else. I kept glancing at a huge rain shower over my left shoulder and probably only a few hundred yards away. It was chasing me around and I hoped silently it would never catch me.

At 2.10 pm, some three and a half hours after I had taken off, I spied land. What started as a grey shadow drew slowly closer until eventually I could make out the outline of Sandbanks to the right and Portland Bill to my left. I still had half my fuel supply left and I felt good. As I crossed the coast at 6000 feet the weather started to clear slightly and Portland Radar asked if I wanted to be transferred to Bournemouth Special Rules Zone. I felt in familiar territory now and I was flying outside controlled airspace, so I was quite happy to cease communications and make the descent on my own. The reply came back that Portland would be pleased to keep me on their frequency. I was obviously an

interesting diversion for the military control personnel. I continued to fly north to make it as easy as possible for the retrieval crew who had been dispatched from the office to collect me. As I passed over Wimborne, Portland said I had gone as far as I could with them so I checked out and told them I would close my flight plan, to confirm safe landfall, by telephone after I had landed. I switched off the transponder and descended to 1500 feet when the retrieval crew called to say they were almost at Salisbury. As I had found a completely stationary pocket of air over Tarrant Hinton, on the main road between Salisbury and Blandford Forum, I literally hung around until they arrived beneath me. I noticed from smoke on the ground that the wind on the surface was from an easterly direction and steady. There was little evidence of that dreaded thermic activity which had been forecast.

I descended for my landing and picked up speed considerably. As I passed over a line of trees I found a stubble field with a good road beside it and decided this was to be my landing place. It was 4 pm and my flight had taken five hours and ten minutes. As I hauled the ripcord I glanced over my shoulder to read my speed: seventeen knots. At that speed any landing by balloon is at best a controlled accident and I stowed everything as well as I could for a bumpy landfall. As I dragged along the stubble on my stomach, struggling to deflate a large and now lightly laden balloon, there was a loud and persistent hissing sound and I started to be enveloped in fabric. In the chaotic landing, a rope had got caught on a toggle and released a small canister of gas. As I climbed out I was greeted by the incongruous sight of a huge, perfectly formed, fluorescent-orange life raft.

The following morning I was greeted at Flying Pictures with a bottle of champagne and I noticed on the operations board that the nameless new balloon I had flown had been christened. It was to be called *Alderney*.

Last-minute checks after taking off. The packed life raft can be seen hanging on the side of the basket.

167

CHAPTER THIRTEEN

SEND IN THE CLOWNS

I N JANUARY 1995 FLYING PICTURES EFFECTIVELY CLOSED DOWN for a week while most of us went off on our annual junket to Château d'Oex in Switzerland. This was the venue for what had been for years the biggest balloon festival in mainland Europe. About eighty balloonists were invited each year, including about ten from Flying Pictures. It was more like a paid holiday floating around in the Swiss Alps.

Our sponsor at the event was the car parts group Unipart. Muir Moffat, who had been a good friend for many years, was number two at the company and a demanding client. Nevertheless, the event was something that we looked forward to every winter. Muir reckoned it was the most cost-effective corporate entertainment imaginable. His key customers were encouraged to relax for the several days they came and he made sure they were never burdened by constant attention from an overeager supplier. It would be an experience none of them would ever forget and it represented Muir's subtle approach to building important relationships. This meant that *we* had to entertain his clients both on the ground and in the sky. Muir would just appear every now and then with a bottle of champagne to check that everyone was happy. We always took at least one television crew with us to ensure we delivered some good media exposure to Unipart.

As an annual entertainment for the guests, Ian Ashpole would jump out of baskets and parachute back to the launch site. No one ever doubted that this was done more for his pleasure than theirs, but it all added to the variety of the occasion. This year there was to be a 'night glow' on the Saturday night. To create this spectacle, balloons would be inflated in the darkness at various points around the mountains. Directed by radio, the pilots would illuminate the balloons by turning on the burners. This theatrical event was synchronized to music which boomed around the village. Ian had the idea of positioning himself on the top of the main Unipart balloon at the principal launch site. After achieving the not inconsiderable feat of actually getting himself up there, he planned to set off some fireworks. It was an interesting idea and everyone thought it would be fun. It was.

Settled into his plastic chair on the top of his huge cushion some eighty feet above the ground, Ian began to organize his equipment. The first thing he did was to place a rocket

Previous spread A bunch of Swiss nuts livening up the opening of the Château d'Oex annual balloon festival. This spread Main picture: a picture-postcard scene from the balloon festival at Château d'Oex in Switzerland. Insets Me and Ian preparing for Alpine flight.

172

Nightglow at Château d'Oex. The burners light up the balloons, the whole spectacle synchronized to music by radio control from a central point to the pilots.

in an empty Champagne Mercier bottle. He lit the blue touchpaper and waited. Just as it ignited, the bottle fell over and whirled around on the chair, spinning the point of the missile around in a circle. Ian dived into the safety of the fabric at the top of the balloon. He was clear of the explosive device just as it fired itself off in a horizontal direction. It was a very powerful rocket, and succeeded in penetrating the skin of a Belgian balloon moored alongside. It went straight through the balloon and out the other side before ricocheting off the Belgian pilot's van. At last it fizzled into the snow, its force spent.

The Belgian pilot, Monsieur Benoît Siméon, is a courteous and charming man. Except when someone sends a rocket through his balloon. His outrage at the unfortunate incident was not unreasonable. Not all stunts work as planned first time, but this time the repairs and apologies cost us dear. We agreed with Ian that this was one trick that he should not try again.

When I got back to England I began planning a wholly different kind of event. The Walt Disney organization was keen to stage a big splash to create some publicity for the launch of the video of the movie *Aladdin*. Disney's promotions company had come up with the idea of a world record-breaking release of toy balloons. They couldn't think of anyone other than us who might have some idea how to do it. 'Sure, we ought to be able to fix that,' I told them.

We were going to have to release 1.6 million balloons simultaneously if we were to beat the record, which had been set in America. This time the CAA was not so keen on our plans. It was such a huge number of balloons that there were genuine fears that they could play havoc with aircraft. This meant that we couldn't stage the event anywhere near large cities or airports. We eventually settled on Longleat, the stately pile in Wiltshire owned by the Marquess of Bath.

We had never done anything like this before, so the first thing we did was to enlist the support of a professional who had done many big charity balloon releases. His name was Colin Renwick and our association with him was the start of a great relationship which has lasted to the present day. Colin had six huge marquees manufactured, we ordered the vast quantity of balloons and BOC supplied three tanker loads of helium gas.

When the day came we had managed to assemble 2000 volunteers, who had responded to radio appeals. It took all of them nearly seven hours to complete the task. Each balloon had to be inflated with helium from a bottle and then tied by hand before it was released to the ceiling of the marquee. When the job was done each of the marquees would have supported a three-ton hippopotamus. It all looked a mad extravagance when the tops of the six marquees were removed simultaneously at four o'clock in the afternoon. I shall never forget the look on my small son's face as the most incredible explosion of colour imaginable hit the sky.

We filmed the event from the ground and Marc was there, of course, in his helicopter. In America the film was shown on CNN coast to coast, every hour for a whole day.

Mission: Impossible came next. The movie, that is. Another great project involving action helicopters, the Channel Tunnel, trains and balloons. This time the balloons were unmanned. Some bright spark came up with the innovative idea that if eight little one-kilowatt light bulbs were put inside a white helium balloon, the diffused softness would simulate moonlight. The big, illuminated, lighter-than-air orbs could be adjusted for height by letting them up and down on a string. In this case the string would be attached to barges moored beside the bridge over the River Vltava in Prague, which was where the scene was set. We had been asked to give the balloons a try because light sources to illuminate the bridge for filming couldn't be installed on the bridge itself. The alternative would have cost a fortune as it called for high towers and heavy lighting equipment, including vast translucent screens.

I went to see Per Lindstrand, but he was otherwise occupied with an ill-conceived attempt to fly round the world in a balloon with Richard Branson. I was allocated a handsome young man called Jo Hansen, who was spending some time working at his fellow Swede's factory. Jo was clearly enjoying his stay. Only the week before, two seamstresses at the factory were having coffee in the canteen with Per when the conversation turned to the subject of the dishy visitor from Stockholm. One of them said to her boss, 'You know what? Me and Tracy reckon that we're the only two girls in Oswestry that Jo hasn't slept with.' When Jo was later told of the girls' claim, his response was, 'One of them is lying.'

Jo managed to tear himself away from his extracurricular activities to put together a very good prototype balloon, although I later discovered the whole thing had been subcontracted to a manufacturer whom Per had promised me he would outperform in quality. When we took it to Pinewood film studios the director of photography strutted around with his light meter and pronounced it brilliant. Four more, please. Another triumph.

In 1996 we started discussions about balloons directly with Sainsbury's, rather than dealing with the supermarket group's advertising agency. Even after twenty years we still had trouble enthusing agencies about the effectiveness of our product. Sainsbury's were currently in the doldrums, as Tesco had just overtaken them to become the UK's biggest supermarket chain, and they needed some activity to shake off their dowdy image and inject a buzz into the brand. One of their promotions managers, Chris Ward, had sent an e-mail to Sainsbury's new marketing director, Kevin McCarten, suggesting a balloon. Chris Ward told me of the client's positive response and a presentation was arranged for the following week. One night I was lying awake at about 2 am, wondering what might work. Suddenly an idea came to me. I woke Susie to tell her not to be alarmed if I went missing. 'I've had an idea and I'm going out to the shed to write it down.'

Main picture Our world-record balloon release. We organized 2000 people for eight hours to manually inflate the balloons. The upward pressure of the balloon gas would have supported a three-ton hippopotamus on each of the marquees.

Above Hijack of the filming helicopter. Archie and Pollyanna, top and bottom centre. Marc Wolff's children, Lily and Henry, are in the front and back seats respectively.

Aladdin. The best video you could wish for.

The garden shed was originally put there as an office for Susie's business, which was marketing board games. It had light, a heater, a desk and a computer. By the time the family woke I had mapped out an idea for an aerial circus.

Sainsbury's were particularly proud of their fresh produce, which was superior to that of the competition. I used this to conceive a number of hot-air balloons in the shape of a strawberry, an apple, a hand of bananas, a bunch of carrots and a bunch of flowers. This would be Sainsbury's Flying Circus. It would be transported around in vehicles painted in lots of primary colours and with attractive branding. It would go on tour to outdoor events and Sainsbury's stores all over Britain. Beyond this, I had a video in mind – something which could be given to staff and possibly even shown in stores. It would be an explosion of colour, complete with jugglers, clowns, stilt-walkers and barrel-organ jollity. The script would be hinged around a gamut of incredible stunts, which Ian Ashpole had already proven possible during previous escapades. This will cheer everyone up, I thought, and it will be a great way to bring a smile back to the brand.

When I went with Chris Ward to present this rather audacious scheme in the inner sanctum of the directors' floor at Sainsbury's headquarters on London's South Bank, I did not have high hopes. British marketing managers are a conservative bunch with a common allergy to taking a risk. Kevin McCarten, God bless him, was not one of them. His experience told him that an advertising agency would quote between £500,000 and £1 million to produce the video I proposed. I said we could do it for under £100,000. There were a lot of sensible and pertinent questions, but I convinced him that we were in the unique position of being able to supply everything required from within Flying Pictures' armoury. Subject to a few details, he was on. Just like that.

This was to be one of the most exciting projects in our history. The balloons were commissioned and the film script took shape. I gave myself the role of ringmaster, who would conduct activities from a Cloudhopper. Richard Mervyn, an experienced film director, who was working with us on a project to film the history of Britain from the air, would direct. Richard Hall, for whom I had worked in advertising at French Gold Abbott some twenty years before, had recently joined Flying Pictures as chairman. Coincidentally, the same David Abbott for whom Richard and I had worked all those years ago, was now chairman of Sainsbury's advertising agency, Abbott Mead Vickers. Because of the coincidence of knowing the agency well, Richard thought it might be worth going to see the Sainsbury's marketing team there. There just might be some potential for cooperation.

Above With cardboard moustache glued to my upper lip I become self-appointed Ringmaster of the Sainsbury's Flying Circus.
Opposite Scenes from Sainsbury's aerial extravaganza.

When we went together to see Adrian Vickers, he and his colleagues had already heard what we were up to and were intrigued to learn about the project. However, as I presented the scheme he appeared more and more bemused. He politely wished us luck and we left. As we walked out Richard summed up his analysis of the meeting. 'They started off interested,' he said, 'and they could see that an event like this could help change the supermarket's image of stuffiness. As you started to explain how it worked they began to suspect a degree of frivolity. You finally lost them when you came to the part about a gorilla jumping after a banana by bungee-jumping out of a balloon itself shaped like a bunch of bananas. After that, they couldn't get us out fast enough. To them this was more like a Bob Newhart sketch than a serious marketing ploy. They don't believe you, Colin. They think you're mad. You'll just have to show 'em.'

So we did.

The first day of shooting was in my local Sainsbury's at Badger Farm, near Winchester. We had the use of the store between midnight and five in the morning. The shoot featured a magician and a clown. My cousin Ian Keable, a full-time professional, was the magician. I was the clown.

For the aerial action we went to Much Marcle in Herefordshire. We had a cast of a hundred, mostly volunteers. There were checkout girls from the local Sainsbury's, plus the local band and choir. We dressed them all up as clowns with red noses. We had professional circus performers and, of course, we flew the balloons. Ian Ashpole had an exhausting two days as he went through almost all the stunts he had performed individually over previous years. He *did* bungee-jump out of the balloon dressed as a gorilla and he tightrope-walked as a clown from one balloon to another, carrying a bunch of flowers to a weeping girl in the other basket. Nigel Rogoff, leader of the RAF Falcons free fall team, was dressed as a rabbit and sat on a trapeze under a carrot-shaped balloon before falling off and skydiving down.

Halfway through the second day the landowner watched utterly gobsmacked as a couple of balloon pilots, dressed in glorious Technicolor, started to take a dinghy off the roof rack of a car. 'What *are* they doing *now*?' he was heard to ask. It was explained that this was just a safety boat for the next sequence, which involved the landowner's pond. 'Would it be all right if Colin Prescot, dressed as the ringmaster over there, flies that Cloudhopper and goes fishing from overhead? The script calls for him to hook a packet of sliced Sainsbury's Scotch Salmon on the end of a line out of your water.' Without the hint of a smile – was he having his leg pulled? – he waved his assent and left us

178

Above Having bailed out of a balloon by diving from an attached springboard at 5000 feet, Ian somehow ended up landing safely in this paddling pool. Magic.
Right Take-off of the Flying Circus from Much Marcle, Herefordshire.
Opposite Fishing for packets of Sainsbury's smoked salmon – and catching some.

180

Ian at 10,000 feet under
450 toy balloons.

to it. When I had completed the stunt a gust of wind caught me off guard. I disappeared unceremoniously into the stinking water, my white breeches ruined and riding boots full of the stagnant, gooey mud from the bottom. It brought gales of laughter and cheering from everyone there.

For the grand finale Ian donned a wetsuit, goggles and flippers. He did an impressive backflip off a makeshift diving board affixed to a basket at 8000 feet. The expert camera parachutist Simon Ward followed him down before the film cuts to show Ian landing safely in a child's paddling pool.

At the end of the final day someone remarked that it was the best staff outing we had ever had and ever would have. It was a fair comment.

Two months later Ian topped off his repertoire in Sainsbury's Flying Circus by performing the world's longest abseil. He descended a 1600-foot climbing rope from the strawberry-shaped balloon flying at 6000 feet over Albuquerque, New Mexico. He fell straight off the end of the rope and parachuted down.

The following year saw Ian performing yet another novel stunt, which would gain him an additional entry in *The Guinness Book of Records*. It was arguably his most ridiculous to date. We persuaded Champagne Mercier to sponsor Ian to climb to over 10,000 feet, carried beneath 500 large, helium-filled toy balloons. He was accompanied through the clouds by a balloon full of journalists floating nearby. The shots from the helicopter, which was flown by Marc Wolff, with Adam Dale as photographer, were to make the national television news bulletins, and a large picture of the ludicrous spectacle adorned the front page of *The Times* the following day.

Towards the end of 1997 we had a rather different kind of staff outing. Lucius Peart, now our marketing director, had been talking to London Weekend Television about *You Bet!*, which was screened nationally on Saturday nights. This was a fund-raising charity show based around the idea of stuntmen being challenged to do something which is seemingly impossible. A panel of celebrities gave their views as to whether the stuntman would succeed or not before the same question was put to a live audience in the studio, who voted yes or no. Then the film was shown. Some stunts succeeded, some didn't. The percentage of the members of the audience who had voted correctly determined the amount of money which went to charity. For the successful stuntmen the prize was the sort of desperately vulgar trophy that ends up on display in the loo. Those who had failed went home shame-faced with nothing.

The show's producers were interested in staging some sort of waterskiing stunt and, without a moment's hesitation, Lucius told them that we could organize one with a helicopter and that I was their man. 'I'm forty-seven, Lucius. I think they will probably think I'm a bit old for waterskiing stunts,' I told him. 'I haven't done one for years.' I took a look at it anyway. After all, I was the only person in Britain who could demonstrate to the CAA that I had previous experience (authorized by them) of waterskiing behind a helicopter. Eventually a scenario was agreed upon where the challenge would be to ski a course in a certain amount of time. The catch was that to succeed I had to be towed by three different forms of transport. We worked out that if I started on a mono-ski with a jump-start off a jetty, a boat could tow me through a slalom course. Then a skier towed by a car from an adjoining footpath could bring me out his tow rope, which I would grab, and he would drop away. Finally I would cut a course to below the helicopter, where a rope would be suspended for me to grab on the way to the finishing line.

The location selected was the Olympic-standard rowing lake in Nottingham, which was straight, man-made, had a towpath and was two kilometres in length.

What I told my colleagues (but not London Weekend Television) was that I had never done a jump-start in my life. I explained my problem to the Thames Valley Ski Club, who had a high jetty and thought they could help. Jump-starts from high up are terrifying. You stand there, one foot on the edge of the jetty, the other planted in a mono-ski. You gather about eight arm's lengths of slack rope, psyche yourself up for the impending terror and shout, 'Go.' The boat does exactly that. It speeds away at thirty miles an hour while you watch the slack rope disappearing faster and faster until the fraction of a second before it goes taut. This is the moment when you wonder what on earth you are doing there and you have an almost irresistible urge to let go and admit, 'Sorry, guys, this is not for me.' If you hold on and jump at exactly the right moment, and get your balance absolutely right, you hit the water with a crash – but you are skiing. Wow.

The first time I tried I went absolutely flat on my face and it hurt. When I pulled myself together and had another go, exactly the same thing happened. I had had enough.

With Ian before filming
You Bet!

I went back to the office and admitted defeat. 'Come on, Col, you can do it.' Lucius had faith. I went back the next day. We went through the whole rigmarole again until my instructor, a teenage junior champion, asked if I would like him to demonstrate. Yes, I would. I stood beside him on the high jetty, listened to him coolly talk me through the procedure, saw the rope go taut and watched him fall flat on his face in the water. 'Well, I never said it was easy,' was all he could offer. I phoned Susie on my mobile phone on the way back. 'I'm not sure I'm up to this.' She was sympathetic. 'You have to practise. Give it time.' So I went back again. And again. On the fifth day I suddenly did it. I can't explain why. I was bracing myself for another painful dunking when I found myself skiing along on the water. I couldn't hear them but I could see the cheering and screaming of celebration from everyone in the boat. I did it again. I had the knack. I was ready to go.

We had one day for rehearsal and one day for the real thing. This was to be a company outing. Just about everyone involved was an employee of Flying Pictures – the pilot, engineer, camera crew and assistants. Ian Ashpole was a competent skier who would be the hand-over man skiing behind a Land Rover Discovery driven by Lucius. The only thing we did not supply was the boat and driver. On the first day the gales were so strong and the weather so bad that we couldn't even get the helicopter up from its base at Elstree. That left us the single day to try everything out, go for the real thing and record it on film. Most of the morning was spent driving a boat round in ever-decreasing circles, trying to grab a line dangled from the helicopter. The downwash and turbulence played such games with the handle that I couldn't get hold of it. We soon gave up and improvised by having another skier start in the water and be pulled by the helicopter before handing over to me in the same way as the car. But there was no other skier. John Marzano, our ground cameraman, said he had done some skiing. He volunteered, adding that his assistant could operate the camera. There was no time to argue.

We did a couple of trial runs of the whole course and the producer timed us. The fastest we had done it was in two minutes fifty-two seconds. It was time to go for it. The

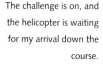

The challenge is on, and the helicopter is waiting for my arrival down the course.

producer explained we could do the event once only and that whatever resulted would be the piece for television. The challenge was to complete the stunt in two minutes thirty seconds. 'That's impossible,' I complained. 'The fastest we have managed is more than twenty seconds longer than that.' 'It doesn't matter if you don't succeed. It's going to be great television,' he replied. Someone suggested that the show had had a run of successes recently and that a few more failures were needed to even it out. Bugger that, I thought. It may not matter to him if I don't succeed, but it matters to me.

The team and I went into a huddle and discussed how we might speed things up a bit. Another ten knots for the boat (I would just have to be a bit more careful on the turns) and the changeovers would just have to be slicker.

The cameras were set, the crowds moved back and the countdown was heard over the PA system: 'Three, two, one, go.' The boat took off and I was grateful to be still upright when I hit the water. I got through the slalom course at the increased speed, dug into the outer edge of my ski and leaned over to get nearer the bank where Ian Ashpole had just surfaced. But however much we both pulled we couldn't reach each other – the boat driver was just too far from the shore. The poor fellow was the only member of the team who was not used to working with us and he couldn't make head or tail of my frantic hand signals. The challenge was blown. I took a gamble. I simply let go of the rope and sank into the water. I figured that, without even the first changeover on film, the producer would have nothing worth showing. As I waded out of the lake to meet him I apologized and explained what had happened. My gamble paid off. 'I saw what happened,' he said, 'would you mind doing it again?'

The final run went smoothly past the first change. As I reached John Marzano, head of our camera department, skiing behind the helicopter he was leaning out as hard as he could in order to reach me. As I approached he was shouting, 'Quick. I can't hold on much longer.' I lunged at the handle and just grabbed it in time before he collapsed into the water. Unknown to me, a radio message was then screamed by Lucius to Terry Neill, who was piloting the helicopter: 'Floor it, Terry.' I was suddenly going a terrifying sixty miles an hour on a short, unstable ski with the pull from above rather than from in front. It felt as though I would lose control at any second, which would cause at least some injury. How I kept going to the finishing line I shall never know.

When I was brought back to shore by the speedboat and stepped exhausted on to the jetty, the cameras were all in position. The presenter, Sarah Matravers, said, 'You don't know if you've done it, do you?' 'No,' I replied. 'Have I?'

'Congratulations,' she said as she produced the appalling plastic trophy from behind her back.

The transfer to the helicopter tow successfully completed, it's a dash for the finish line.

183

CHAPTER FOURTEEN

TOUCHING THE FACE OF GOD

P ER LINDSTRAND AND I HAD ALWAYS HARBOURED AN AMBITION to break the world altitude record for balloons. For most of the many years we knew each other there was rarely an occasion when we met without talking about it. It would be the ultimate adventure. By 1997 we agreed that if we were ever going to get such a project under way we had better get a move on.

Per had always been different. I suppose we were all different but he was *very* different. Every time he got difficult I would chide him, 'You're not only an old bastard, you're a bloody-minded old bastard.' This always brought him down to earth with a smile. He was unusual in that he was a Swede with a wonderful sense of humour. It would serve him well at awkward times, of which there were many. Quite often he would promise one thing and deliver something quite different, by which time it was too late to do anything about it. These shortcomings were often compensated for by his easy charm. We all had a lot of fun with him and he produced some very good balloons for us over a number of years.

However, when the cock-ups did happen they were often spectacular. The most notable in my case was the lethal spreader rig on *Superman III*, which collapsed on the first test. They didn't only happen to me.

Mike Kendrick, at that time the director of Lighter Than Air Limited (and now Chief Executive of the Virgin Airship and Balloon Company), once ordered a hot-air airship from Per for the makers of Peter Stuyvesant cigarettes. It was completed so late that the first test flight had to be made in front of both the new client and the press at the same time. The new airship was supposed to have a vectored thrust system (in which air is ducted out of the envelope near the aerodynamic stabilization fins at the rear of the ship) to give it more control. It never worked in repeated tests, which was why it was delivered late. However, it was apparently airworthy and it had a flight duration of two hours, which was considered acceptable.

Previous spread An artist's impression of the biggest manned balloon in history on the Edge of Space.
Above With Per Lindstrand in Switzerland, discussing our ambitions with the press.

At least that was the theory. As the new ship flew off to the popping of champagne corks, the pilot was to radio back that he was running out of fuel only a few minutes after take-off. The majestic craft bounced ungraciously on the roof of a house before crashing into a field. One enterprising photographer scooped an excellent picture of the mishap at the moment when the tiles were being dislodged from the roof. The picture was splashed across a local newspaper the next day with the headline 'SMOKING CAN SERIOUSLY DAMAGE YOUR HOUSE'. The tobacco company did not consider this the sort of publicity they wanted and immediately fired the operators. The next time the airship was flown, this time by a different pilot, he put his hand too close to the propeller and lost a finger. (Welcome to the Nine Finger Club, Mr Kirby.)

Per is a big, tough man with incredible guts. Although many of his projects did not work first time he did notch up some very remarkable achievements. This can be put down to some contrary qualities, including determination, enthusiasm, self-belief and luck. As I write, he still holds the world record for altitude, distance and duration for hot-air filled balloons. The first of these records he achieved on his own, the others with his long-term benefactor, Richard Branson. We all had our hearts in our mouths when the pair used to set off across oceans. Richard was not an experienced balloon pilot and Per was not – in the opinion of many – an appropriate partner, in spite of his experience. Nevertheless, they survived and have trophies and certificates to prove it. If ever there was an odd couple this was it. 'Don't you fear for your life?' I once asked Per, and his reply was, 'I think that if the Almighty wanted me, he would have got me by now.' He had a point.

Richard was very loyal to Per, continuing to employ him through three major projects (which involved a much higher number of attempted flights). This was in spite of several public outbursts by Per and a joke about his Labrador dog, Charlie. Per told reporters that there would be a crew of three crossing the Pacific – he to fly the balloon, Richard to work the video and Charlie to bite Richard if he ever dared touch a single control.

Mike Kendrick, as flight director of the Branson adventures, was to react robustly to the sniggers that resulted from Per's irreverence. He pointed out that, apart from providing funding, Richard had in fact made some key decisions that had averted imminent disaster on several occasions. In particular Mike was convinced that the Pacific crossing would not have ended happily but for Richard taking control during a period of several hours when everything was going alarmingly wrong. Per was apparently behaving strangely at the time and one theory was that he was incapacitated by hypoxia. Mike also felt compelled to refer to Per's crash-landing off Scotland after crossing the Atlantic. It left Richard safely aboard the balloon while the pilot jumped in the water without an immersion suit or even a life jacket. 'It was a miracle that he was stumbled upon by a passing dinghy,' Mike said.

Whatever they said about each other, Richard and Per could hardly be called a team. At best there was an uneasy truce on the rare occasions when they were actually together. Interestingly, in his autobiography Richard was to describe his long-term flying partner as a 'loner'.

In spite of all this Per and I had had a lot of fun together over the years, I knew him well and I thought I could work with him on a high-altitude flight, provided he employed properly qualified engineers to run the technical side of the project.

An attempt at the world altitude record appealed to my sense of theatre. It would be visually breathtaking stuff. The balloon would be more than ten times bigger than any manned balloon in history. I had long dreamed of seeing the world from the Edge of Space. And a flight at the start of the new millennium would evoke the bygone age of space exploration and capture the imagination of millions. After all, most people didn't even know that manned ballooning in the stratosphere once *was* the American space programme. There were many forgotten heroes who risked their lives in the quest for scientific knowledge. The main purpose of these flights was to find out how man could survive in the hostile environment that exists outside the world we live in.

For me this flight was the ultimate challenge. I was attracted to the idea of recording, with the benefit of the best of modern technology, what could be one of the most intriguing images ever made. The holy grail would be a picture of the biggest manned balloon in history in an ink-black sky with the curvature of the earth and a 650,000-square-mile view below. Most bizarre and compelling of all was the theatrical element of two little spacemen on an open, flat-platformed deck in the vast arena of space. Obtaining such an image was not going to be easy, but I felt sure there must be a way of taking with us a piggyback balloon which could be floated off into space with remote cameras on board.

The first high-altitude flight of any significance took place in 1927, when Hawthorne Gray, a US Army Air Service captain aged thirty-eight, flew from Belleville, Illinois, to 27,000 feet. Unable to absorb oxygen into his lungs, he passed out with hypoxia. Fortunately he came to before landing. He made two further attempts, on the second of which he braved his way to 40,000 feet, but he was to be found dead in a tree after this final descent.

In early 1931 Auguste Piccard and Charles Kipfer, both Swiss, made the first flight into the stratosphere using a closed capsule and passed 50,000 feet. They lifted off from

187

On an open deck on the edge of space. An artist's impression of me and Andy Elson (with whom I was later to form a partnership).

Augsburg in Germany and landed in the mountains near Obergurgl in Austria. In September of the same year the Russians joined in the fun when the Red Army launched a balloon, enabling Georgi Prokoiev to set a new world record at 62,304 feet.

In early 1933 Tex Settle and Chester Fordney made a flight to 59,000 feet from Akron, Ohio, and they made the first live transmission from the stratosphere to the earth. Settle described the journey as being to the region of night beyond the earth's atmosphere. This was followed in July of the same year by an attempt by Kepner, Stevens and Anderson. Sponsored by *National Geographic* magazine and the Army Air Corps, the three Americans reached 60,000 feet when the balloon started to fall apart. As it descended to 5000 feet the hydrogen ignited and the balloon exploded. All three men jumped clear and landed safely in parachutes.

Josef Stalin was irritated by Settle, Fordney and the others upstaging Prokoiev. He therefore ordered another Soviet attempt, this time by three civilians called Fedosienko, Wasienko and Vyskin. They claimed to have reached 67,585 feet at the end of January 1934. However, they used too much ballast to attain their altitude and did not retain enough to slow their descent. They were killed on impact, which caused national grief, described universally as the greatest since the death of Lenin. Their ashes were entombed in the Kremlin wall.

In 1937 Stevens and Anderson (without Kepner) reached a new record of 74,000 feet. They were the first human beings to report seeing the curvature of the earth with their own eyes. They also shot the first motion pictures in the stratosphere.

In the dismal thirties such flights had a dramatic effect on public morale in the United States and the Soviet Union alike. The historian David De Vorkin saw them as 'compelling symbols of the romance of the human spirit with which every citizen could identify and vicariously experience'.

There were no more attempts for two decades.

In 1956 Lieutenant Commanders Malcolm Ross and Lee Lewis of the US Navy flew a balloon to 76,000 feet, the first flight into the stratosphere for almost twenty years. Now the USA and the Soviet Union had their sights firmly on space and the manned balloons became the focus of serious scientific experiments rather than of sporting glory.

That same year, under the command of Colonel John Paul Stapp, the Man High project was initiated by the US Air Force to research the effects on human beings of living in an environment devoid of atmosphere. The programme's first flight was made by Joe Kittinger to a new record of 96,000 feet in a pressurized capsule.

A year later Ross and Lewis improved their own altitude (now overtaken by Kittinger) to 86,000 feet. The flight was made shortly after the Russian's first *Sputnik* flight into outer space, so it hardly got a mention in the media. In August 1957 David Simons of the United States set a new record of 102,000 feet and was the first man to remain in the stratosphere for a whole night.

The third of the Man High flights was made in October 1958 by twenty-six-year-old Clifton McClure. Probably the most remarkable of all the balloonists to fly into the stratosphere, he had reached over 100,000 feet when he reported very high temperatures on board. (These were later discovered to be due to the fact that a ground-crew member had forgotten to replenish the cooling system with de-icer before take-off.) McClure was immediately ordered to descend as quickly as possible. Due to the extreme heat, he had already developed a fever and reported his body temperature to be 104 degrees Fahrenheit. It is widely acknowledged as a near miracle that, despite some lapses in concentration, he managed to retain consciousness during the necessarily long descent. The arriving helicopter emergency services witnessed a perfect landing high up in the San

Opposite At launch the 'Edge of Space' balloon will stand six times the height of Nelson's Column.

189

190

The American team of Kepner, Stevens and Anderson start their ascent to 60,000 feet in 1934.

Andres Mountains of New Mexico. The pilot was capable of firing the explosive bolts to eject the balloon from the capsule at precisely the correct moment. McClure was ordered to remain completely still until help arrived, to which he replied that he hadn't come all this way to be carried off in a stretcher. He actually climbed out and walked to the arriving crew, where his temperature was recorded at an almost unbelievable 108.5 degrees, which, until then, had been considered unsurvivable. Within an hour his temperature had been brought down to an acceptable 100 degrees and he was pronounced perfectly fit by the next day.

In November 1959 Joe Kittinger made the first of a series of US Air Force flights using an open gondola and with the pilot wearing a partial pressure suit. He endured a number of serious difficulties and parachuted out at 76,400 feet. He blacked out during the descent but regained consciousness in time to land safely. One month later, with all the technical problems of the previous flight satisfactorily resolved, he made a further ascent to 75,000 feet. Then, in August 1960, he flew to 102,500 feet to record the highest-ever parachute jump, which has stood for forty years. Kittinger endured excruciating pain caused by a failure in the pressurization of his right glove. His hand had swollen to twice its normal size at the point of jumping. His incapacity meant that he was unable to detach his heavy backpack near the ground and he had a very heavy landing, which he survived with no more than unpleasant bruising.

In 1961 Commander Malcolm Ross and Lieutenant Commander Vic Prather of the US Navy rose from the deck of an American aircraft carrier in the Gulf of Mexico to reach a world record height of 113,740 feet, an achievement which has never been surpassed. The flight went with no hitches and a perfect landing was made a few miles from the carrier. Tragically Vic Prather had his visor open when the helicopter came to pick him up. He missed the line, fell in the water, disappeared beneath the surface and drowned.

A year after this tragedy the Russians decided to rejoin the competition. Andreyev parachuted out at 20,000 feet on the first Russian ascent for twenty-eight years and the last one ever staged. His co-pilot, Dolgov, stayed aboard to reach 93,970 feet, at which altitude he also jumped. For some unreported reason, instead of allowing him to freefall to a safer environment, his parachute immediately deployed. His in-suit pressurized oxygen supply would have been limited and he lost his life during the long descent.

The flight which Per and I started to plan would entail a target altitude of 132,000 feet (twenty-five miles) and to achieve this we would have to build the largest balloon in history. The huge balloons used in the round-the-world attempts of recent years had been in the region of 500,000 to 750,000 cubic feet in volume. Our balloon would need to have an almost unimaginable volume of 40 million cubic feet. The maximum altitude, or 'ceiling', as with all gas balloons, is the point at which a balloon is completely full. If the balloon is still rising at the ceiling, the helium expanding as a result of decreasing atmospheric pressure causes gas to dribble out of the bottom (where an opening is left as its only automatic means of escape). The loss of gas means that the balloon will fly no higher. To reach a ceiling of twenty-five miles we could calculate the size of our balloon by taking into account a number of factors. These included the all-up weight (the total weight of the balloon, fuel and passengers), the decrease in atmospheric pressure during the ascent and the outside temperature at the ceiling. The balloon would be fabricated from a clear polyethylene film, which is extraordinarily light yet tough enough to withstand a high-altitude temperature in the region of -100 degrees Fahrenheit. The material was to be similar to the plastic which freezer bags are made of – but thinner. The gas bag would be filled with a big bubble of helium which would expand as it rose and the air got thinner. At the Edge of Space it would occupy some 300 times the volume that it had at launch.

A clear and calm day would have to be selected for the flight and the ascent would be made at a rate of about 800 feet per minute and take approximately three hours. The deaths of previous explorers of the higher regions provided a sharp reminder of the dangers of our planned journey. In particular, weather balloons of the kind we would use still had a ten per cent failure record. This normally meant that the ill-fated ones shattered in the sharp increase in wind speed caused by the tropopause, a band of temperature change normally found at around 50,000 feet. However, with modern weather forecasting, we were confident we could avoid such a disaster. After reaching the ceiling at the Edge of Space many hours would be spent creating lasting images for the media, which had never previously been possible.

Captain Joseph Kittinger of the US Air Force in a partial pressure suit at over 100,000 feet, just before he made the longest jump in history, on 8 August 1960.

Unfortunately our plans to fly to that exalted region were short-lived. It was not long before Per decided to immerse himself in a project where there was immediate money on the table. Pursuing a logical extension to his successful crossings of the Atlantic and Pacific, he had been attempting to fly around the world with Richard Branson since 1996. They now decided to have another go. My plan to fly to the upper atmosphere was put on ice.

At this point I had to acknowledge that much had changed since Clare Francis asked me eleven years earlier if it was possible to fly around the world in a balloon. Weather forecasting was more sophisticated, balloon technology had improved to give longer flight potential and small lightweight GPS navigation systems gave instant updates of position and speed. In spite of all this it had never really occurred to me that I might get involved in the challenge to circumnavigate the globe, preferring instead the allure of the Edge of Space, which had always fascinated me.

And then, out of the blue, I received a phone call from someone whose name I knew but whom I had never met. His name was Andy Elson.

CHAPTER FIFTEEN

BOY GENIUS AND THE NON-FLYING SCOTSMAN

RICHARD BRANSON'S COCKTAIL OF COMMERCIALISM, irreverence and guts never failed to dazzle. No one could miss his adventures. And none of this was lost on James Manclark, a millionaire living in grand style in East Lothian, Scotland. He had watched the reports of Branson, Lindstrand and (Alex) Ritchie launching from Morocco in early 1997 as the bearded wonder's team had another go at flying around the world. From behind his morning newspaper, James Manclark was hatching a plot.

James's early background included Harrow and the Life Guards. Since then he had been a landowner and, in his words, he dabbled in property. Now in his late fifties, he had previously participated in many rich man's games such as powerboat racing, luging (representing Britain in the 1968 Olympics in Grenoble), bobsleighing (representing Britain in the 1972 Olympics in Sapporo), horse racing and polo. Most intriguing of all, he was co-founder and Chairman of the World Elephant Polo Association. Every year he would set off for Tiger Tops in Nepal for the elephant polo season.

Now he resolved to take on Richard Branson at his own game and beat him to the prize for completing the first circumnavigation of the world in a balloon. Andy Elson was working as a design consultant for Cameron Balloons on the day when James came bowling into the Bristol factory. He had come to meet the owner, Donald Cameron, and Alan Noble, a veteran organizer of big balloon adventures and a consultant to the company. James simply said he was going to be the first person to fly around the world in a balloon and what were they all going to do about it? He had never flown a balloon in his life but he had made up his mind.

Don Cameron had been steadily building a solid business out of supplying balloons and equipment for the round-the-world attempts and he was keen to facilitate James's new quest for adventure. James asked who he should fly with. Alan introduced him to Andy. 'This is James Manclark. He wants to fly around the world.' 'Oh really?' was the engineer's simple and uninterested response. He was later persuaded to take more notice. Andy's girlfriend, Jackie, was also working in the factory. 'There's money there,' she told him. The two men were chalk and cheese. But when James and Andy eventually talked they got on well.

The silver spoon was missing from Andy's mouth when he was born in 1953. However, he was lucky to be adopted at an early age by his new and loving parents, Don and Phyllis Elson, with whom he grew up in Somerset. By all accounts he was a difficult child who regularly played truant from school. At the age of fourteen he went dinghy sailing with a girlfriend (whose name he can't remember) at Salcombe in Devon. When they got out into the Channel they kept going until they got to Cherbourg. Andy telephoned his concerned parents to say where he was and, not surprisingly, he was told to come back immediately. So he simply turned around and sailed back.

At the local school, Wellsway Secondary Modern, they failed to spot that he was a gifted boy with a frighteningly high IQ but severely dyslexic. His exam results were not good, he wasn't interested anyway and he was prone to wandering off to do what he felt like doing. It was a bonus for his English teacher one day when Andy was prepared to recite a poem to the class. His chosen piece was *Eskimo Nell*. He had learned the unabridged version, which is usually omitted from schoolbooks. He was doing well until he came to the verse which reads:

Back to the land of the Eskimo
Where spunk is spunk
Not a trickling stream of lukewarm cream
But a solid frozen chunk…

'ELSON. OUT. OUT OF MY CLASS IMMEDIATELY,' bellowed the teacher.

Downcast, Andy sloped off to find work on a building site, not to be seen much at school thereafter. He finally left Wellsway at the age of sixteen with no qualifications.

Later he attended the Royal Technical College at Filton, in Bristol, where he took an interest. In fact, to everyone's surprise, he excelled. He went on to read aeronautical engineering at Bath University.

In Andy's professional career he built up a successful engineering business before being distracted by the allure of hot-air balloons. His business disappeared and he became a professional balloonist before reverting to being an engineering consultant for Cameron Balloons, the largest balloon manufacturer in the world. His most significant feat in flying to date had been the first crossing of Mount Everest in 1991.

Andy and James came to an arrangement whereby

Andy would build the capsule and Cameron Balloons would manufacture the balloon envelope. James would give some money to Andy to start work and he would be back with a sponsor in short order. That was in the summer of 1997.

When Andy called me in September he said he hadn't received any money and James had failed to secure a sponsorship. He wondered if I had any ideas and could help. I told him it was too short notice and I didn't think it was realistic.

The Elson/Manclark project was postponed to 1998 while James gave himself more time to secure the funding required. At the same time Bertrand Piccard and Wim Verstraeten asked Andy if he would join them on *Breitling Orbiter 2*. Swiss-born Piccard and the Belgian Verstraeten had made an attempt the previous year but had survived in the air for only six hours. As they approached the Mediterranean after their launch from Switzerland they smelled kerosene on board; it had seeped into the capsule, which Andy had designed for them. They were reluctant to continue. This year they were anxious not to have any repeat of technical problems they were not qualified to solve. Therefore it made sense to take along the engineer who had designed the system. James Manclark willingly released Andy, taking the view that the experience he would get would come in useful for their flight the following year. Neither Andy nor James seriously considered that the flight of *Breitling Orbiter 2* would have much chance of succeeding in getting all the way round the world.

Piccard, Verstraeten and Elson set off from Château d'Oex, Switzerland, in January 1998 and landed almost ten days later in Myanmar (formerly Burma). A few weeks after the flight Andy came to Flying Pictures to meet Lucius Peart, our Marketing Director. The purpose of his visit was to discuss a totally different project, involving the RAF's Red Devils. When I bumped into him outside the front door as he arrived, I congratulated him on a great achievement. We then chatted briefly about the fact that he had resumed work on the Manclark project with a view to launching at the end of 1998. He had at last received some seed money and had started work on the capsule. As he was called into his meeting I simply said, 'Let me know if I can help.' The next day he called me and said I could. 'Could what?' I asked. 'Help,' he replied. He had no faith that his partner was ever

'Look at my new baby.' James Manclark with his newly-welded pressurized capsule shell, designed for a flight of up to a month in the stratosphere.

195

going to raise the funds required and besides, there was more time to get organized this time around.

With a twinge of interest, I agreed to go and see him at his workshop in Glastonbury, Somerset.

When I arrived I found Andy in his overalls. I was introduced to Glenn Fairley. 'It's just the two of us,' Andy explained. 'We are building the gondola together. We do everything. And we both clean the toilet,' he added. This was Andy's way of emphasizing that it was a democracy, which it wasn't. After an hour of looking around the basic aluminium shell that would become the capsule, I was impressed. I said I would think about it all. As I drove home I alarmed myself with the sudden realization that I was thinking about it all quite seriously. I discussed it with Susie, who was at first reluctant to endorse my enthusiasm. 'If you go and kill yourself, I'll never forgive you,' was her humorous, though completely serious reaction. After more than ten years together she knew me well enough to know that I was already unstoppable. Just why I was unstoppable was a question I couldn't answer. The old cliché 'because it was there' is probably the best explanation I could offer. 'OK,' she said, 'but let's get it over with quickly.'

When I called Andy the next morning he was not expecting to hear what I had to say. I told him that the sponsorship funding required was substantial enough for any interested company to insist on investigating the project very seriously before proceeding. In my view there were only three ways to get money for this sort of high-risk adventure:

1. You are very rich and subscribe the funds yourself. (If your name is Richard Branson and you have made several hundred million pounds this is not so hard.)

2. You have an amazing stroke of good fortune. (Breitling is a Swiss company, it has a historical association with aviation pioneers, Bertrand Piccard is Swiss and his grandfather, Auguste Piccard, was the first European to fly into the stratosphere – that's a pretty lucky set of circumstances.)

3. You find someone who is personally passionate and obsessed enough about the project to be *desperate*.

I told him that option one – self-funding – might be a possibility, although I knew his partner was a reluctant investor of further funds. Number two – luck – couldn't be counted on. That left number three. If he wanted *me* to be passionate and obsessive about getting the sponsorship I would have to be one of the pilots.

Andy took in what I was saying and said he would have to talk to James. There then followed a few days when Andy and I checked out each other's piloting credentials with the same experts. When I spoke to Don Cameron and Alan Noble they were amused to be answering the same questions that had just been put to them by Andy. Don told me that after the last Breitling project he had resolved never to work with Andy again, adding, 'But I must say it was only momentary. He's a super chap.' Alan told me that Andy was completely unmanageable. He recalled a critical time in France during the preparations for the Breitling flight when Andy complained about a dirty hotel room he was occupying. He insisted on moving to another one the following night. When he discovered he was still booked into the same hotel (Alan had had the problem rectified) it just wasn't good enough as far as he was concerned. Without saying anything to anyone, he simply disappeared, hitch-hiking to Paris and then catching a flight home. No one could find him anywhere for three days. Several other people had no hesitation in advising me that Andy was unreliable and dangerous – to work with, that is. When I talked to him about his reputation he made no effort to defend himself. 'It's all true,' he said simply.

In spite of all this there was a point about which everyone was unanimous: 'He's a brilliant engineer.'

I now had a picture of someone who clearly liked things to be exactly as he wanted. I surmised that Andy possessed justified self-confidence and focus. However, if any irritation or distraction upset his concentration he would simply go crazy. I thought I could handle that. After all, the characteristics seemed to me to be very similar to those of several creative directors I had worked with in advertising. With anyone who is creatively brilliant there is almost always a price to pay.

What I liked about Andy was that he was determined to do a good job and he had a reassuring sense of humour. He enjoyed his work, he had an easy charm and we got on well. I was also reassured that several balloonists had told me that he was dead honest and he was that rare breed of engineer who did not go wildly over budget as a result of failed experiments being discarded along the way.

I made up my mind. If James and Andy would have me, I was in.

James was due to visit Bristol on 8 April and Andy suggested we all met for dinner afterwards. We agreed on Warminster, which we calculated as being roughly equidistant between them and me. 'We'll meet at the first pub we find on the left as we leave the A303,' I suggested. I arrived a couple of minutes before the other two. Andy drew up beside me in his Lotus rocket ship and climbed out of the driver's seat. 'Not this pub,' I said. 'Let's go into Warminster.' Andy said that as James was six foot five and had extreme difficulty getting in and out of the car, he had better not get out to say hello. Instead, an arm appeared from the passenger window, rather like a tentacle from an octopus. I took the hand on the end of it and shook it.

Over prawn cocktail and lamb chops I was interviewed by James, while Andy kept disappearing to talk on his mobile phone. He asked me what made me think I could find a sponsor when he had been unable to do so. 'Well, it's my business,' I said. 'It's what I do.' Even so, I explained, I didn't think it would be an easy task and there were no guarantees. I wanted no payment for seeking a sponsor but I would aim to include a reasonable profit if I was successful. 'I gather you want to fly with us,' James said.

'Yes.'

I explained that my first port of call would be Cable & Wireless because the company had just sponsored a very successful round-the-world boat trip, setting a new world record for ships under power. This would be a very obvious extension to that success. 'They're not interested,' said James positively. 'I've already approached them right at the top and the answer was no.' I suggested respectfully that approaching all his chums who were chairmen of the big multinationals was not necessarily the right way to go about the problem in this day and age. The old-boy network was out of fashion. 'I don't have your contacts, but I do know how to run a professional project, the selling of which should be pitched at below board level,' I said. James was unimpressed. However, he was prepared to let me have a go.

'How much did Cable & Wireless spend on their boat project?' James asked. I told him that I believed that it was probably in the region of £1 million. Later on I was amused that James told me he needed £1 million for the balloon flight. Curious that. Andy had told me only the day before that James required just half that amount on top of his investment to complete the project.

I learned from Andy the next morning that I had passed my test and James had accepted that if I raised the sponsorship I could join them on board the balloon. This was a relief to Andy, who was fast coming to the conclusion that there had to be two pilots on board anyway. James just wouldn't make the grade.

Cable & Wireless Adventurer, which set a new record for circumnavigation of the world in a powered vessel – 74 days, 20 hours and 58 minutes – in 1998.

That same day I called Karen Earl, who ran a sponsorship agency which was the largest independent company of its kind in Britain. I had known Karen for many years and we had always said to each other that one day we must work together. Karen had also managed the Cable & Wireless boat project with masterly PR skill. 'I need to meet you,' I said.

'When?'

'Today.'

By chance she was free at lunchtime and we met at the Sugar Club restaurant in Notting Hill. I told her my story and by the time I had finished describing my two new partners we had both got the giggles. 'You're really serious about this, aren't you?' she concluded. Karen had never in her career gone out and sold a project to anyone. Her business was essentially taking on the management of projects that companies had already committed to. Nevertheless, she said she would think about it. In the meantime she would be happy to set up a meeting with Catherine Barton-Smith, Cable & Wireless's sponsorship manager, to get a reaction.

I went into overdrive. First I spent several days with Andy thrashing through every technical detail until I understood it all. Then I set about putting a prospectus together. In early May James, Andy and I met at Flying Pictures for a photographic session in the studio. I had a brochure printed entitled 'The Science of Success', a line provided by Richard Hall. The slogan was to become the soundbite by which we were to differentiate ourselves from the other teams.

I had met Catherine Barton-Smith before. We had talked about the Edge of Space project when I was planning it with Per Lindstrand. On that occasion she got me all wrong. 'You're mad,' was her reaction then, so I was a little apprehensive about how she would view this new caper. In the event she took a great interest and had probably decided that with this plan I had at least a chance of coming back alive. Even so, she didn't hold out great hope. Her boss, Adrian Moorey, was away, and besides, there was no budget and the timing was wrong. The boat adventure had only just ended and Cable & Wireless would not be planning another major sponsorship until the summer of 1999 at the earliest. However, given that the jet stream winds in the northern hemisphere are only suitable for a round-the-world flight in the winter months and our attempt was scheduled for the winter of 1998–9, we would be unable to fit in with Cable & Wireless's timetable even if we wanted to delay the project.

I wrote to everyone I knew. I wrote to everyone I did not know. I made trips to America and Europe when anyone showed the slightest interest. I got more and more cross with every rejection. Once a week I would spend a day with Andy going over his steady, focused progress. I had said to him at the outset that it was by no means certain that I would succeed in getting a sponsor and that even if I did it might be at the very last minute because time was short. He remained completely relaxed and philosophical every time our hopes were raised, then dashed. 'I think you're doing a brilliant job,' he would say encouragingly after each failure.

199

In the meantime Andy and James weren't getting along well. Andy considered, quite rightly, that James would have to start concentrating on training and safety if he was serious about climbing aboard the balloon. He was also irritated that James remained in Scotland, offering little help to the project. 'What do you think you contribute to this adventure, Mr Dolittle Manclark?' he faxed him bluntly. 'The money,' came back the reply. 'Even that never arrives on time,' replied Andy.

Russell Brice had now joined the team full time to run all the logistics. A calm and modest man with huge mountaineering achievements behind him, Russell was a New Zealander living in Chamonix, in the French Alps. As well as coordinating and running countless expeditions to the Himalayas, he had climbed Mount Everest twice and would have done so many more times if he had not had to bring team members down when it was clear they weren't going to make it. Also, he had supplied invaluable local information to Andy for his successful balloon flight over Everest in 1991. In July James Manclark had a meeting in London for which he would be flying down from Edinburgh. He suggested we all meet at Heathrow to review progress. As Andy was too busy and didn't want to waste a whole day, Russell and I

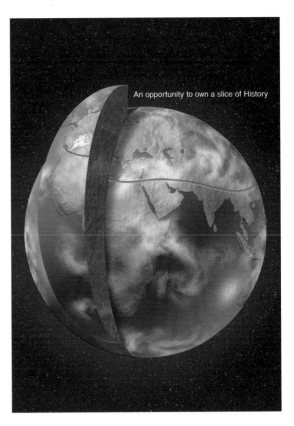

An opportunity to own a slice of History

The front cover of the brochure designed to seduce a sponsor into supporting our attempt at round-the-world flight.

went along together. James was steaming: 'You can tell Andy that if he puts the phone down on me one more time there is no more money.' Russell was sympathetic in his quiet, diplomatic way, which carried great authority. We talked about the problems – there were many – and the fact that Andy was under great pressure. Russell then said he thought Andy, James and I should have professional help and counselling as we hardly seemed like a team that was about to embark on a serious expedition.

James was perplexed but accepted that Russell could arrange a team-building expert to accompany us to the French Alps the following week, for a few days' training in mountain survival. 'I should probably warn you that I get very cold hands due to circulation problems,' said James. When Russell reported this to Andy, his dry response was that he would probably also have cold feet by the time we launched this adventure.

We asked James to meet us at Heathrow so that we could all fly out together, to which he replied that he would rather make his own arrangements. Having done this, he was due to meet us in France a couple of hours after we arrived. As it happened, he either missed his flight from Edinburgh or it was cancelled, so that he didn't make the connection from London. He didn't arrive until the following day, which ensured a frosty atmosphere before we started. In between climbing mountains and attending lectures we were subjected to professional team-building techniques. We were bullied into declaring what we thought of each other. It made an interesting few days.

In the meantime James was getting concerned about my lack of success in finding a sponsor. Time was not on our side and he was beginning to lose faith. 'I have always said it could go down to the wire,' I reminded him. There were several companies interested and I was doing my best. He was also getting concerned about cost control and lack of information about what was being spent. I said that this was none of my business. This was his project and I was providing my services for nothing until a sponsor was found. I had been through all the budgets with a fine toothcomb but I didn't think it was my place to manage the project. I had never been asked to. He would have to talk to Andy. There was no real conclusion to these discussions and we all returned to England to carry on as before. Andy and Russell went back to the workshop in Glastonbury, me to my office in Chobham, Surrey.

Mr Micawber flew home to Scotland.

By the time of the annual Bristol Balloon Fiesta in the first week of August 1998, there was still no sponsor. However, Tim Pethick, the UK Managing Director of *Encyclopaedia Britannica*, had decided he was definitely interested. On the Friday evening there was a good gathering on our hospitality stand. Among those present was Ian Hannah, who had sponsored the Cloudhopper at Smirnoff nearly twenty years ago and was now the Big Cheese at Allied Domecq. He was saying nice things about us. We were teasing Catherine Barton-Smith from Cable & Wireless about what a huge opportunity she was missing by not sponsoring our flight around the world. Tim Pethick was drinking in the atmosphere and he was well primed for his visit to the workshop in Glastonbury the next morning.

Marc Wolff wanted to come along to see the capsule as well. 'Just to check up on what you're up to, Col.' Andy gave Marc and our prospective sponsor the conducted tour. As Andy was explaining all the instruments on the front panel, Marc fell fast asleep as he sat at the flight deck. Andy and Tim looked a bit puzzled, so I reassured them that I had seen Marc drop off to sleep in the most unlikely places all over the world. He never could get enough sleep. As he breathed gently in and out through his nose I recalled a time in America some years before when he had nodded off during the main course at dinner. He had still not come round when it was time to leave, so I persuaded the restaurant manager just to turn out the lights and lock up. Marc eventually woke at 3 am with no idea where he was. Now he was to wake up inside a balloon capsule. He was impressed. He told Andy so, adding that if he wanted a reserve pilot in case of illness or mishap, he would willingly comply. Andy's response was that the expedition needed pilots who could stay awake.

Marc was not the only one to fall asleep in my presence. Tim Pethick wanted me to present the project to his board in Chicago the following Wednesday. *Encyclopaedia Britannica*'s president would be there, and he would make the final decision. I arrived at the appointed time, just after lunch. The president's eyelids were getting heavy after less than five minutes. By the time I had finished he was struggling to remain conscious. I was adamant that the one thing my presentation was *not* was boring. Yet the man had barely taken anything in. As I flew back to London I knew that *Britannica* was a dead duck.

Over the next few weeks I hooked several potential sponsors, only to see them all slip off the line. I was getting pretty despondent when Karen Earl talked again to Cable & Wireless now that Adrian Moorey, the Director of Corporate Affairs, was back in harness. They just might be interested after all. Karen and her colleague Alison Moor decided they would also like to show my presentation to Gallaher, the tobacco company. On 18 September, just six weeks before we wanted to be on standby for launch, Andy and I went along with them to see Barry Jenner, who ran the Silk Cut brand. He listened patiently without saying a word – apart from correcting my mistake over the date when man first set foot on the moon. Afterwards he asked a lot of very perceptive questions before pronouncing: 'I think you are both barking mad. It's a very exciting adventure. I'll come back to you in just a few days.'

Marc displays his frequent habit of falling asleep in mid-conversation over dinner.

Karen and Alison knew Barry well, having looked after Gallaher sponsorships for many years. 'I think he's going to go for it,' said Alison. We were in high spirits when, on the same day, Karen took us to see Cable & Wireless. It was a good meeting which was attended by around six executives, although Karen felt compelled to warn them that the sponsorship might not now be available.

Back at Glastonbury Andy was horrified to discover that several suppliers had had their cheques bounced. James Manclark now came to Flying Pictures to tell me that time was up. There would be no more money unless Flying Pictures wanted to keep the project alive by injecting some funding of its own. 'What about the balloon envelope?' I asked. A deposit had been paid to Cameron Balloons for the huge balloon, which was almost complete and on which several hundred thousand pounds would soon be payable. Silence. After a protracted discussion I agreed to take over all payments for an unspecified period provided he unbounced the cheques to Andy's suppliers. The potential problem with Cameron Balloons was a matter between them and James. In any case I was now fairly confident of sponsorship and all would be well. If Cameron Balloons got wind of the precarious situation they would be apoplectic and completion would be seriously delayed. We would have to move fast.

I reported to my board what I had done. In effect I had taken a sabbatical for several months while I worked on the project. I had handed over all my work with the exception of a filming project for Marks & Spencer in partnership with Channel 4. My colleagues were therefore understandably nervous that their chief executive was about to commit the company to a further period of uncertainty as well as now incurring real costs. Nevertheless, they gave me unanimous support.

On Wednesday 23 September I went to the Empire Test Pilots' School at Boscombe Down, near Salisbury, to do some hyperbaric training. This meant being put in a pressure chamber under the supervision of a doctor. First the air was pumped out to simulate an altitude of around 25–30,000 feet. Then the doctor removed my oxygen mask and made me perform a number of simple tasks in order to learn the symptoms of losing consciousness due to lack of oxygen (hypoxia) before it was too late. The oxygen mask was not replaced until I was almost unconscious. It was a relief to get out of there.

We had still had no decision from Gallaher, so after the hyperbaric session I called

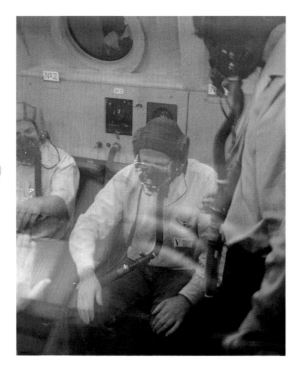

202

In the hyperbaric chamber at the Empire Test Pilots' School, Boscombe Down, Wiltshire, the moment before they removed my oxygen supply at a simulated 25,000 feet. The supervising doctor is standing beside me.

Alison Moor on my mobile phone in the car park. Still no confirmation, but she was ninety-five per cent sure it was on. I called James Manclark to give him an update but it was clear he had severe doubts – quite reasonably, given the results to date – that I would achieve anything. He was already looking at a substantial financial loss and by now he seemed to be somewhat detached from the project anyway.

When Karen called me on the morning of 25 September I could tell even before the 'Hello, how are you?' bit that she had bad news. 'Barry's not going to do it.' With this news even Andy showed the first chink in his armour of confidence. 'This is getting boring, isn't it?' he said. I felt at my lowest ebb. 'Come on, Lucius, let's go down to the pub,' I suggested. Lucius had been a great friend for ten years and he was a sympathetic marketing director who was used to taking the knocks. I decided to take the afternoon off to reflect. Just as we were about to leave the Sun Inn in Chobham, the lady behind the bar asked if there was a Colin Prescot in the pub. The office had been ringing around every hostelry in the area to track me down. Karen Earl needed to speak to me urgently. When I called her she was cross.

'Where have you been?'

'In the pub.'

'Why isn't your mobile phone switched on?'

'Because I left it in the office.'

'What? Colin, if you and I are going to work together, we are going to have to have words.'

'Sorry.'

'Cable & Wireless want a meeting next week and they have asked a lot of questions.'

'Wow.'

'You and I have work to do.'

'I'm on my way.'

I turned to Lucius. 'You can stick your pint of Guinness. I'm off.'

After my meeting with Cable & Wireless I spoke to James and reported that I believed they would support the project. I also had to explain that some of their sponsorship advisers were recommending that they only back a sound, scientific project with a serious and professional approach. In their view, the inclusion in the team of a millionaire with no experience, who didn't even have a pilot's licence, was inappropriate. It all smacked too much of a gung-ho yuppie trying to take on Richard Branson at his own game. It would be fair to say that Andy and I would at this stage have been very uncomfortable about James coming with us. He had barely been training, he really knew very little about the technical side of the project and, to be fair to him, all he ever wanted was an adventure without the hassle. That is what he considered he had been paying for.

James was unfazed by my news. Not long before, he had asked if I knew anyone who would pay £100,000 to take his place, which would at least provide some money to keep the project rolling. He was sceptical about Cable & Wireless. On the other hand, if I was right about getting a sponsor he could at least negotiate selling out.

Cable & Wireless had recently bought all the internet interests of MCI, a communications company in America, and C&W's chief executive, Richard H. Brown, was keen on our project provided MCI came on board and contributed from their budget. We had a video conference with America at Cable & Wireless's London headquarters in Theobalds Road, Holborn. It was the first time I had made a presentation to another continent by telephone and the link kept going down. It was difficult to tell whether we had won MCI over or not. Another week went by while everyone deliberated. Karen thought the clincher would be to get all the key people from Cable & Wireless in London down to Glastonbury to see the capsule – they would be impressed. However, they were busy people and getting them to agree to travel there at short notice was proving impossible. On 6 October Karen called me. There was a gap in the diaries of the bigwigs the following day between mid-morning and mid-afternoon. 'I want you to take a deep breath and hire a helicopter to take them down to you and back.'

203

With Andy at the press call to launch the *Cable & Wireless* balloon project.

I did, they came and they *were* impressed. 'It will now be down to America and a main board meeting on Friday,' said Adrian Moorey as he left with his party.

The meeting went on all day, much longer than expected. Afterwards Adrian had to go straight out to dinner, and didn't contact us. Andy and I spent a weekend on tenterhooks as to whether the project was dead or alive, for this was surely our last chance. On Monday we were told the almost unbearable news that Adrian was out of the office all day. The only tiny bit of hope we had left was based on his delightful secretary Angela's remark: 'I'm sure he would have let me know if there was a problem.'

On Tuesday mid-morning my patience gave out. I called Karen. She was on the phone. I spoke to Georgina Cooke, who managed the Cable & Wireless account. 'Hasn't Karen got hold of you?' she said. 'Oh, hold on, she's on the other line trying to get you.' Before she handed me over she whispered, 'It's good news.'

Negotiations of the deal were conducted over a number of weeks, mainly by James Hunter Smart, our finance director, and a very patient Nick Folland at Cable & Wireless. At midnight on the eve of the press conference to announce the adventure some details of the contract were still being thrashed out. James woke me from a deep slumber to say there was a problem. The insurance brokers had finally admitted defeat – no one was prepared to quote rates for all-risks cover for the balloon and equipment. 'That's OK,' I told him. 'We've budgeted to lose it all anyway.'

'I can only get £10 million of third-party liability,' he went on.

'What's wrong with that?' I asked, trying to wake up and concentrate.

'If you hit a jumbo jet, Flying Pictures is bust,' he said.

'Yes, and I am also *dead*,' I said.

He paused to take in what I was saying. 'So you want me to go ahead?' he asked.

The contract was finally signed at nine o'clock the following morning, just half an hour before a flying champagne cork signalled the start of the press conference, which was held at the Honourable Artillery Company's HQ near the City of London.

CHAPTER SIXTEEN

PLEASE GOD, MAKE MR BRANSON GO *SPLOSH* IN THE SEA

B Y OCTOBER 1998 THERE HAD BEEN nineteen attempts to fly around the world in a balloon. Some were more successful than others but all had ended in failure. Only one had managed to travel as much as half the distance. The amazing fact is that, of the nineteen attempts, four never even took off and only six stayed airborne for as long as twenty-four hours.

The 1978 transatlantic crossing by Anderson, Abruzzo and Newman was described by the international media as the last great aviation record to enter the history books. However, in 1981 Maxie Anderson was to make his first attempt to fly around the world solo. It was something which would have seemed completely unimaginable a few years earlier. He took off from Luxor in Egypt and landed in India three days later with an envelope leak. He had the same problem a year later, when he managed to fly just sixty miles. In 1983 he made his final attempt, when he flew from Rapid City in South Dakota and landed in eastern Canada. For the third time in a row he was plagued with a leaking envelope.

Three years later John Petrehn of the United States announced that he would be making an attempt in the southern hemisphere from Mendoza in Argentina. The launch failed.

Barron Hilton of the Hilton Hotels chain famously predicted that the sponsor of the first global circumnavigation by balloon would get $100 million of media coverage. Between 1992 and 1996 he put his money where his mouth was by sponsoring a number of Americans to take part in the Earthwinds project. The principal pilots involved were Larry Newman (one of the trio that first crossed the Atlantic), Richard Abruzzo (the son of Ben Abruzzo, who also made the first Atlantic flight) and another experienced balloonist, Dave Melton. The team made five attempts during those years, the first based at Akron, Ohio, and the others all at Reno, Nevada. Sadly those five projects can be summed up as follows:

1. No launch.
2. Balloon destroyed at launch.
3. Balloon hit mountain soon after launch.
4. Safety valve failed after the balloon had flown 250 miles in the wrong direction.
5. Anchor balloon burst soon after launch.

A complex and ultimately overambitious project, Earthwinds expired with barely a flight to its name.

The American balloonist Steve Fossett's first flight was in 1996. Steve is a remarkable man who has achieved some extraordinary things. He has sailed oceans, climbed most of the highest mountains in the world, swum the English Channel and flown across the Atlantic in a balloon. He has made a personal fortune out of stock trading and he preferred to manage his sporting endeavours without the distraction of sponsors and, if at all possible, solo. With the exception of the last one, in 1998, he made all his round-the-world balloon attempts on his own. A solo effort takes incredible strength of character and is not something that most 'extreme' balloonists would even contemplate (me included). Also, Steve preferred to take a low-tech, unpressurized gondola even though this restricted his altitude capability. Pressurization of a capsule adds considerable complexity and danger to a balloon flight. For example, sudden decompression at over 30,000 feet can cause unconsciousness and death within minutes from lack of oxygen. To train for the handicap of using an unpressurized gondola at altitude, Steve would acclimatize himself for several months before take-off by sleeping at night in a specially made chamber with the air pumped out.

For his first flight Steve took off from Rapid City, South Dakota, and was soon in difficulties in thick fog over the Atlantic near Newfoundland. He activated the emergency beacon on board his gondola and the coastguard immediately sent planes to search for the ditched balloon and pilot. The coastguard's personnel were perplexed that the readout of the beacon seemed to indicate a speed of twenty miles an hour, but then Andy Elson, who was technical adviser on the project, realized what was happening. 'Get the planes out of the area. He's still flying.' Steve eventually limped into a field near Halifax, Nova Scotia. There had been a fault in the manufacture of the balloon's outer skin, which had gradually shredded.

In 1997, with the fault rectified, Steve took off from St Louis, Missouri, and made an amazing flight all the way to north-west India. He was refused permission to enter Libya but flew south until Colonel Gaddafi relented. He then ascended back into the jet stream and overflew the south-eastern corner of the country before being forced down by bad weather a couple of days later.

Early in the following year Steve again took off from a stadium in St Louis and set off across the Atlantic at great speed. Somehow he managed to fly over one of the worst storms to afflict Britain that winter and carried on down into Germany. He eventually arrived at the Russian border, where he had no permission to fly. However, he was granted approval to enter the airspace provided he landed as soon as possible. The wind forced him further into unwelcome territory and he put down at Krasnodar, a fair distance across the border.

By now Steve was fed up with all the diplomatic problems in the northern hemisphere. Libya and Russia had denied him access, although he had somehow got away with entering the airspace of both countries. The Chinese had also resolutely forbidden him to enter their airspace if he ever got that far. Without China, the conventional wisdom went, it was virtually impossible to get around the world. The jet stream is fragmented and uneven. Although it moves throughout a band hundreds of miles wide, it never leaves China. Indeed the core of the jet stream blows straight across the region, which is why a balloonist needs to be in it to speed around the world and why it is so important to gain permission to overfly this vast country.

By contrast, in the southern hemisphere there were no diplomatic problems at all – just vast tracts of lonely oceans. Steve decided to have his gondola refurbished for a flight during the southern winter. In early August 1998 he launched from Mendoza in Argentina. While Andy and I were in the French Alps doing our mountain training we heard the astonishing news that, after eight days flying, he had crossed Australia and was now over the Pacific for the enormous last leg, which would have no land between him and victory. He lasted just a few hundred more miles. The last thing he remembers is tracking away from a thunderstorm. Exactly how he ended up in the sea is open to conjecture. He recalls waking up in the water and abandoning his gondola for a life raft. A ship diverted from its course to pick him up the following day. 'Frankly, it's good to be alive,' were the words he used when asked to describe how it had been.

Two other American attempts were made in the winter of 1997–8. The first was by Kevin Uliassi on New Year's Eve, whose solo ascent lasted no more than a couple of hours. He flew too quickly to high altitude and heard a loud explosion as the bottom of the balloon blew out. In panic he put out a Mayday call but he eventually managed to land safely in spite of the gas escaping from the burst envelope.

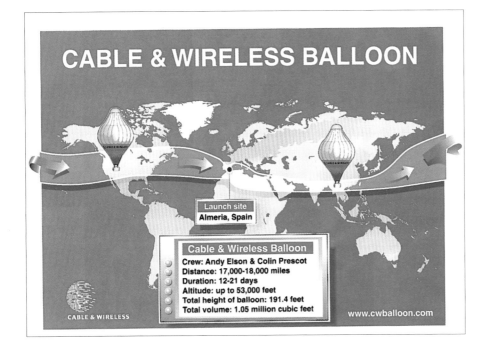

The planned route in the jet stream for our flight in *Cable & Wireless*.

The second attempt was by Dave Melton of the Earthwinds project and Dick Rutan. A flyer since the age of fifteen, Rutan had completed more than 105 missions over North Vietnam as a US fighter pilot. In December 1986 he and Jeana Yeager made the first non-stop fixed-wing flight around the world, travelling some 25,000 miles in an ultra-lightweight plane called *Voyager*. Now he aimed to add balloons to his record book. Dick and Dave (Duck and Dive might have been more appropriate names) took off from Albuquerque, New Mexico, on 9 January 1998 on a flight which was to last just a couple of hours. They encountered precisely the same problem as Uliassi a few weeks before. This time the two pilots had no hesitation in bailing out in parachutes. Rutan displayed a cut nose during the interviews after the event, but Melton had sustained more serious injuries as a result of a hard and fast landfall in high winds.

The balloons of both Uliassi and Rutan–Melton had been manufactured by Cameron Balloons in Bristol to the design of Andy Elson and Don Cameron. There were suggestions that the manufacture was faulty. *Breitling Orbiter 2* , flown by Bertrand Piccard, Wim Verstraeten and Andy Elson, was a similar balloon, which was to launch from Switzerland on 28 January 1998. (*Breitling Orbiter 1*, piloted by Piccard and Verstraeten, had flown for six hours into the Mediterranean the previous year.) The Americans were keen to see if the Breitling team would suffer the same fate as they had. Andy was dismissive, believing that both American attempts had been launched with far too much lift. His conclusion was based on the rate of ascent by both doomed balloons. Overfilling the balloons with helium gas would have caused them to ascend rapidly through their ceiling. At this point the build-up of pressure would have been too much for the envelope's safety valve. The inevitable result would have been that the balloons would have burst when the strain became too much.

In the event Andy was correct that *Breitling Orbiter 2* would not have the same problem and it flew for more than nine days to Myanmar. During this expedition the world watched with their hearts in their mouths as Andy abseiled over the side to repair a pressurization leak in the capsule while at 6000 feet over the Adriatic.

To date Richard Branson and Per Lindstrand had not yet had much success. They failed to launch in 1995–6 after they announced their first attempt. A year later the third man, Rory McCarthy, was suffering from pneumonia and was forced to withdraw on launch day, 7 January 1997. His place was taken by the project engineer, Alex Ritchie. The trio set off from Morocco but abandoned the attempt in the Algerian desert eighteen hours later, after a rollercoaster ride over the Atlas mountains during which they had to jettison a high proportion of their fuel.

During their next attempt, at the end of the year, a gust of wind broke the *Virgin Challenger* balloon away from its moorings. It sailed away majestically, leaving Richard still in his hotel room and the rest of the crew on the ground at the launch site. More tragically Alex Ritchie suffered multiple injuries on the run-up to this project while parachute-jump training at the launch site in Morocco. They were injuries from which he would die a few months later.

By the summer of 1998 the challenge was attracting burgeoning worldwide attention. There was a growing belief that this final frontier would be breached before too long. Richard Branson's highly efficient publicity machine was also an undoubted catalyst for the snowballing interest. Now the race was really on. No fewer than six teams announced their readiness for the winter season of 1998–9.

Bertrand Piccard would be making his third attempt in *Breitling Orbiter 3*. His team mate this time would be Tony Brown, a British Airways Concorde engineer who had been flying balloons for pleasure for several years. The pair were later to fall out. Brian Jones, who was working on the project as project manager at Cameron Balloons, stepped in to take Tony's place.

I spoke to Alan Noble, the experienced flight director of the Breitling project, at the time the change was made. I asked him why he didn't take Tony's place himself. He replied that he considered himself too old to put his life at risk at high altitude in a prototype pressurized capsule for possibly days on end. A strange thing to say to me.

The next team to declare was Richard Branson and Per Lindstrand again. Steve Fossett, who had lost all his equipment in the Coral Sea off Australia a few months before, had no time to rebuild for the winter season in the northern hemisphere. Richard Branson asked him if he would like to join him on his attempt. Sure he would. The balloon was to be called *ICO Global Challenger* as ICO had replaced Virgin as its main sponsor, although market research later indicated that everyone associated it with Branson's company.

An Australian team, led by John Wallington and sponsored by Remax, the world's largest chain of estate agencies, planned an ambitious flight into the stratosphere in a pressurized capsule, wearing pressure suits. They believed their successful circum-navigation would take about ten to fourteen days from Alice Springs, Australia.

Kevin Uliassi planned his second solo attempt from Rockford, Illinois. It had limited funding and the balloon was to be called *J Renee*, after his wife.

The fifth announcement was from a team planning to launch from Albuquerque, New Mexico, in a privately funded adventure. Two of the pilots, Mark Sullivan and Jacques Soukup, were Americans. Mark was a veteran balloonist of the Albuquerque Balloon Fiesta, the world's largest ballooning event. Jacques was an amusing character who in his earlier life had been a Dominican friar. Both chastity and poverty bothered him, so he abandoned the cloth. He now lived in great wealth in a huge manor house in Wiltshire with his friend Kirk Thomas. The third pilot was a Briton, Crispin Williams, a former RAF flight lieutenant, who was now working for Cameron Balloons. Williams had a fine record of competition flying. The balloon's name was *Spirit of Peace*.

Last to announce their intention to fly were the Cable & Wireless team, the only team with an all-British crew. The pilots were to be the dynamic, dashing duo of Andy Elson and Colin Prescot.

We had had a considerable debate about what name we should give our balloon. Most expeditionary craft tend to have the words 'Voyager', 'Explorer', 'Discovery' or 'Challenger' as part of their name. Certainly Richard Branson had adopted this technique in his boat and balloon projects to create an air of adventure. *The Times* had recently commented that balloons, like boats, now all seemed to bear the name of their sponsor. The newspaper remarked that if the owl and the pussycat went to sea in 1998 it would most probably be in a Heinz Peas Multihull. Eventually we came down on the side of simplicity. Our craft was named simply *Cable & Wireless*.

Andy, I and the team now pressed forward with a renewed urgency. It was different now that we had proper funding; a huge weight was off our shoulders. Martin Hutchins, Glenn Fairley and Ian Bishop were the only engineers Andy trusted to get on with the job of building the capsule in his absence, while we were off training. We had both used the project to get much fitter than we would otherwise have been. I ran several miles every day with Norman, Susie's West Highland terrier. For the last three months I was on my own as the wretched animal got bored of the routine. Andy took to his mountain bike and assaulted all the hills near Wells, where he lived in the old cricket pavilion.

The only training we did with most of the other teams was to spend a morning in the swimming pool at Swindon Leisure Centre, organized by Cameron Balloons as a sea-survival exercise. We had both undergone this training before and we had already

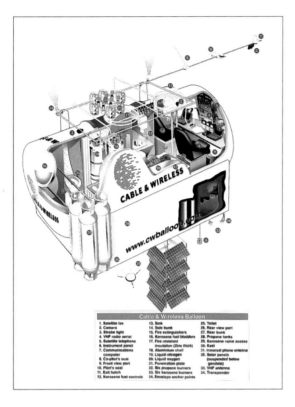

Cable & Wireless Balloon

1. Satellite fax
2. Camera
3. Strobe light
4. VHF radio aerial
5. Satellite telephone
6. Instrument panel
7. Communications computer
8. Co-pilot's seat
9. Pilot's seat
10. Front view port
11. Exit hatch
12. Kerosene fuel controls
13. Sink
14. Side bunk
15. Fire extinguishers
16. Kerosene fuel bladders
17. Fire resistant insulation (Ziro thick)
18. Aluminium shell
19. Liquid nitrogen
20. Liquid oxygen
21. Penetration plate
22. Six propane burners
23. Six kerosene burners
24. Envelope anchor points
25. Toilet
26. Rear view port
27. Rear bunk
28. Propane tanks
29. Kerosene valve access
30. Keel
31. Inmarsat phone antenna
32. Solar panels (suspended below gondola)
33. VHF antenna
34. Transponder

Above top The layout of *Cable & Wireless*'s capsule.
Above A view through the top dome of Andy and me on the flight deck.

arranged to have much tougher drills with the RAF in the sea. But we went along anyway. We bought a couple of pump-action water pistols from Toys 'R' Us (Andy's idea, not mine) and when the exercise was over we had a field day with our unarmed (and largely unamused) rivals. We were both surprised how many people were taking part in the course. The *Spirit of Peace* team had a reserve pilot for each member and the *Breitling Orbiter 3* team (then including Tony Brown) had Brian Jones as a reserve. We were asked who our reserve pilots were. 'I'm not flying without Andy,' I explained simply. 'And I'm not flying without Colin,' Andy added.

They looked at us with pity.

We also took a first-aid refresher course and attended lectures on world meteorology as well as on survival in deserts, jungle and snow.

I spent at least three days a week in the workshop helping the team put together the 3000 working parts that went into the capsule. Everything was brilliantly thought out and made. It was all down to Andy's vision. The only item I argued with was the man-made Kevlar flying wires (coated in a plastic sheath) which were to hold up the entire capsule and many tons of fuel. These would save a considerable amount of weight compared with the stainless-steel alternative. 'What happens if we have a fire?' I asked. 'The material is non-flammable,' was Andy's reply. I told him that my experience suggested otherwise, remembering the filming of *Green Ice,* when the Kevlar lines had gone ping one by one as the flames licked at the Cloudhopper. Andy promised to think about it. A few days later I came in to find stainless-steel wires engineered beautifully into place.

On 25 November the internal fit of the capsule was almost complete. Karen Earl Limited, as Cable & Wireless's sponsorship agent, wanted to take full advantage of any opportunity to keep the publicity rolling. We had told them that we planned a trial twenty-four-hour lock-in in the capsule to familiarize ourselves with the interior. It would also give us a chance to try living in the small space. The media loved it. We did a number of live radio interviews. Television crews made us enter the capsule for the last time about a dozen times over while they got the angles right. Tim Shearman shut the plastic dome behind us. It was planned that Helen Rumbelow of *The Times* would stay in the capsule for the first hour and interview us. However, she immediately felt claustrophobic and had definite second thoughts about the scheme. 'Don't worry, we'll look after you,' I said, but she was unimpressed. She had to file her report early, she lied, before making a fast exit.

By eight o'clock in the evening everyone had left and we were bored. The workshops were shut up and we were cocooned in our capsule with nothing to do. 'Why don't we go out for dinner?' I suggested. The fact was, we weren't locked in at all, so it would have been very embarrassing if anyone from the media spotted us. We felt like two naughty schoolboys as we lurked in the shadow of the front of the unlit building to make sure no one was looking. We then made our way furtively across the scrubland to the Little Chef on the roundabout a few hundred yards away.

When we got back we had a glass of wine and went to bed. The bunks were very comfortable and we slept soundly. The whole exercise was somewhat futile because there was no way we would ever be able to sleep at the same time once we were airborne.

We were both woken at 7 am by the sound of the dome opening. There was then a dull thud as Russell Brice dropped the morning newspapers on to the floor under the flight deck. Any semblance of a serious exercise was now well and truly shot to pieces.

I decided I wanted to get comfortable with freefall parachuting, so that I would have no hesitation about abandoning ship in an emergency. I had made only three jumps in my life and these had been many years before. Andy had also done a few in the past but he never planned to jump again, except in very extreme circumstances. So Ian Ashpole came to hold my hand in Florida while for three intense days I psyched myself into completing an accelerated freefall programme.

Almost all the skydivers I trained with were twenty or thirty years younger than me. I think I was the only one who was not having 'a real good time'. The interminable journey to 14,000 feet, crammed in with up to twenty other parachutists, was not a pleasant affair. Apart from the sheer terror of what was in store, the thinness of the air caused an unexpected problem. At ground level the atmospheric pressure is about 14.7 pounds per square inch. At skydiving altitude it is only about half this amount. This means that any gases inside the body expand almost twofold and consequently have to escape somewhere. The flatulence on board was quite appalling and the rattling Twin Otter plane was more like a flying stink bomb as its inmates discussed who had had the vindaloo curry the night before.

In a photograph of the experience, the expression on my face looks like a cross between that of a condemned man and one who has a nasty smell under his nose (which, of course, there was).

Some jumps had been cancelled because of the weather, and I had to make six jumps on the final day in order to collect my skydiving qualification. For five of these the instructor would jump out with me and follow me down, to observe my exercises and

Above top Ian Ashpole arrives to help me with a crash course in skydiving. **Above centre** My first freefall jump (with two guardian angels). **Above** With my instructor, centre, and Ian after our first descent.

Landing at sunset after my final solo jump to gain my skydiver's certificate.

help me if I got into trouble. The sixth jump had to be solo. In order to get to this stage I had to succeed in all the previous five skydives. By the time I had completed the five jumps (it never got any less frightening) I was tired. My instructor suggested we call it a day but I didn't want to leave without my certificate. The chief instructor was called to adjudicate. He told me it was almost unheard of for a novice to complete that number of jumps in a day but if I was sure I felt confident enough he would let me go for the solo. At this point Ian Ashpole got shirty. He considered he was there partly to make sure (at Susie's request) that I didn't do anything stupid and he resolutely refused to let me go unless I discussed it with her first. He frogmarched me to the phone. When Susie answered the call at our home in England, Ian was momentarily distracted by someone who wanted a form signed. I told her it was going well and I just had the solo jump to do to complete the course. 'Sounds great,' she said. I hung up and told Ian she was just fine about it.

When we got to 5500 feet the door was swung open and my heart was in my mouth. My instructor hovered for ages in the doorway before coming over and telling me we would have to circle for a while to wait for a gap in the clouds. Silently, I prayed we would have to abandon the jump. We didn't and several minutes later I fell out of the door. In my tiredness I didn't concentrate hard enough on getting my body stabilized in the arched position. I tumbled out of control, arms and legs flailing as I saw in turn sky, sea, land and then sky again. I had to yell at myself in the shouting wind and at last became stable. I pulled the ripcord and landed safely. When my instructor returned with the plane he looked ashen. 'I was seriously worried about you up there for a while,' he declared. '*You* were worried?' I replied. 'You should have been with me.'

Freefall parachuting was not for me, but I was glad I could now call myself a skydiver and that I would have some degree of confidence if I ever had to use the skill in an emergency.

Back in England, I found a copy of the new 1999 edition of *Guinness World Records* on my desk, which pleased me greatly. Inside there were two new entries. The first, under the heading 'Biggest number of stunts', read:

Flying Pictures of Surrey, UK, has planned and coordinated air stunts for more than 200 feature films, including Cliffhanger *(USA, 1993),* Goldeneye *(GB, USA, 1995)*

and Mission: Impossible *(USA, 1996), and coordinated the aerial stunts for hundreds of TV shows and ads.*

The second entry, headed 'Most expensive aerial stunt', concerned an achievement planned and coordinated by Flying Pictures:

Simon Crane performed one of the most dangerous ever aerial stunts when he moved from one jet plane to another while flying at 4.752 kms (2 miles, 1480 yards) for the film Cliffhanger *(USA, 1993). The stunt was performed only once because it was so dangerous and cost a record $1 million (£568,000). Sylvester Stallone, the film star, is said to have offered to reduce his fee by the same amount to ensure that the stunt was made.*

Our balloon and capsule finally left Britain for the selected launch site in early December 1998. Martin Harris, our weather expert, had found a selection of suitable locations in southern Spain. Andy and I went out to look at the options. The seventh fairway of La Envia Golf Club in Almería won by a country mile. The golf course was owned by a fabulous gentleman by the name of Don Francisco Mendoza (or Paco for short). He was excited about the project and nothing was too much trouble. The seventh hole changed from being a par five to a par four while we occupied the tee area for quite a few months. A large tent was erected for our final assembly of the capsule, which took several weeks.

On 14 December Sky Television organized an amusing split-screen live interview between me in Spain and Per Lindstrand in Morocco. We enjoyed some good banter. We were still not ready to fly, but Per claimed he was shipshape and that the weather was looking favourable for their launch in a few days. I wasn't sure I believed the propaganda

Our capsule being prepared on the launch pad – the seventh tee of La Envia Golf Club, Almería, southern Spain.

Per Lindstrand, Richard
Branson and Steve
Fossett talk to the press
before lifting off from
Marrakesh on 18
December 1998.

but I was wrong to doubt him. He departed from Marrakesh with Richard Branson and Steve Fossett just four days later. We were puzzled by their decision. We looked at the forecast trajectories and concluded that if they went straight up into the jet stream it would take them too far north, towards the part of China all teams were banned from entering.

A couple of months earlier the Breitling team had very sportingly gone to Peking to negotiate permission to fly in Chinese airspace on behalf of all the teams. We all now had a piece of paper authorizing entry and overflight anywhere south of twenty-six degrees north. This was not ideal but we all considered it manageable. China had never given overflight permission before and everyone believed that a circumnavigation could only be possible by overflying the territory.

When I returned home for Christmas the Branson team had been flying for three days and were heading exactly where we thought they would. As they approached China at a point which was indeed too far north, Mike Kendrick, the flight director at Mission Control in Middlesex, put out a statement that China had refused permission to the team to enter their airspace. They were ordered to land. The next statement put out was that he had apologized to the Chinese but the balloonists were going in anyway. To land now would be life-threatening. The Chinese response was that they would not endanger life but the balloon must land as soon as possible. Between Richard Branson and Mike Kendrick a very skilful and public display of diplomacy ensued as the Prime Minister and Sir Edward Heath were dragged into the crisis. To everyone's amazement the next statement put out by Mike Kendrick was that the Chinese had granted permission for the team to fly on through the country to the Pacific.

'My God, the bastards have got away with it,' fairly sums up our sentiments at the time.

Mike Kendrick later told me that the team had been given the impression on the approach to China that they were going to be allowed to fly in but that the Chinese changed their minds at the last minute. This may or may not have been a diplomatic distortion of the reality of the situation. It sounded highly unlikely to me. The information we soon received from the British Embassy in Peking was that the Chinese government was furious that a gaggle of millionaires should enter their airspace without permission and that as a result it would now be reviewing the permits for all the other teams.

On Christmas morning I was at home with the family. Richard Branson and his team were still flying merrily along across the Pacific and had just about covered half the world. People were starting to talk about them making it all the way. We set off for the Christmas Day service at the local church in Stockbridge. As we went in through the porch Susie said to the children, 'Now, remember, we have all got to pray that Mr Branson goes *splosh* in the sea.'

When we returned to the house the phone was ringing. Ian Ashpole was trying not to be gleeful. 'They're coming down, Col. They are landing near Hawaii in the morning.'

'It worked,' commented my eight-year-old son matter-of-factly. Richard and his team had almost run out of fuel and they had no hope of making the coast of America. The sensible thing to do was to put down while there was land nearby. The Hawaiian coastguard effected a textbook recovery of the crew. The balloon and capsule sank in the Pacific and Richard lost his address book.

I had a flood of phone calls from the media, asking for my reaction. I was sorry they had to come down. I was pleased they were safe. The first part was a lie and the second part the truth. There was not the least doubt that all the teams quietly wished the same ill luck on each other whenever any rivals were airborne.

Within a few days the Chinese government withdrew permission from all other teams to overfly any part of their airspace in any circumstances. The wording of the letter from the British Embassy left us in no doubt as to the serious consequences of disregarding this instruction. For Cable & Wireless this was an embarrassing development. Perfectly reasonably, it was made clear to us that if we had even the tiniest thought of imitating the Branson flight we should forget it. A very high proportion of our sponsor's business was in China and for a branded balloon to flout that country's instruction was quite unthinkable.

I called Catherine Barton-Smith at Cable & Wireless with a regular update. 'Are you beginning to regret you sponsored our project?' I asked her. 'Right now, yes,' was the blunt response. Nevertheless, she and Adrian Moorey were enormously supportive and put no pressure on us whatsoever to withdraw from the race.

As a result of China's clampdown, Kevin Uliassi decided to call off his launch. The *Spirit of Peace* team abandoned their plans altogether. The Australians had failed to get off the ground, while Breitling said they had no intention of flying unless China allowed them in.

Andy and I had other ideas. I had put the best part of a year into our project, and Andy even more. We were determined not to follow everyone to the exit.

In the six weeks after China overturned our permission we completely revised our strategy. If we could not fly over China we had to fly around it. Martin Harris considered this almost impossible to achieve but he was prepared to investigate the best way of trying. Eventually we came up with a plan to penetrate deep into the Sahara desert and fly slowly out of the jet stream towards the south. It would mean flying as low as we dared during darkness and it would take far longer than we originally planned. Our new strategy went completely against the conventional wisdom that the only way to circumnavigate the earth was to wait for the jet stream to be strong enough and in the right direction and then go like hell.

Andy had suggested we could carry a lot more fuel if we sacrificed our height capability for the first few days. We briefed Martin on the basis of 'no more than 24,000 feet for the first week'.

216

Chinese takeaway – Andy and I being given the news that permission was withdrawn for our flight over China.

Several surprising things came out of our new research. First, the reduced altitude was unlikely to seriously compromise our options for finding the right direction at the latitude we were aiming for. Second, the traditionally accepted end of the flying season no longer appeared to stand up to close investigation. It seemed to be feasible for us to delay for at least another month. Third, the amount of extra kerosene we could carry if we restricted our flight ceiling for the first few days was a staggering three tons. Andy devised a way of simply piggybacking nine barrels of fuel on each side. After reanalysing the stress the boy genius had ordered a new, reinforced crown ring to hold the load-bearing nylon tapes, along with a new set of flying wires with a higher breaking strain. He worked out that we could probably now fly for a month. It was worth a go.

And so, to the astonishment of most experts, we announced on 13 February 1999 that we would be launching in three days' time.

In fact Andy and I made our decision against the advice of Martin Harris, though not seriously so. Martin thought the weather pattern would improve if we waited. It looked good enough to us and we wanted to get on with it. Conditions at the time of the launch, scheduled for sunset, were forecast to be calm and the medium-level winds would take us south, though backwards to the east. As long as we were going south we didn't mind about that, although a trip to the Canary Islands had never previously crossed our minds. We would then swing round to the east and track slowly across Africa with a view to positioning ourselves to make an assault on the Pacific from south of Hainan Island, the southernmost part of China.

I had a call on my mobile phone from Don Cameron, who is one of the most respected men in world ballooning. He asked me if we had taken professional meteorological advice. It was an extraordinary question. Alan Noble, the flight director of the Breitling team, told me that everyone was convinced we would end up going in a circle up to the

Caspian Sea. 'No we won't,' I said. He told me that he and his meteorology experts couldn't see it and he bet me a pint he was right. The website of a film company making a documentary about the race around the world even suggested that the flight might be going ahead purely because the crew were under pressure from the sponsor and that there might be financial implications in not launching. The wild assumption about pressure from the sponsor could not have been further from the truth. Cable & Wireless had been wonderfully supportive and at no stage did they put us under any pressure whatsoever. The simple truth was that no one could fathom out our new strategy.

Within twenty-four hours the world descended upon us – news crews, Karen Earl's PR team, documentary makers, journalists, Spanish dignitaries and all manner of spectators. Cable & Wireless chartered a special plane to fly our families and invited media down to Almería. I left the apartment which had become my second home for the past months to move into a nearby hotel with Susie and the children. My brother and sister, Jeremy and Caroline, had also come, together with my niece Gemma and mother-in-law, Heather. It was enormously cheering to have them all there. At last we were on our way.

On the day scheduled for the launch Andy had his hands more than full checking all the final technical details, so I took an early-morning news conference at

the La Envia Golf Club, aided by Russell Brice and Lucius Peart. I explained that the weather pattern was moving slightly slower than we expected and that we may have to postpone the launch by a day. No one seemed to mind. At 4 pm we confirmed that our departure would take place on the following morning, Wednesday 17 February.

An enormous team of some thirty people were already preparing the massive and complex envelope. The important thing now was for Andy and me to get some sleep. Andy was unavoidably going to have a disturbed night preparing the balloon for launch, but we agreed that I should be left in peace. I would then pilot the balloon after the launch while Andy caught up with the zzzzs.

As my family and I had our last supper in the hotel, the butterflies had already invaded my stomach with a vengeance. I had a couple of glasses of red wine to calm me down. Everyone incessantly remarked on how cool I was. I must be a great actor. To my surprise, when I got to bed, I slept. I woke again after a couple of hours but then I slept again. At around 4 am I woke and strode outside to look at the weather. The flags were blowing proudly in a stiff breeze. What the hell's going on up at the launch site? I wondered. It looked like far too much wind to me. As I stood there, Andy appeared from the room next door. 'Err. We got problems,' he said.

'Wind,' I volunteered.

'No,' he said. 'It's calm up at the site. They can't get the top insulation tent fitted to the main balloon. I'm going up there to try and sort it out.' This sounded like bad news. Two experts from Cameron Balloons were there and if they couldn't make it fit, it probably

Above top Andy and I, flanked by Susie and Andy's girlfriend, Carrie. Paco Mendoza, owner of the La Envia Golf Club, and his wife are in the middle.

Above The last press conference before launch, La Envia Golf Club, 16 February 1999.

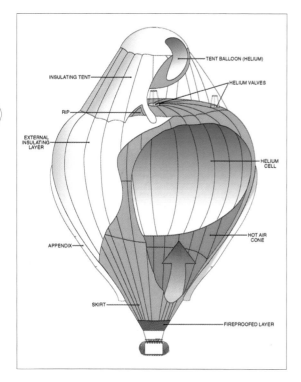

TENT BALLOON (HELIUM)

INSULATING TENT

HELIUM VALVES

RIP

EXTERNAL
INSULATING
LAYER

HELIUM
CELL

HOT AIR
CONE

APPENDIX

SKIRT

FIREPROOFED LAYER

218

Above A cross-section of our *Rozier* balloon shows the helium cell at centre with a second skin, providing insulation at the top and a hot-air chamber at the bottom.
Below left With Susie and our three children, Polly, Archie and Lara, the day before launch.
Below right A final farewell to Susie.
Opposite Pre-dawn inflation of *Cable & Wireless*. The Sainsbury's strawberry hot-air balloon shows the scale of one of the biggest manned balloons in history.

wouldn't. It also meant that the helium filling process (which was scheduled to take several hours) could not be very far advanced if they were still trying to deal with the top of the balloon. If we were not ready to go by about 9.30, when the strong sea breeze was due to set in, it would be all over before we started.

There was nothing for me to do except go back to bed and hope Andy could solve the problem. Amazingly, I slept again until my mobile phone rang at 6 am. It was Andy. To my dying day I shall never forget the relief of hearing his words: 'It's going remarkably well.' Without saying anything I thought to myself: You bloody genius.

I kissed Susie gently as she woke. 'I'll see you up at the site. Someone will pick you up in a car at 8.30.' She held me for a second before releasing me. 'It's going to be fine,' I said.

Lucius, along with Chris Ward (who had come from Sainsbury's to coordinate the on-board food and drink), were waiting downstairs to take me the six miles to the site. They looked more nervous than I was. I cracked a few jokes to lighten the atmosphere.

When we came round the hillside at La Envia, the sight that greeted us in the darkness was awesome. The massive gold and silver balloon was standing upright, quivering in the floodlight as the helium rushed in from the tanker standing alongside.

Everything was set. Cool as a cucumber, Andy went up to our apartment for a shower. He reappeared at nine o'clock. Precisely an hour later the complete calm was disturbed by a gust of wind and the balloon lurched sideways. 'Come on, Andy,' I said, 'the sea breeze is starting. We've got to go.' I hugged Susie and the children warmly. 'I love you and I'll see you in a few weeks,' I told them confidently as I climbed the ladder.

CHAPTER SEVENTEEN

HELLO, EUSTON

I CLIMBED THE LADDER TO THE DOME at the top of the capsule and with a final wave I disappeared inside to get things organized on the flight deck. Andy was to follow and supervise the launch from the top. Ropes were released and that left the balloon tugging at the line which led to Paco Mendoza and Antonio Bonilla, the Mayor of Vicar, both of whom had beaming smiles. The mayor held the rope taut against the block of wood while Paco swung his ceremonial axe.

Missed.

There then followed what seemed an interminable few seconds as Paco wobbled the axe head back and forth to ease it out of the wood. Having done so he took another swing with a huge arc over his body. This time it worked and the balloon heaved upwards. To everyone's horror it became apparent that two mooring lines tied to the capsule were separately still attached to a vast block of concrete which had been anchoring us to the fairway. Andy leaned over the side of the capsule and quickly cut one of the lines. The suspended concrete block descended like an Exocet missile past the head of one of the ground crew. The other block was still attached and we were now trailing it towards the crowds of people. Andy slashed at the rope with his knife and it fell mercifully clear without hitting anything. It was 09:47 GMT on 17 February 1999. There were cheers and screams from the crowd but I could see nothing from inside the capsule, where I was already calling the control tower at Almería Airport to let them know we were airborne.

When we reached 2000 feet I noticed that our ascent rate had slowed and we started to descend. What we had not known was that there was an inversion in the atmosphere, a phenomenon in which the temperature of a band of air increases rather than decreases with height. This caused the helium gas to be less efficient at raising the amount of weight it was trying to lift. The normal procedure with a balloon which is filled with lighter-than-air gas is to let it go when it has a predetermined amount of lift and allow

222

the gas to expand during the climb until it fills out the entire gas cell at the ceiling. Then the balloon dips and climbs within a narrow vertical band no deeper than 1500 feet. A temperature inversion upsets all this completely.

We now had to start the burners, which we had not planned to use until nightfall. The back-up propane burners were the only ones which could be lit quickly by means of a pilot light started with a sparker. However, we now found that the supply was turned off at the taps on the tanks, which were at the other end of the capsule from the dome.

As Andy clambered along the top of the capsule I urged him to put on his harness. 'There's no time for that,' he said as he slid along the guard rail. I passed him the long pole designed to reach over the side and turn the taps of the individual propane cylinders. Soon we could hear the roar of the burners doing their job. At 8000 feet we sealed the dome to pressurize ourselves at that altitude as we continued to climb. We had to keep burning fuel up to the top of the inversion layer at 16,000 feet and let the balloon float up to its ceiling, which turned out to be about 21,600 feet. As we burned fuel by night and so reduced weight, the ceiling would get higher and higher as the days went by. Andy had worked out that if we ever got down to the last barrel of fuel our ceiling would be well over 50,000 feet.

We started a steady stream of conversation through the satellite fax to and from our Control Room in London and by 12:30 GMT the atmosphere was relaxed enough for a bit of humour to start creeping in. Andy typed into his computer:

> *Question. What time did we take off? Colin is having trouble with his Breitling. When the big hand is on Mickey and the small one on… We are just having Chicken Noodle soup. Cracking stuff, Grommit. Place looks like a tip already. Parachutes discarded in the gangway, toys on the desk.*

He also apologized for the first and last time about his appalling spelling, which was to flood all his transmissions. He is quite seriously dyslexic, a surprisingly common problem in highly intelligent people.

We soon got word of the first piece of drama at Mission Control in Holborn. It concerned the heavily pregnant Catherine Barton-Smith. Her waters had broken just before our take-off and she had been rushed to hospital. Robert was born as we set off across the Mediterranean.

When the ITN chase plane arrived we set up our microwave link for the first time. This meant we could relay sound and pictures direct to the television crew for broadcast on the evening news. There was a brief conversation between Andy and his mother Phyllis, who was on board with the ITN reporter Terry Lloyd. Phyllis said we looked absolutely magnificent – just like a bauble on a Christmas tree. Andy reminded her that whenever they had had baubles on their Christmas tree they had always fallen off and broken, but he was sure we would be all right. As soon as the ITN plane left, Andy retired for a well-deserved rest. We had been so busy in those first few hours getting ourselves organized that it seemed only minutes before we saw the Atlas mountains of Morocco.

Andy went straight to sleep and didn't wake until sunset. We were tracking south-west as planned and everything was under control as we lit the burners for the night. I soon got word from Mission Control that the worldwide news coverage of the launch and our subsequent progress was nothing less than sensational.

As we talked to the Moroccan air traffic controllers we ran into a problem that was to haunt us everywhere we went. Having established who we were, the type of aircraft and the fact that our destination was unknown (all pretty unusual for routine controllers to

handle), they asked us constantly for our next reporting point and estimated time. Lacking any ability to steer towards a fixed point, we could never do this. Whenever they pressed us we would make something up to keep them happy. This usually meant we had to tell them something quite different later on. Early in the night we had our second meal and discovered that we had forgotten the plates, a very basic omission which was to cause quite a few problems for the duration of our voyage. Andy was in good form and let Mission Control know:

Cuisine improving. We have found the Almeria avocados and Brie and biscuits. Just missing the Rioja and dancing girls.

Tim Cole came on duty at Mission Control just as Andy turned in for a second rest. I faxed him:

Currently Flight Level 180 tracking 218 degrees at 25 knots. 32dg N, 7.75 dg W. Marrakesh is 29 miles to run. Now there's a coincidence.

This was the city from which Messrs Branson, Fossett and Lindstrand had departed just eight weeks before. My enduring memory of that first night was lying by the bottom dome on the floor and watching the lights of Marrakesh go by as I listened to the light puffing of the kerosene burners outside our capsule.

Andy took over the hot seat at 06:30 GMT and I was asleep as soon as my head hit the pillow. I woke briefly as Andy shut down all the burners when the sun came up but otherwise slept for several hours.

Ascending slowly over the foothills of the Sierra Nevada before turning south across the Mediterranean to Africa.

When I woke I remarked to Andy that I considered it a real privilege to be there. He agreed and said that it was worth making the most of. After all, it doesn't happen too many times in life that you get given £1 million to go on holiday. I brushed my teeth, washed and shaved, using the small electric shaver I had bought for the flight. Normally I wet-shave with a razor and I couldn't get on with this chopping machine, so I never used it again. By the time we landed I had quite a beard. We then received a message that Steve Fossett had called and wished us the best of luck. Andy replied:

Please give him our thanks and tell him we will forgive him for messing up China provided we make it all the way round.

On the subject of China Ian Ashpole had something to tell us:

The British Embassy in Peking has just spoken to the Foreign Office. The Chinese are now aware that you are in the air. They know we have declared our intention not to fly through their airspace but the embassy describes them as 'jittery'.

Per Lindstrand also sent us a missive:

Watch out for the Yeti. He is 25 miles south of K2. Fluffy white with blue eyes, red feet and gets bigger when you take your oxygen mask off.

Always full of banter he later sent another:

While you are out there over the desert would you mind looking for the fuel tank we lost there in 1997 along with 100 litres of French mineral water and Richard Branson's underpants? The first item is white, the second clear and the third brown.

By late afternoon everyone wanted to talk to us on the satellite telephone and Ian asked if our workload would permit any interviews. Andy replied that my favourite programme was *Today* on BBC Radio Four and that he would like to be interviewed by a Spice Girl (or even two). *Today* was not interested and the Spice Girls were out of the question, so we had a quiet discussion about who was going to talk to *Blue Peter*. The BBC TV kids' show was the only one on offer that interested us both. I suppose we both just wanted to impress the children in our lives.

At 01:06 GMT on 19 February we were in the Canary Islands Control Area but Andy was having trouble making radio contact:

Still cannot raise them. I am knackered. Must be time for my sleep. I'll go throw a bucket of water over Colin. On second thoughts we don't have water to spare.

Just thirty minutes later I sent a position report containing details of track and strategy, together with the following news:

Boy Genius retired to bed and snoring happily.

Opposite On our way at last. The gleaming landscape is a massive area of plastic greenhouses where vegetables are cultivated for export to northern Europe.
Above The later result of my fight with the electric shaver – two bearded explorers in their tiny capsule after weeks in the air.

225

226

It probably took about another five days for our competitors to fully work out what we were up to. During most of that period we had seen no sign of life whatsoever as we sailed further and further into the desert. Not a road, a house, nor a camel – just breathtaking nothingness as far as the eye could see. We had been through countries that most people have not even heard of and for which we had only recently bought maps – Mauritania, Burkina Faso, Niger. By that time we had got thoroughly used to life on board, but considerable frustration set in at having to settle for interminably light winds in order to hold our course.

Our diet was fine, although we ran out of fresh food on day four. Thereafter we had to settle for things like hot water poured on soups and dried pasta, or muesli accompanied by powdered milk mixed with cold water. Variations on this diet included cheese and biscuits, and dried ham provided as a present at the take-off by Paco Mendoza. Water could be boiled and the higher our altitude the lower the boiling point. Typically it would be about 85 degrees Fahrenheit. We had to be careful to prevent condensation escaping from the kettle. Also, this could only be used during sunlight because it was a drain on the power supplied by the array of solar panels suspended under the capsule. In addition to water, we drank Coca-Cola and vast quantities of Ribena and lemon-and-ginger herbal tea, which we both liked. We also had on board two boxes of Sainsbury's wine, one red and one white. Pilots are not supposed to drink alcohol but we took the view that it would relax us during what was necessarily a high-stress marathon flight. In fact it never occurred to either of us to drink any of the wine during the first week aloft. After that we would normally have a measure in a paper cup before turning in for a sleep. It was nectar.

The most common question asked was how we went to the loo and kept clean. Our loo was a small space with a curtain across it. It was similar to an airline loo except that we were unable to keep any waste on board. This meant we had to be careful where it got ejected. The desert was fine, of course, as was the middle of the ocean. The loo had a wooden seat. Plastic was out of the question because at –55 degrees it becomes brittle and breaks and, as Andy put it, 'it bites'. We flushed it by placing a piece of rubber-covered wood over the top, kneeling on this to create a vacuum and then opening the valve at the base. The difference in pressure simply sucked out the contents into space. There was one thing we had to be very careful about. If we were flying low there were times when the cabin pressure was higher than the outside air pressure. If the valve is opened in these circumstances the horrendous result doesn't bear thinking about. The timing of loo visits is a personal question, but I usually made them when Andy was asleep and snoring or had his headphones on.

As far as cleanliness was concerned, we used wet wipes. Every morning and after a strenuous session outside the capsule, we would strip off and take a full bath using these. It worked fine and neither of us emitted any unpleasant body odour at any time during the flight. Washing our hair was a luxury we couldn't afford. After three days the scalp becomes itchy, but after that we simply got used to it. After sixteen days we recalculated our water supply and indulged in the only hair-wash we had. This was done by carefully pouring the water over each other's heads at the tiny sink in the galley space.

After three days the heating had broken down irretrievably. 'Buggered' was the word Andy used. The boy genius had simply designed it too well and the

Andy washing his hair in the tiny on-board sink for the first time in sixteen days.

motors melted. It was never going to be a luxury cruise and we coped. There were some occasions when it was so cold that I would hop around in my Arctic sleeping bag to keep warm. In our tiny living space it was just three jumps from my sleeping compartment to my chair at the desk on the flight deck.

Did we take any exercise? No.

Communications consisted of Inmarsat M and Inmarsat C. The first is a voice telephone via satellite, which is expensive to use. In fact this worked only very rarely after the first day. The second is a satellite fax system, in which the Capsat (C for short) is the on-board hardware. Apart from the occasional hiccup, this system worked perfectly throughout the flight. We simply typed the message into one of the two computers on our flight deck, dialled the number and transmitted. When incoming messages arrived from Mission Control a green light appeared on our instrument panel and we retrieved them without difficulty.

Boredom was very rarely a problem. By and large we were very busy. There was no autopilot because it would consume too much fuel. This meant that one of us was actively flying the balloon all the time. There was a rare time on the fifth day over the Sahara Desert when Andy was able to fax Mission Control:

> *I haven't touched a single control in the last five hours. The balloon is flying itself so I'm going to set the altitude alarm and go to bed. Bet Colin will be surprised when he gets up to find it on self-fly. Andy.*

Above top The interior of the capsule from my bunk. Andy's bunk is on the right and the flight deck at the end. The cylinders hold our supplies of oxygen and nitrogen. **Above** Andy at the flight deck, repairing the satellite telephone.

At that moment I woke up to spoil his joke. We plotted our position on on-board maps every thirty minutes and we were constantly reviewing strategy and weather forecasts. Andy, who normally devours books at a furious rate, started but never finished *Snow Falling on Cedars*. I did one or two coded crosswords and read the short book *Longitude*. I had suggested taking the game of Scrabble for odd moments when we had time to kill but Andy vetoed this because he can't spell.

Life-support systems consisted of a large canister of liquid oxygen and one of nitrogen. When we sealed the dome we would live in the pressure environment of the altitude prevailing at the point when it was sealed, no matter how low or high we went thereafter. We could open the oxygen valve to enrich the atmosphere, but no higher than twenty-five per cent because of the fire risk. We could squirt nitrogen into the capsule to increase pressure if we had a slight leak. There were times when we would be out of breath, even getting out of the chair, and this was an indication that there was too much carbon dioxide in the mix. Andy would then check our Draeger measuring device, which would tell us what proportion of our atmosphere was made up of oxygen, nitrogen and carbon dioxide. The Draeger unit drove us mad because when the atmosphere got to dangerous levels it would set off an alarm, which refused to stop even after we had remedied the situation. We used to bury the damn thing in the bottom of one of our sleeping bags and roll it up in a futile attempt to drown out the piercing noise. The final piece in the life-support jigsaw was a scrubbing system to take out the carbon dioxide released by exhaling. Headaches were a good indication that the scrubbing system had been switched off for too long or that the filters needed changing. This happened on several occasions.

By 13:30 GMT on 21 February we were well into our fifth day and we had still not gained a single degree of longitude from our take-off in Almería. We had gone so far west in order to fly deep into the southern Sahara that it had taken this long to retrace our steps in the easterly direction we needed to travel clockwise around the world. I saw on the map that we were just thirty-five miles from Timbuktu in Mali. I remembered being taught in school that this was one of the most remote places on earth. So I called them up on the radio. No answer. I tried again. This time I heard a crackle as someone came on the airwaves. I explained that we were a balloon on our merry way around the world, after which I sent a message to London:

Such joy. We just spoke to Timbuktu. Frightened the life out of the poor devil. They have no conflicting traffic today (surprise, surprise). We will pass 6 miles to the north. River Niger coming up soon just to reassure us that there is more than just sand in this world.

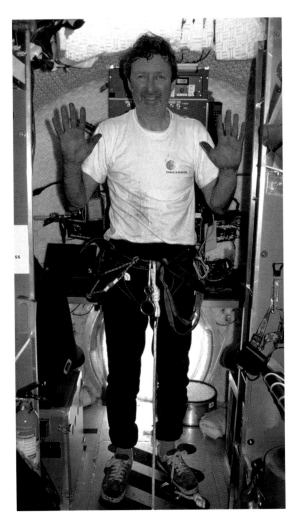

After hours outside transferring fuel, hot from the sun and reflected heat of the Sahara desert, I'm bathed in sweat, oil and grime, which took a whole box of baby wipes to clean up. My clothes just went overboard after sessions like this.

Ian Ashpole replied:

The girls have found this topical note:
Tim and I a-hunting went.
We came upon three women in a tent
Since they were three and we were two
I buk one and Timbuktu.

Later that afternoon we had our first refuelling session. This entailed transferring kerosene from the piggybacked barrels into the in-board tanks, from where they could be pumped through the burners. I let them know down below:

We are outside refuelling, so don't phone – we have no answering machine on board.

We fitted our harnesses and Andy took his black London brolly with him. I had seen this for several days crooked over the oxygen tank and I had meant several times to ask my partner what it was there for. 'To keep the sun off,' he said. I knew him better than that. It was a ridiculous idea but the photograph I took of him sitting on the barrels with refuelling pump and umbrella was to be seen by millions around the world after I transmitted it by Inmarsat M for syndication by the international media. I warned London:

Stand by for great pic for tomorrow's newspapers. Andy over the side refuelling with desert below

Left Shaded by an English brolly, Andy on the outboard fuel barrels over Africa. We sent this picture back by satellite and it was syndicated to newspapers all round the world within hours.

and holding brolly for shade (or rather for posing effect). The caption should read: 'Explorer Elson 6 miles from Timbuktu.'

A day later, after more steady progress, I called Mission Control:

Hello, Euston. Er, Euston we have a problem. Andy has just spotted the River Niger and he has asked me if I think the tide's out. I am getting a bit concerned about him y'know. It might be the early stages of swamp fever. Colin at 9,400 feet over the River Niger.

It was the first and last time I used the 'Hello, Euston' joke while airborne. Cable & Wireless's headquarters were only just down the road from Euston Station in London and I thought it would be a good device to jolly the media along. We had even thought of building in an electronic beep to our telephone interviews in order to ape the *Apollo* missions of the sixties and seventies. Unfortunately the joke had worn so thin by the time we launched that my faxed transmission was probably seen as a somewhat feeble revival. Well, it had amused me anyway.

It quite amused Andy too. *The Times* had earlier described us as the odd couple. Andy's response was: 'There's nothing odd about us – it's everyone else.' It was true that we were very different characters and from different backgrounds, but one thing we did have very much in common was the giggles. We both had a fit of them when he sent his next message:

Above Tim Cole and Ian Ashpole at Mission Control.

Thetideisoutatrivernigerbutithasgotahellofabeachwhichistwothousandmileswide. Nothingmuchnewhereexceptthatthelastcupofcoffewastoomuchforthecomputerandnow thespacebarwon'twork.I'lltakeittobitsnextandseeifIcanfixit.Andy.15.44N01,09W105 Deg15.2knots8,980feetornearenough.

In complete contrast to this jollity I woke up on the seventh day with an attack of shingles. I didn't feel at all well and Andy was in a bad mood. I sat lethargically at the flight deck. Andy was concerned but I assured him that I had medication for it and he already knew that I had a history of suffering such attacks. He started firing off furious messages to London about I don't know what. He was the fiery one while I was the diplomat, he once told a journalist. Mission Control had set up a baby's pram with a large number of teddy bears in it. The level of Andy's mood was demonstrated to new people coming on shift by the number of teddies that had been thrown out of the pram. Today they were all on the floor.

Russell Brice later came on duty and he too expressed concern about my condition. He asked if there was anything I wanted. Yes, there bloody well was. I faxed him back:

> WISH LIST
> A replacement satellite phone that works
> Paper plates
> Sponge
> Faster winds
> A refuelling plane with two tons of kerosene
> My wife
> An engineering genius who does not snore.
> Colin.

Above top Resembling a scene from *Kelly's Heroes*, Andy appears comically out of the hatch, pointing to the horizon. I snapped this as I was harnessed over the side.
Above An exhausted Russell Brice after months of coordination.

He did not know how to respond, so he didn't. But he did put it up on the internet site for the one million-plus subscribers who were logging in every day and I had many comments about it after the flight.

We had set ourselves a number of waypoints on our route to aim for. One of them was the joint border of Chad, Libya, Sudan and Egypt. In the early hours of 24 February I was feeling a little better, though not much. We were approaching the southern tip of Libya and, if we could miss it, it would make life simpler. We had received written overflight permission but the country's record in honouring such documents was not promising. Steve Fossett had been refused entry three years earlier only to have that denial rescinded as he was tracking south of Libya. Just eight weeks before our flight, Richard Branson's team had got permission to fly through only after considerable difficulty. I sent the news:

> *Andy to bed. Just reviewed everything. All looks good. Currently 17,200 feet and my calculation now is that we will miss Libya by 75 metres. Colin.*

This was followed an hour later with:

> *Just entered Sudanese airspace at 17,800 feet. Missed Libya by 0.15 degrees (less than 200 metres). Cannot raise Khartoum (must be asleep). Colin.*

'Bullseye,' came back the message from Martin Harris. It was a crowning moment.

The tempo stepped up a beat as we approached Egypt and the air traffic controllers got busy with us. After almost ten days of empty desert the busy areas came as something of a shock. However, we were having trouble for a while making contact with the right frequencies and we were floating around in darkness listening to an incessant chatter from aircraft all around us. Our short-wave radio was not working (it never did) and the VHF could transmit over only short distances. We were able to find several very helpful 747 pilots flashing past us at 600 miles an hour who would relay messages with our position, track and speed to air traffic control. This helped but we asked Mission Control to ask Heathrow to fax our flight plan to Cairo for us. When we got it sorted out at last Andy sent the following:

Thanks. That's just what we need – more airways. Yes we have a squawk (allocated radar number) and we are being handed on. Wow, at last they got it together. Colin now a gibbering wreck but the boy done good, it was his turn on the radio. Now how do I arrange the shift rota so he gets the next lot as well? From Andy – sanguine and cool as usual. Well nearly.

Bullseye. Our Global Positioning Satellite system shows that we missed the target of the four-way border between Chad, Sudan, Libya and Egypt by less than 200 metres.

We crossed the Red Sea in darkness before speeding up over Saudi Arabia on day nine. We even saw the GPS speed indicator briefly touch sixty-one knots. It was the fastest we went on the entire flight. More sand greeted us but it was paler and appeared flatter. I watched many huge oil wells pass by underneath through the dome beside my bunk.

Over Oman we were again busy with air traffic control before the long trek over the Indian Ocean to our next waypoint – Mumbai (or Bombay as it is better known). During this period several aircraft asked to speak to us and wished us luck:

Are you the Cable & Wireless balloon? We have been reading about you in the newspapers.

Our Inmarsat M satellite telephone, which had been so temperamental at picking up a usable signal, now broke down completely. We seemed to be permanently faxing messages back and forth, trying to analyse the problem with Anthony McQuiggan, who had done such an amazing job coordinating all our communications and computer equipment for the flight. Andy now insisted on taking the whole thing apart. The flight deck was soon covered with hundreds of bits and pieces, from circuit boards to soldering irons to tiny screws, and it all remained there for two days while he tried to repair the phone. I occasionally urged him strongly to forget it. We had better things to do and the Capsat would see us through. But he was determined. He eventually told me that he had had an idea which involved taking a capacitor out of one of the lights on board. He was going to have to disable the light in the loo or the galley space, and which one did I think was least important? This was getting ridiculous. He was never going to get the phone fixed but there was no stopping him. I resigned myself to the fact that there would be no illumination in the loo, which was not too serious, I decided. Two hours later the phone worked again. I was amazed and not a little impressed.

There were literally hundreds of messages of goodwill being sent to either Mission Control or direct to the internet site. We were drip-fed the occasional greeting but there were unfortunately just too many to get them all. They were rationed to us by whoever was on duty at Mission Control. One of my favourites among those I did receive was from one of my greatest friends of the last twenty years. Geoffrey Cheetham, who was now the director of marketing at Energis, a competitor of our sponsors, Cable & Wireless, wrote to me:

> Colin, I panic enough about your mad exploits without seeing pictures of you in the newspaper waving an umbrella out of a balloon at 8,000 feet over Africa. Trust the Primus stove is still functioning to make enough tea and I expect there is an open fire for the crumpets too. Since you ignored my advice twenty years ago to get into this ballooning malarkey, just enjoy. Your adventure is certainly giving me and many many others much pleasure. We are right behind you. Geoffrey at your favourite telecommunications company, not your financing one.

There was one for Andy too, although whoever sent it forgot to sign his name:

> Elson you old bugger, you better succeed – I've got a FIVER riding on it.

It was clear we were going to arrive north of Mumbai but not enough to be seriously off course. We were on our way to another milestone. On 27 February 1999, flying over India, we beat the world endurance record for the longest flight of any aircraft in the earth's atmosphere. Andy was dismissive. I was chuffed. We had just broken his own record of a year before. Then he had narrowly surpassed the nine and a half days that Dick Rutan and Jeana Yeager had spent in the air in December 1986.

Day Eleven over India. After several days inside we descended to open the dome and get some fresh air. We had just broken the world endurance record for any aircraft in the earth's atmosphere.

Mission Control said that the girls from Karen Earl were desperate for a photograph of us together which they could issue to the media to celebrate our setting a new world record. This was easier said than done, but we tackled the problem as a team. The boy genius rigged up the electronic Agfa digital camera to his computer so that a picture was shown on the screen for framing purposes. On the morning of 27 February we descended to 6000 feet and opened the dome. It was the first time we had been outside in five days. With my harness on I scrambled across the top of the capsule with the camera, trailing wires behind me. I felt unmistakably queasy as I leaned right out into the flying wires at the far end to tape the device into a position to get us both into the shot. I returned like a professional cat burglar to pose with Andy, who clicked a remote-control key on the computer. Within hours of our sending the image down the wires to London it was all around the world.

There was a flood of messages of congratulation. Most of these we never saw, but notable among them was a very generous one from Bertrand Piccard, who was still contemplating the possibility of taking off in a couple of days on the same mission.

We crossed India without mishap and flew on into the Bay of Bengal. Alone on the flight deck early in the evening of 28 February, Andy sent a few reflections to London:

> *Well how are we all?*
> *What is new in the world?*
> *Are Breitling going to launch?*
> *Will the Bracknell Met Office computer break down every weekend?*
> *We are poodling across the Bay of Bengal.*
> *It's dark and a full moon.*
> *The satellite reception is awful. Both C and M.*
> *Rumour Control says that Martin Harris has bought a new fir cone to go with the seaweed so maybe we'll get some useful weather. He says that Breitling won't catch us up. Is he doing their weather as well?*
> *I could give you our position, height and speed but then you probably know better than me. Andy – here or there.*

Some hours later, at midnight GMT, he was snoring again and I faxed London:

> *I am going to start the descent as the first tinges of light have appeared on the horizon so there may be a gap of a few hours while I wake Andy and we refuel. Wind seems to be dropping all the time but we have made good progress south. Colin.*

As dawn broke on the first day of March we descended to 1500 feet, where I volunteered to carry out the main fuel transfer of our journey. Just before I went outside we got the news from London that Breitling was preparing for launch – there had just been a press conference on TV.

The refuelling took six full hours. Unfortunately the fuel bag in the forward tank had sunk so far down that I couldn't reach it through the handling hole on the side of the keel. Harnessed to the top rail, I had to use a hacksaw blade without the handle to patiently

More fuel transfers over the Bay of Bengal.

Over western Thailand on the morning of 1 March 1999. The early signs of thunder clouds are already forming in the distance.

carve my way through the aluminium honeycomb before I could reach the bag. I must be one of the few people who has vandalized the fuselage of his aircraft while in flight. Unknown to me, Andy had tape-recorded this episode, during which my arm was repeatedly cut by the jagged metal. There is now an undeniable record of some pretty fruity language that my colleagues on earth never even knew I was capable of. Andy, who stayed on board, periodically sent back reports, one of which I did not see until after the flight. It read:

Have cut up the redundant heating system to make extra refuelling pipe to help Colin reach the bags. It's great to see someone else covered in dirt and struggling. Andy now at 6,000 feet.

During this period Andy had been busy passing me tools from the capsule and concentrated on keeping the massive balloon at no more than 6000 feet above the sea. When I eventually climbed back inside I was sweating from the extreme heat, exhausted and sunburned. I threw my kerosene-stained T-shirt overboard and took a double ration of baby wipes to get clean.

Back at Mission Control they could only watch bemused as the automatic position reports came through. We had spent all day going backwards in a south-easterly direction towards India again. We were soon on our way, though. We crossed south of the mouths of the Irrawaddy, and entered Myanmar. We had taken a horrendous amount of time to get there, but we were on course and we still had even more fuel left than we had intended to carry on the flight before the China crisis.

As we crossed the border into Thailand I remembered that Marc Wolff and our team were filming there. They were shooting the aerial sequences for the movie of Alex Garland's novel *The Beach*. Leonardo DiCaprio was there too, having reportedly trousered half the $40-million budget. I wondered what they were all thinking of us as we flew overhead.

We had now been flying so long that we began to wonder what was going on in the world. Therefore we were glad to be fed snippets of news by the BBC via Mission Control:

Euro doomed to failure say group of British politicians.
Japanese doctors perform the country's first heart transplant in 30 years after a law was passed allowing such operations.
A white contestant representing South Africa in the Continent's Face of Africa beauty contest has sparked a row over her colour.
Two British hot-air balloonists are on course to circle the world non-stop avoiding Chinese airspace but could face a challenge from a rival balloon with permission to overfly China.

Back in England, Lou de Marco, the retired head of the CAA's helicopter flight operations, who had been negotiating all our permissions, tried just one more time to see if the Chinese would relent. The message he got back, and sent to us, was:

The Deputy Director has stated that any attempt by Cable & Wireless Balloon to violate Chinese Airspace will result in very serious consequences for which the British side will be held responsible.

CHAPTER EIGHTEEN

THE TASTE OF FEAR

THE *CLOCKWORK ORANGE*, AS ANDY CALLED THE BREITLING BALLOON – it had a horological sponsor and the capsule was orange – took off from Château d'Oex in Switzerland at 09:10 GMT on 1 March 1999. We had just completed our refuelling in the Bay of Bengal when they departed. The launch looked a bit rough on TV, we were told, but they were away. In the meantime we were approaching an area where we knew there was a risk of thunderstorms. This was the hazard we had always feared most. It made the whole strategy of flying south of China a hairy one.

Martin Harris sent us an ominous briefing headed 'PILOTS THUNDERSTORM WARNING':

> *The probability of large CBs [cumulonimbus clouds] and thunderstorms developing close by to the track of the balloon over Myanmar and parts of Thailand is very high during the next 72 hours...*

We were obviously concerned but Andy's reply tried to make light of it:

> *Looks like we will be going cloud spotting tomorrow. By the way Chinese food is banned for the whole team until further notice.*

A chase plane with a film crew from Bangkok came to find us on the first morning of our flight in Thai airspace and the cauliflower clouds were already building around us. After the plane left, Andy and I discussed what we could see ahead over the mountains. It was not a welcome sight. We desperately wanted to avoid flying over the top of these towering castles of white vapour because the upper winds were forecast to be backing north, which would carry us into China. We had three choices. We could take on the thunder clouds (which, together with flying into power lines, is one of the two most dangerous things you can do in ballooning); we could fly high into China and get shot down; or we could abandon the flight by landing in the jungle below. There was no question of giving up and China was out of the question. On the other hand, we didn't want to get into an argument with a cumulonimbus cloud. Not under any circumstances.

Two messages came up. One was from Steve Fossett, who was impressed by our stamina and thought we were setting an endurance record that would never be beaten. The second was from Mary Fagin, Lord Lieutenant of Hampshire:

Congratulations from everyone in Hampshire. Keep going, we are all watching you.

I saw Mary several months later and told her that hers was one of the few messages to get through. 'They do tend to,' she said.

I sent a request to Mission Control:

When Martin wakes with his harem of helpers in Oxford could you please mention to him that I estimate arriving at 97 E at approximately 1130 UTC and not at 1700 UTC as he suggested in his briefing last night. The latitude at that point will probably be around 1520 N. If this looks dangerous to him I need to know before he cleans his teeth. Colin at 17,550 feet.

Andy had more experience than me of bad weather and he thought we would be all right if we stuck at 18,000 feet. I was not in my most relaxed state of mind (come to think of it, I was scared as hell) but Andy seemed happy and retired to bed. I was soon becoming very uneasy listening on the radio to the consistent requests by aircraft to divert because of the weather. Nevertheless, everything seemed to be working fine for the time being as we floated along, tiptoeing between the huge columns of whiteness.

And then suddenly (seemingly out of nowhere) it hit us. We were engulfed in thick black cloud, there was a deafening roar and we were swung violently from side to side. The variometer needle showed us shooting upwards at 2000 feet a minute (we had never climbed at more than 500 feet a minute before then) and almost as quickly it indicated 1500 feet a minute downwards. Andy tumbled out of his dreams. Clad in nothing but his underpants, he rushed to start the burners as we tried to burn and burn and burn our way out of trouble. We were totally out of control.

I screamed out the instrument readings incessantly as Andy kept the burners blasting heat upwards. There were frightening pauses as we lurched uncontrollably and then accelerated upwards while the whole envelope flapped and tore above us. (We never knew just how much damage had been done to the balloon until we saw pictures of the landing several days later.)

It was difficult to know when to start burning again. But the target was most definitely *up*. So the burners just burned and burned. Every time we thought we might have begun to stabilize or have got back a degree of control, there was another violently vibrating rumble. We would then be hurled downwards again as I watched the dial on the variometer swing in a way it was never designed to. There would then be a pause as we hurtled skywards all over again. My heart was thumping against my chest wall as I imagined what could happen at any moment. If the balloon were to split it would be terminal. I glanced at Andy's bare feet

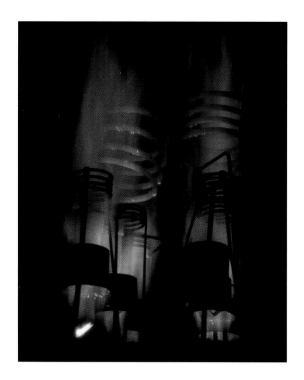

Previous spread The first of the bad weather to hit us – at 32,000 feet above the Thai jungle. **Below** The reassuring glow of the kerosene burners through the top dome.

beside the flight deck, his head being high up in the dome to see what was going on around us. His near nakedness made a nonsense of our perilous state. We had had no time to get our parachutes on. Even if we had managed to get them on and were about to plummet out of the sky, we would have had the desperate problem of getting the dome fastener open. And if we had, it would have caused explosive decompression. We would then have to work out how fast we were descending in order to make a rapid decision as to whether or not we could get down to a safe altitude without losing consciousness. If we couldn't, we would have to don our oxygen masks. If the decision was to make an immediate emergency exit, we would then have to climb one after the other up the ladder, which was so narrow we could put only one foot on a rung at a time. Finally we would have to force ourselves out of the dome – impossible at speed.

My partner was utterly calm and I tried to put my imaginings out of my mind. I realized that he would survive no time at all in the jungle in the unclothed state he was in even if he managed to don his chute. (There certainly wasn't going to be time to get dressed and assemble the survival gear in these circumstances.)

'We got real problems here,' he muttered with masterly understatement.

'Fifteen hundred feet a minute upwards,' I said as a deathly whistling signalled another rush of violent force outside our stricken craft.

Yet again the ascent would slow and the capsule would lurch and swing and creak as I kept hold of the laptop computer in front of me. These movements were completely alien to a balloonist and we were both trying to formulate in our minds what to do if the final crack of noise heralded a burst balloon. At the same time we both knew full well our chances were minimal if that happened. We were on our way down again in a ferocious downdraught which tested the instruments to their limits, before coming to an abrupt stop. Once again we reversed skywards for the next rollercoaster. Judging by the heat that was being forced from the burners towards the main helium balloon above us, we should have been moving strongly upwards. But there were no rules in this weather and we prayed that the violent forces within the cauldron of cloud would smooth out and that our balloon could tough its way through the battling air currents.

We remained calm and found ourselves exchanging only essential information. Finally we had a prolonged period of climbing, fast at first and then slowing to a steady 400 feet a minute. It was almost beginning to feel normal again, although I was now seriously concerned at our altitude, as we were still surrounded by the murky greyness of water vapour.

We were now at 29,000 feet and I asked Andy if we were yet clear of cloud and he confirmed we were just emerging over the top. This was at least a profound relief because I knew we were only about 2000 feet lower than our ceiling. Timing the shutdown of burners was a fine judgement in itself, because to burn through the ceiling would have spilt a lot of gas and sent us plunging downwards again – back into the maelstrom. We levelled out at last. There then followed a few minutes of uneasy calm while neither of us breathed a word. All we could hear in the eerie silence was the occasional clank of the stainless-steel burner coils as they contracted on cooling.

At last Andy dared to step down from the dome. Then he went back with his camera to record the almost unbelievable sight below. The pictures of the

Looking down at the thunderstorm that miraculously spared us. Remnants of the torrential rain are still spattered on the plastic as we finally emerge over the top at 29,000 feet.

cloud tops around us were distorted by the curvature of the dome, but they serve as testament to our terrifying ordeal. Andy asked if I wanted to have a look. Cowardly, I simply declined.

It took a terrifying ninety minutes – an experience neither of us will ever want to repeat. We agreed we had felt fear in a way that neither of us had ever done before. Both of us cleaned our teeth afterwards to wash the disgusting taste out of our mouths.

At 06:55 GMT (now mid-afternoon in Thailand) I sent a fax to Ian Ashpole:

> *Just got entangled with several CBs and have had a very bad 90 minutes. Very nasty indeed. We think we are clear now but keeping alert. Now at our ceiling over 32,000 feet trying to overfly remaining towers of thundercloud. All stable for the moment. Good speed and direction away from the enemy. One more underneath us to pass over. Monster to our south with serious anvil top (which hopefully means it is decaying). Should be OK now. Colin at 31,650 feet.*

He replied:

> *I've just had the shivers reading your last message. We are keeping everything crossed for you down here for a safe transit. We are all thinking of you both. Ian.*

We tracked away from the storms into persistent calm at 31,000 feet and to our surprise the wind direction was only marginally further north than at our lower level. We were travelling just north of east. We now contemplated the next danger area for thunderstorm activity – the mountains between Laos and Vietnam, where we would arrive at nightfall. It took little discussion to agree on a course at maximum altitude and we just had to hope the westerly wind that was helping us to avoid China held out.

No sooner had this gut-wrenching experience reached a conclusion than we heard a female voice from Bangkok Control announce:

> *Stand by for an important message.*

After a few minutes a second lady came on the line, again speaking perfect English:

> *Permission to overfly Laos and Vietnam is refused. Please state your intentions.*

This was ridiculous. Had we really come all this way, over all this time and through the cauldron of eastern skies just to find we were refused further progress? We explained patiently that we had seen our written authority before departure, but the reply came back that it had expired at the end of February.

Time to wake up Lou de Marco in England. Before working for the Civil Aviation Authority, which he had left a year earlier, Lou had been our inspector at Flying Pictures. In that capacity he ensured that we adhered to all the procedures required of us as holders of an Air Operator's Certificate, the licence we needed for our helicopter filming activities. A calm, sensible and intelligent man, Lou had always been very fair. We had had a difficult time back in 1989 when, in what was thankfully our only serious accident, stuntman Clint Carpenter was killed on location in Greece. Throughout the aftermath of the tragedy Lou kept a sensible grasp on the situation, investigating exactly what had happened and at the same time looking at how to operate in the future to reduce the risk of such a thing ever occurring again.

In the late nineties Lou had a serious motorcycle accident. As a result he failed the mandatory medical examination undergone by pilots, lost his flying licence and had to retire early from the CAA. As he had time on his hands I had no hesitation in inviting him to manage both the acquisition of diplomatic permissions and search-and-rescue operations for our round-the-world project. Andy, who is always deeply suspicious of (and often hostile to) anyone who has not been thoroughly tried and tested by him personally, took to Lou quickly. Lou had worldwide contacts and a lifetime experience of the ways of governments, aviation authorities, rescue services and other relevant procedures. In addition he had an enormous network of international contacts whom he knew on first-name terms.

Tonight Lou rubbed his eyes and digested our problem. Meanwhile, in our balloon some 10,000 miles away, we flew on at our almost statutory twenty knots (I think the needle was stuck on this figure for most of the eighteen days). We had time to consider if this really was the end.

Little time passed before Bangkok Control came back on the radio, Lou having made a very speedy and effective intervention:

> *Golf Charlie Whisky Charlie Whisky, you have been cleared to proceed through Laos and Vietnam.*

There followed a period of enormous relief where we took stock of our situation. I poured us both a small paper cup of red wine. We thought it would be good to calm the nerves. Normally this amount would have little effect but what we had not considered was that we had both lost more than six kilograms in weight since the start of our flight. We got the giggles over something futile and realized that we were already just very slightly drunk. The green light flashed on the console and we retrieved a message from Ian Ashpole saying that he knew we were busy but he had not had a position report for two hours. We thought this was hysterically funny and put the wine box firmly back in

its locker. I reported back our apologies that there were now two (hic) drunks on board having a philosophical discussion about a hell of a day (hic), something Ian clearly rejected as a joke:

Two drunks on board. Tracking away from the enemy towards Laos and Vietnam.

> *What a day you have had. If you ever experience anything as bad as the thunderstorm again it might be worth toning down your description to Carrie and Susie. They love you very much and will only worry more and make their part in this great adventure even more difficult. Your description scared the pants off me. God knows what they are making of it. I know I have said it before but you are both real heroes. Ian.*

In my haze I replied that we should just tell Susie that it was the closest she got to the life insurance and leave it at that (hic).

Andy went to bed. I knew I was slightly tipsy because now that Andy had retired I found I was giggling to myself. As he started his customary deep snort, followed by more regular snoring, I checked our altitude and set the burners to cruise at the level I wanted.

I also plotted our position on the map and checked it. I was in a very jolly mood and taking some time to perform these now familiar tasks. And then inexplicably I had an idea.

Two hours later, when Andy awoke, he peered through the chink at the end of the curtain and was perplexed to see no sign of me at the flight deck. He drew the curtain back further to look for me. On looking left (instead of right to the flight deck) he was astounded to see me sitting cross-legged on my bunk with a pair of binoculars pressed to my eyes. I had worked out that I could focus on the instruments perfectly to keep track of our progress. I was comfortable there with my pillow propped up against my back. Only occasionally did I have to stagger the few paces to readjust the burner levels.

Andy suggested it was my turn to grab some sleep and I accepted the invitation enthusiastically.

I slept soundly after the drama of the thunderstorm of that day and Andy woke me at dawn. He was exhausted and wanted me to take over again. 'Did you manage to keep us in an easterly direction?' I asked. I hopped the three steps in my sleeping bag to the flight deck (rather as if I was in a sack race at my children's school sports day). Better than that, he had actually found us a wind slightly to the south and we would soon be crossing into the South China Sea at Da Nang on the Vietnamese coast.

Wise advice to my old friend Pooh from Geoff Thompson of *The Times*.

As Andy retired to his bunk for his traditional four hours of respiratory rumbling a new air traffic controller came on watch at Ho Chi Minh City. He told me it was an honour and a privilege to have us in his airspace. Oh, now that's really nice, I thought.

And so I had the privilege of ascending to an altitude of about 16,000 feet, which flew us neatly around Hainan Island, China's most southerly point. It was an extraordinary period of several hours when I found a freak and very narrow band of wind which was no more than about 400 feet in height and had the perfect direction. To stay within it took razor-sharp concentration as my heart thumped in my chest.

By the time Andy woke up the job was done and we had a fair wind right up the Chinese coast towards Hong Kong. For me it was the most satisfying time of the whole flight and we allowed ourselves a few moments of self-congratulation. Wow, we had achieved the impossible – we had got round China.

The next day we were to receive a message from the British ambassador in Peking congratulating us on our achievement. He was either genuinely impressed with our skill (as he claimed) or more likely relieved that he was not going to have to handle a major diplomatic incident.

Ian was back on shift early:

Just seen a wonderful sight – the plot of your track around Hainan Island – what an amazing feat after 15 days flying. Ian.

I responded:

I must say you are great for morale, I am not sure I am going to be able to live like a normal human being after this (probably never did anyway). I've forgotten what it's all like down there. Colin at 22,420 feet.

We were heading almost due north. This meant we came within a couple of miles of the

Asian Buffer Zone and consequently Chinese airspace. Twice a very strange radio intervention came on the Hong Kong frequency. We never did find out what that was all about.

Golf Charlie Whisky Charlie Whisky, this is China.

It took me completely by surprise and I paused a couple of moments before deciding not to reply. In both cases the Chinese ladies had been interrupted by the Hong Kong controller. We never did work out if this was done to stop us talking to the Chinese, and in any case they should not have been transmitting on the Hong Kong frequency.

As we flew up past Hong Kong we heard that the Breitling team had actually flown over our launch site and were following our own course down into the Sahara. Where we were, some 9000 miles ahead, the air traffic airwaves got very busy again. We had to talk our way apologetically through a danger area (we really had no option at that point). But, as was usual throughout our journey, the controllers were incredibly helpful and patient with this huge, slow-moving object that seemed to take for ever to clear out of their airspace. Several aircraft asked if they could circle us to give their passengers a view and we gladly welcomed them to do so. Andy spotted a 747 circling us with flaps and gear down at 24,000 feet. Its pilot came on the radio and told us in his broad Aussie accent: 'It's koinda difficult to floi this thing when everyone's on the same soid of the plane.'

A British Airways captain asked us how long we had been flying. 'Sixteen days,' I said. 'Good grief,' was his only reply.

We carried on through the gap between China and Taiwan and on Martin Harris's advice we aimed as close to a northerly direction as possible. As we passed the northern tip of Taiwan Andy snapped his favourite picture. It was sunrise with the island poking its nose above the mists. About this time we received some rather depressing weather predictions about the Pacific crossing. It was clearly going to be touch-and-go as to whether or not we could get to the north of Japan quickly enough to beat the weather. We could not afford to hang around.

Still intact after the violent storm, our solar array, the power source for all our electrical needs, is seen suspended from the capsule as we fly up the Straits of Formosa.

Nevertheless, there were still three barrels of fuel to transfer into the main fuselage, so we descended before dawn and opened the dome. We were now virtually becalmed at little more than 1000 feet and I could see a whole line of fishing boats below. God knows what the fishermen must have made of this big fiery dragon descending over their ocean. As day broke I climbed out with my harness and completed the task of emptying the barrels as soon as possible. Once this was done, Andy handed me the specially sharpened ice axe we had brought along in case we had to land in mountains. I proceeded to lean over each side and pierce a large hole in the base of each of the eighteen empty barrels. (The loud clang as the sharpened tip ruptured the thick metal wall resounded all around me. The reason for holing the barrels was in order to make sure they sunk properly if and when we decided to drop them to save weight.)

I was most of the way through this task when kerosene suddenly spurted out of the hole I had just made in the last barrel. I had obviously missed one in the process of transferring the fuel. It was still full. I shouted for Andy, who was inside the capsule, and

Fixing some additional solar panels to the side of the capsule at 5000 feet over the Straits of Formosa.

his head appeared comically through the dome. I had already cut the pump away from the refuelling hose to throw it away, as it would not be needed any more. (We thought the hose might come in handy for something or other and decided to keep it.) On seeing my error, Andy immediately started as hasty a repair job as he could on the pump and hose. In the meantime I carefully checked all parts of my harness and had to lean right down, head first, over the barrel to stick my fingers in the hole to plug the leak. For thirty-five minutes, while Andy screwed, bound and soldered, I hung there staring at the waves below. It was one of a few moments on the trip when I seriously queried what on earth I thought I was doing.

We were now approaching the area north of Taiwan that Martin Harris described as Coffin Corner. He never promised that he would be able to find us a wind up the Chinese coast and in fact he had seriously doubted it was possible. We were still not getting the speed we wanted. We had hundreds of gallons of fuel left but now the Pacific winds were slowing from their previously predicted accelerating speed. Because of the time we had already taken, we had started to doubt that we could now get all the way round the world. Looking ahead, we were confident about reaching the east coast of America, but we now felt we would be unlikely to make the final hurdle of the Atlantic.

As we crossed the southern tip of Japan on the night of 6–7 March, Andy was snoring happily. Our long-awaited Pacific crossing was just starting and I pinched myself to keep fully awake as the first rays of light appeared over the horizon. Sadly, the grizzly bear had come to get us. The bad weather behind had already caught up with us and I broke the news to Andy as he shuffled out of his bunk.

We both knew it was all over. The only thing I wasn't sure of was whether or not Andy would argue that it was worth proceeding because there was no immediate danger and a remote chance that we might get through to better weather to the north. We went through the motions of turning up the burners in an attempt to climb through the upper level of cloud. At least then we could recharge our batteries through the solar panels, for the fuel pumps would not last a day without sunlight. As we expected, the wind veered sharply east, and as it was not the strand of the jet stream that best served our purposes we didn't even get through to the sunshine by 18,000 feet. We could have continued our climb with the help of our back-up propane burners but we knew this upper wind would take us straight out into the southern part of the north Pacific. This was where more thunderstorms were forecast in the area around Hawaii. So we simply called it a day.

Not surprisingly, Andy was now fully awake. When I showed him the weather briefings his disappointment turned to anger. He took over the computer to fax London:

URGENT URGENT URGENT URGENT
Martin, you may have overlooked one thing. Our batteries are not charging under the cloud and we have to burn all the time to stay in the air, so we are running our fuel pumps. We will not be able to stay in the air for more than a few hours more.
You have blown it.
Yesterday before I went to bed you said how well we were positioned between the

weather systems etc.
So why are we in cloud? We will have to land in the next 3 or 4 hours.
What are the surface conditions?
Is there no way we can get into sunshine for 3 or 4 hours to recharge? Andy.

I told Andy I didn't think it was appropriate to tell the weatherman he had blown it but he was insistent. But then he was like that – everything had to be just so and if there was the slightest flaw to any element in the meticulously planned strategy the frustration grew in his mind to the point of fury. It was as though there was a demon he needed to expunge from his brain before he moved on.

Almost immediately Andy followed up his message with another just to emphasize the seriousness of our position:

Get on the phone to Martin Harris. Get him out of bed and get him to read my fax
and to reply. Please also call Tim C and tell him we ain't going to make it. Our
battery voltage is 11.2 V so the Capsat will stop working in about half an hour.

Tim C was Tim Cole, the highly experienced American balloonist who was heading our operations team from Mission Control. He had made an early flight across the Atlantic with Steve Fossett. After that he went on to be the mission director of all Steve's solo attempts to fly around the world. We very fortunate that, as a great friend of Andy's, he had agreed to join our team.

Now at the north of Coffin Corner, Andy and I were calm but nervous as hell in our somewhat sudden predicament. The one great uncertainty had always been how our adventure would end. Now that it was about to we had to start working out what to do.

Back in London there was pandemonium as everyone was woken and put on full alert. It was the middle of the night there and I could imagine the normally quiet late shift at Mission Control buzzing with emergency reactivity. Everyone was phoning everyone while both Tim Cole and Ian Ashpole were rushing into their clothes to get over to Holborn as quickly as possible. Tim Shearman, our chief administrator, and our chief support engineer, Glenn Fairley, who had both now worked full time on our project for almost a year, were doing their best to hold everything together. They sent us the short-term forecast for the area in which we found ourselves:

SURFACE CONDITIONS
Surface wind 10 knots veering and increasing to 18 knots within next few hours.
Wind then veering WNW 20-25 knots by 06Z and to 30-35 knots (gale force) by 18Z.
Cloud layers spreading from SW with rain becoming heavy. Ship 32N 134E reporting
cumulonimbus and squall 30 knots southerly wind with falling pressure in last 3
hours. Near 126E there are CBs reported. UP is only option. Tim S/Glenn.

This was very alarming. 'CB' is the shorthand for cumulonimbus, which is a thunder cloud. This told us there was horrendous weather about 100 miles behind and it was catching us up. The situation was deteriorating fast and we could expect winds increasing to gale force by the end of the day. The last comment about the only option being up was worrying. It indicated to us a degree of panic down on the ground. High above the Pacific, some 12,000 miles away, Andy and I had another quick exchange of views and reaffirmed our conclusion that the only sensible option was *down* and down fast.

Meanwhile Andy had discovered that between the two layers of cloud we were actually getting enough ultraviolet light from the sun for there to be a small charge in our batteries. On his side of the flight deck he typed into his computer:

We are proposing to stay at a recharging height for an hour. Then descend and fly low level towards Japan if that is possible. Will land either on sea or land depending on weather and assuming the low level winds will do this. Suggest you send Russ/Glenn NOW to Tokyo. Best leave Susie and Carrie in the UK … If you approve this plan and think we can fly north at low level we propose on our descent to shut down Capsat and switch on every 30 minutes on the hour and half hour. Will you send message via Heathrow to Japan ATC [Air Traffic Control] … We are not in immediate danger. Andy @ 13,760 feet climbing slowly.

We were creating a short delay so that everyone could concentrate on what was happening. At the same time we were beginning to think that it was somewhat futile still being up so high and gambling on vague hopes of something turning up. Andy typed to Tim Cole, who had just arrived at Mission Control:

What do we get if we go up? Do we just end up a long way from land and then have to ditch anyway? The surface conditions described look landable if we do it soon. Andy @ 13,220 feet struggling with all six kero burners on.

The final morning. Considering options on the flight deck, 7 March 1999.

We had all six kerosene burners on full throttle and the fact that we were having to use so much power indicated that we had been accumulating weight in the form of snow or ice on the vast envelope. We were soon to see great sheets of it falling off under their own weight during the descent. Tim quickly replied that as we were still in sleet he saw little point in being at altitude, where our direction was straight out into the Pacific, away from the Japanese mainland. He followed this advice with:

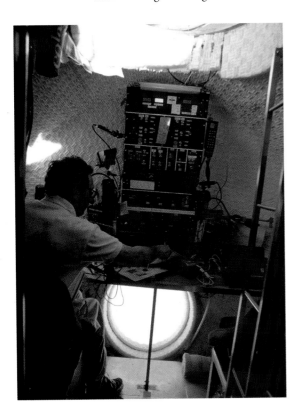

Do not see any immediate improvement in weather and direction. You are 70 miles from land and any altitude will push you out into Pacific. We need intention as to whether we should notify rescue services. Transponder should be set at 7700 (emergency radar trace). Surface conditions only deteriorate and you have 7 hrs daylight. Please advise intentions. TS.

Now that it was clear that the Japanese mainland was unattainable I studied the map with an eye on our direction and speed as we started a careful descent. I took over the computer connected to the Capsat and with one final thought I typed:

If we can fly for 90 minutes and then descend we can get close to the island of MIYAKE-JIMA. Will the weather deteriorate significantly in that time or should we go down and ditch immediately? Colin. 14,000 feet.

At this late stage Mission Control did not like this suggestion and in any case found it overoptimistic. So we decided to forget all other options and concentrate on getting down safely as soon as possible. They asked us to put out a Mayday call immediately.

One of the first people to come through the door of Mission Control after the general alert about our plight was Lou de Marco. This was to be his big day. Lou took out his book marked 'Japan' and started to dial the emergency services.

Tim Cole then called Susie at our home near Stockbridge, where she was fast asleep. Only a few hours before I had managed to have a quick conversation with her on the satellite phone in one of its rare moments of cooperation with a signal. I had told her that I was just fine and we were well organized for our imminent Pacific crossing which would take us three to five days. We had now been airborne for almost three weeks and Susie was at last beginning to get used to the journey. She might even have been settling into a more relaxed frame of mind. While she continued to run her board-games business, Susan Prescot Games, as well as get the children to and from school, there had rarely been a day or night when there was not a satellite van from one of the many news networks parked outside the house. She had given countless interviews and patiently invited journalists and technicians inside for endless glasses of chilled Chardonnay, only to be asked the same questions over and over again. Now, for the first time, she had left the answering machine on, confident that nothing would happen in the night and determined to get some sleep.

When she woke suddenly (as she always did several times a night) the message on the answering machine played back Tim Cole's voice an hour after he had made the first call: 'Come on, answer the phone, please. Come on, honey, we need to talk. Where are you, Susie?' She frantically dialled Mission Control, sensing that something terrible had happened.

As we descended through the lower cloud layer, snow flurries started flying past the dome above us and I put out a PAN call on the radio on 121.5, which is the international emergency frequency on VHF:

Pan Pan Pan. This is Golf Charlie Whisky Charlie Whisky. Charlie Whisky is a balloon in adverse weather seven zero miles east of Japan. Ditching in Pacific Ocean as soon as possible. Over.

A Pan call has less immediacy than the more famous Mayday, which Mission Control had suggested I make. A Mayday call means imminent danger and is often put out as a final piece of information before a crash with fatal consequences. On the other hand, if you put out a Pan call it is taken very seriously but the emergency services monitoring the frequency will know that, although the pilot transmitting the message has serious problems, he and his crew are not in immediate danger.

After a few minutes I sent another message to London:

Please notify rescue services as well as ATC and we will set transponder to 7700. Trying to put out a Pan call. So far no response. Colin.

The Japanese coastguard at last responded to my calls. I calmly explained our problem:

We are commencing our descent with the intention of ditching in the sea.

A quick check on the readout from the GPS satellite confirmed that we were now about seventy-five miles east-south-east of the ancient trading port of Yokohama.

Please advise the expected sea state, wind speed and direction at surface level.

By now we had everyone's full attention. It is not often that any coastguard gets an emergency call concerning anything as high-profile as a balloon flying around the world. I was asked to repeat my request, and I did so in the ridiculous way in which so many people speak to others of foreign tongues – very slowly, very deliberately and (in this case) with a pseudo-Japanese accent. Fortunately they understood what I was saying and I was told to stand by while they checked for information. Soon a voice came back across my radio and advised light to moderate winds, low cloud and rain. The light to moderate wind came as an enormous relief. Landing one of the biggest manned balloons in history was never going to be a picnic but light wind was the piece of luck we were praying for to have any chance of a reasonable end to our adventure.

I passed the information to Andy. While exhibiting his trademark calm, he was almost too preoccupied with controlling our flight level to take it in. We now believed we could make a safe splashdown, cut the envelope away by pneumatic release and remain aboard our newly converted boat until recovered. We would be seasick as hell in our unstabilized craft until a ship came along, but it seemed to us there was no need of helicopter rescue, and this I reported to the emergency services by radio.

We allowed the balloon to descend through the 8000-foot level and I depressurized the capsule by opening the valve in the loo. This allowed air to escape gradually from within so that the atmospheric pressure inside became equalized with the air outside. We opened the dome above the flight deck. Andy had his head through the top of the capsule and was using the blast valves to operate the back-up propane burners. Up until that point in our flight we had rarely used these in preference to kerosene. The highly efficient kerosene system works by a constant flow of fuel, adjusted by opening and closing the valve to give a bigger or smaller flame. However, the burners must be kept going (even if at the minimum rate) because the start-up takes a long time: the burner coils have to be heated to red hot and then the kerosene must be dribbled through to heat it enough to achieve a flame. The flame can then be increased only gradually; if this is done too quickly the cooler liquid follows too fast and the flame is extinguished. In this respect propane is much easier to use. The liquid simply turns to gas as it passes through the heated coils and is ignited (just as in a domestic gas boiler) without any difficulty as it comes out of the jets. Therefore it can be turned on and off in blasts whenever necessary.

While Andy was using the blast valves in just this way, I stayed below and shouted out the instrument readings to help him guide us down. We switched on the video and watched our descent on the television monitor, which received a dramatic picture from the boom camera on the exterior.

We then heard from London that aircraft and a ship had been sent out to us in spite of my assurance that a ship would be enough. We were asked to stay flying below cloud, out of the sea, if possible, until rescue arrived. I responded:

Will fly level if we can. Fully in touch by radio with Tokyo. Descending through severe turbulence at 7,400 feet. Colin.

Fifteen minutes later I followed this with:

4,000 feet descending. 11 knots track 094. Colin.

Andy, whose head was still poking through the top of the capsule, soon reported that he could see several aircraft. 'Wow. It's like Vietnam out here,' he shouted down. We descended steadily until there was a big bang as we struck the waves. I stayed below on the flight deck to concentrate on the instrumentation. I was also very keen to keep London informed as much as possible about what was happening. In particular I was anxious that if we had to evacuate the capsule suddenly I didn't want our families to remain on tenterhooks for several hours, not knowing whether or not we had survived. I deliberately kept the messages flowing in between helping Andy with the descent. One read:

Just landed the solar array in sea. Bounced to 790
feet. Coming down for second go. Clever old
Andy.

I added the last sentence to convey calm and soothe nerves in London. All the empty kerosene barrels on one side of our capsule had now been forced away from their supports and floated in the sea. I hoped they would sink quickly as the lightened balloon heaved us back into the sky. It was apparent it wasn't going to be easy to nail our craft in the sea. Our huge size meant that loss of weight when we touched the surface would keep sending us soaring skywards again. As all the empty barrels on one side of the capsule were wrenched away by the power of the sea, we now witnessed the truth of this assumption. The next transmission read:

Rescue planes circling. Second bounce. All OK. Colin at 550 feet.

We valved gas aggressively. I continued to shout out the altimeter readings so that Andy could get a feel for the rate of descent and control it accordingly. The large solar array was dragging in the water again and acting as an anchor. This had the effect of slowing us down from the mean windspeed of fifteen to twenty knots. As I craned my neck sideways to watch the sea out of the dome under the flight deck I yelled out the numbers. One hundred feet, ninety feet, eighty feet, at which point there was a crash as we hit the water. Whoops, sorry. I could get no real reference for the distance down to the sea by looking through the distorted hemisphere of plastic. In addition it is not reasonable to expect an altimeter set vaguely to the atmospheric pressure of the day to give inch-perfect accuracy. The capsule had been designed by Andy to withstand crash-landing conditions, so there was no serious damage, but the resultant bounce off the water took us back up again with no further action whatsoever.

However, the final descent was more positive and we frantically released gas through the pneumatic valves as we landed. Andy clambered out and hauled on one of the riplines, which are used to tear a panel from the top of the balloon to allow the gas to rush out. We had ditched seventy-six miles east of Japan in a huge, drizzly expanse of the Pacific Ocean.

Andy came back to find me typing a message to Mission Control saying that we were down and safe. Acutely aware that Susie and Andy's girlfriend Carrie would be in a high state of tension while they anxiously awaited news of our fate, I was determined to get the 'we're safe' message to London. This process was not easy as I was now sitting at an angle of about seventy degrees to vertical. My left hand held the computer up against gravity while I frantically tapped away with the forefinger of my right hand. As I pushed the button to transmit the important news I could already feel the awesome power of what amounted to a spinnaker of about eight times the sail area of a huge round-the-world yacht above us. We were being hauled through the water in our capsule at a speed of more than ten knots.

Mission Control never got my final transmission. The aerial was probably submerged when I sent it. It was almost two hours before the news got back to London from the Japanese authorities that we had been picked up alive and well. Susie was later to tell me that if I ever felt like being cross with her about anything trivial I should just ponder what she went through for those two hours between 3.30 and 5.30 am on 7 March 1999. All she got throughout this period was: 'No news yet, I'm afraid.' When the news did finally come through she sat down and poured tears of relief while the children slept on.

Andy was trying frantically with repeated messages to the aircraft to clear the area so that we could eject the balloon envelope. The envelope was dispensable and had been designed with one flight in mind and one flight only. We had always known that it was highly unlikely to be reusable in any form. Nor could the capsule ever be used again as a pressurized vessel now that it had been immersed in sea water, but we were anxious to save it with all its valuable contents. We were unable to wholly deflate the main balloon and an upper smaller balloon still held the main envelope structure upright. Clearly, we couldn't separate the balloon envelope from the capsule by pneumatic release for fear of bringing down one of the aircraft which were flying close at hand.

I doubt that the awful irony of this would have started the Third World War but it might well have left the remaining rescue teams feeling somewhat less kindly towards us and our safety.

Andy could raise no response at all from the circling aircraft and it may well have been that the radio was no longer fully operational. The capsule was still being dragged relentlessly through the waves and it looked as though it was only a matter of time before the water would start slopping into the dome, which was now almost at a right angle to the sea.

With the dome fully hinged open, Andy at last clambered out of the dome above the flight deck. At close quarters he could still see at least two aircraft flying around us and a huge rescue helicopter poised to pick us up. 'Come on, Colin, get the fuck out of there,' he yelled down through the opening. The power of the wind on our vast scalloped spinnaker was awesome. There was a six-foot bow wave at the front of our heavily listing capsule, which had become an unstoppable yacht. Andy had all the bolts and the Allen key with which to secure the dome back into place so as to seal the capsule and make it watertight. I climbed up the narrow steel ladder into the open air to join him.

Andy and I, escaping out of the ditched capsule, are snapped by the military photographer in the Chinook rescue helicopter.

Try as we might, it was physically impossible to lift the heavy dome back into place in order to push the many bolts into the slots. We debated the idea of one of us going over the front in an attempt to get enough of a footing to lift it into place while the other screwed in the bolts, but it was clear that one slip and we would drown. It would not be long before the water would start rushing through the dome opening. We had to give up and clambered out over the back and on to our empty kerosene barrels on the side where they were still attached. There we sat for several minutes discussing what to do next.

In spite of the seriousness of the situation I recall a wave of calm befalling me at this point, the like of which I had not experienced for many months. It was over. We were exhausted and while we were obviously disappointed that we had not flown all the way around the world, all those months of planning, training and flying which were always pregnant with anxiety about how it would all end had finally produced a safe conclusion. There was nothing left to fear. To others it would look as though we were in a highly precarious situation aboard our stricken vessel many miles from land. But rescue was there in front of our eyes and we were comfortable in the knowledge that we had been fully and professionally trained by the experts at RAF St Mawgan to assist the rescue crew in scooping us out of the sea.

There was now nothing we could do apart from abandon ship and leave the whole wonderful craft to a probable ocean grave. We agreed that, once we were on board the helicopter, we must explain what needed to be done to try to save the capsule. There was just no way of communicating with our rescuers from where we were.

Suddenly a diver was in the doorway of the helicopter. He was beckoning frantically and then descended on the winch line to the ocean surface. I seem to remember we had a somewhat comical dialogue about whether to pull the cord on the automatically inflating life jacket before or after we jumped. 'You go first,' I said. Andy pointed out all the various ropes and solar panel lines dragging in the water. 'Whatever you do, watch out for those and make sure you jump clear,' he said. He then leapt overboard, pulling the inflation cord as he went. I simply sat and watched as he disappeared into the distance while I ploughed onwards through the surf. After almost three weeks confined in a tiny sealed space we were now separated for the first time. He looked smaller and smaller in the water as the gap between us widened. I watched the winchman lower a diver to assist him.

At this moment I reflected on what vital equipment might have been left on board. We had had a hasty packing session on our descent as we struggled into our emergency immersion suits, fully expecting that at least the capsule would survive. It suddenly sprung to my mind that the flight log and the landing sequence recorded on video was still in the machine on the flight deck. I really would have liked to retrieve these important testaments to our adventure. I was about to clamber back aboard to quickly recover them when I came to my senses. I even thought of poor Lieutenant Commander Vic Prather of the US Navy, who in 1961 had set the (still current) world altitude record in a balloon, only to drown after a calm landing when the helicopter came to pick him up. It was a daft idea to go back in and I quickly returned to my perch on the empty kerosene barrels. When I related this to Andy later he triumphantly produced the missing tape (though not the log) from his immersion suit pocket. It had been immersed in salt water, but eventually we managed to save some of the footage with the help of ITN.

When Andy was safely in the helicopter it was more than a mile away. All the news reports said that we were in the water for no more than thirty seconds. In reality it was a great deal longer. The videotape recordings from the Japanese rescue craft show that it was nearer to fifteen minutes, which is fairly normal.

The helicopter returned for me so I jumped overboard for the repeat performance. As I turned in the water I had a brief glimpse of a surreal sight I shall never forget. A majestic scalloped golden balloon was sailing away from me, framed by the dramatic greyness of the rain and mist stirred by the downward rotor wash of the huge Chinook helicopter.

CHAPTER NINETEEN

HEADRINE NEWS

W E WERE NEVER TO SEE ANY PART OF OUR BALLOON AGAIN. As I was hauled up out of the water I was struck by the immense damage to the outer skin. This had been shredded by the terrifying currents we were subjected to in the thunderstorm in central Thailand a few days before. How on earth did we survive that? I thought.

'You OK?' I was asked as I was hoisted into the helicopter. '*Hai*,' I replied, that being the only word I know of Japanese. As I collapsed in a heap on the floor of the aircraft in my exhausted and bedraggled state, I lifted my arm to shake the hand of my rescuer. The film of this gesture of gratitude was to be to be broadcast all around the world a few hours later. All the girls at Mission Control were in tears when they saw this pictorial evidence of our safety on the giant TV screen.

The helicopter crew were not prepared to hang around to listen to Andy's requests to stay and secure the capsule. I don't believe they understood anyway. The vast vertical doorway was rolled shut and we returned at frighteningly low level to the Japanese mainland. If we had been flying any higher the two pilots would have had no vision at all through the lowering cloud. They clearly had orders to return us immediately to base. We flew for about forty-five minutes with no idea where we were being taken and unable to communicate with the very well-trained Japanese rescue team. Andy was seated some way behind me on the other side of the helicopter, too far away for us to be able to talk to each other. I glanced around at him a couple of times. He looked serenely calm and reflective and, I thought, perhaps a little sad as he gazed out of the window. After lengthy consultation among the crew the winchman came up to me and shouted his carefully rehearsed message into my ear: 'Good charrenge. Better ruck next time.'

Slumped in our seats, we were given blankets to put over our wet and collapsed bodies. This was quite unnecessary because during our descent we had both put on warm clothes and the full waterproof immersion suit had kept them almost completely dry. We were tired but not cold.

One of the crew pointed out a Japanese Air Force plane flying in formation with us at close proximity. He and his crew mates kept slapping their hands together in mutual congratulation at the success of their rescue mission. It would not be often that they would be dispatched to pluck a couple of balloonists out of the Pacific – particularly

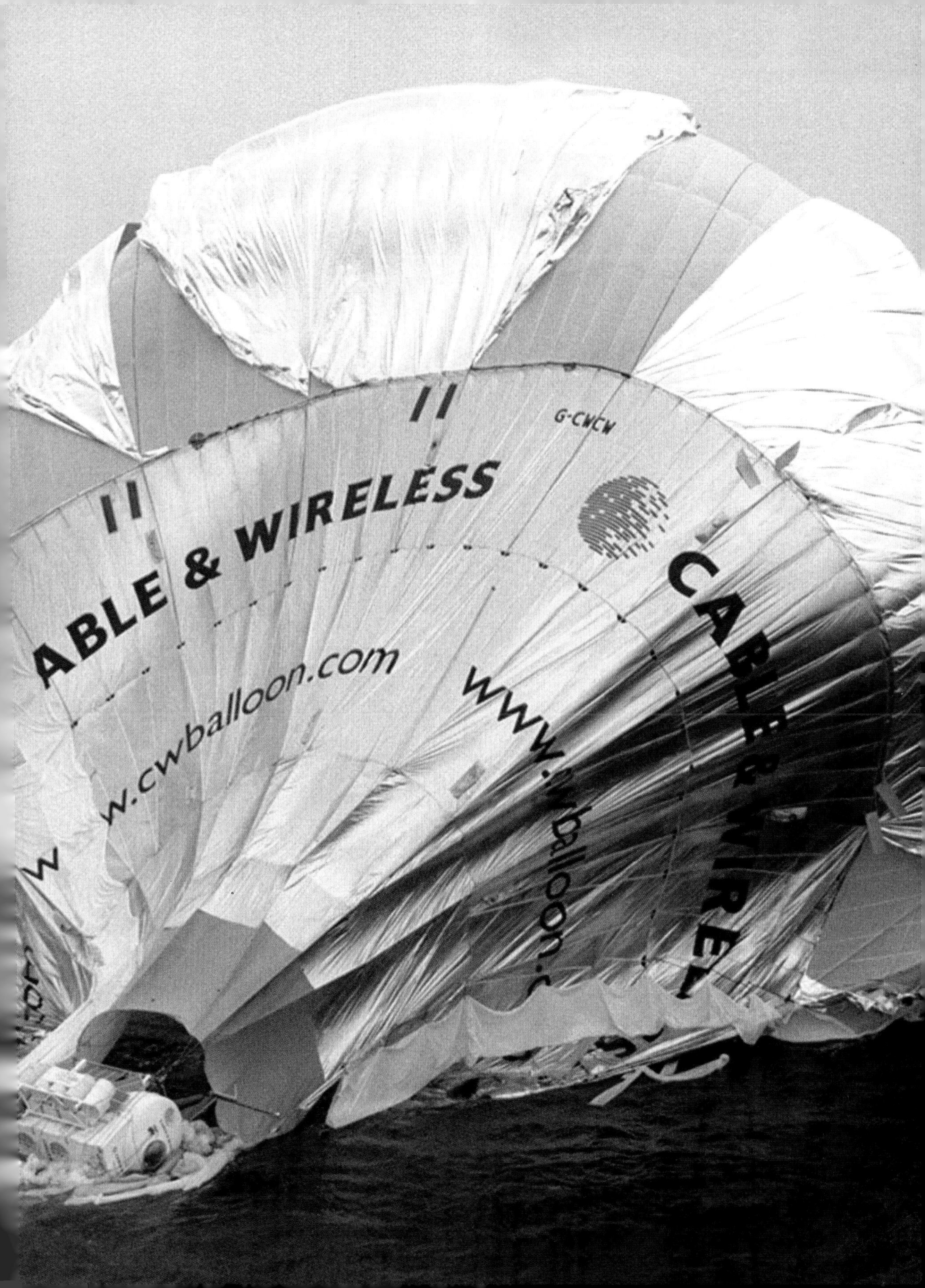
ABLE & WIRELESS
G-CWCW
w.cwballoon.com
www.cwballoon.c

from an adventure which had already been made famous by newspaper reports of our progress. I felt embarrassed at the trouble they had been put to but I consoled myself that it had been a useful real-life exercise for them rather than the simulated training that they were more used to.

After flying over the shoreline we descended into the air force base of Hamamatsu. We swooped down the runway past the three neatly parked AWACS planes and came to a standstill beside a waiting medical crew and van. I wondered why it was the military – the self-defence forces as they are called – rather than the coastguard that had come to rescue us. It was later suggested to me, perhaps a little unfairly, that the rescue services had been pilloried by the world's press for the shambles of their efforts at Kobe following the earthquake there a couple of years before. Maybe they needed a high-profile PR success.

The only completely inscrutable crew member on board was the man with the stills and video cameras. He looked as though he was on his way back from the most mundane of exercises and from time to time he covered his mouth with his hand to mask a yawn. I suppose he considered he was just doing his job, but he probably had no idea of the enormous worldwide media coverage his handiwork was about to attract.

At the medical centre we met the boss, who introduced himself with an unpronounceable name. 'Call me Dr No. Just like in James Bond,' he said, breaking into peals of laughter at his joke. After completing the formalities and filling out a form asking questions such as 'Do you have any injuries?' and 'When did you have your last meal?' we were asked if there was anything we wanted.

I simply suggested that we had not had a beer for three weeks. This caused a certain amount of perplexity. I wasn't quite sure if this was because our hosts considered my response outrageously cheeky. I needn't have worried. Several cans were produced with great gusto and everyone toasted our safe return.

We were also offered the most spectacular hot bath in the biggest tub I have ever seen. Sunken into the floor, it was made of polished aluminium and had already been filled with water at the perfect temperature.

We were desperate to make at least one phone call to let everyone know where we were and that everything was OK. Strangely, our request was stalled for about an hour. Then we were asked politely if we would mind attending a brief press conference, after which they would arrange for us to speak to whoever we wanted to in the outside world. As we were shown into a small room along the corridor we were astonished to see an enormous array of Japanese TV cameramen and photographers. Not much was said or understood and they appeared to want visual scoops rather than anything erudite. Someone mumbled something about failure. It was then that Andy first came up with that great line 'We didn't fail. We simply found another way that doesn't work.' Nobody smiled. In the sheer relief of it all among these serious, sombre-looking journalists I found it very hard to repress an attack of the giggles.

Our reward for cooperation was to be fed with calls from England, including one from Susie. She told me she was proud of me, it was an amazing achievement and she was looking forward to me coming home. When would it be? I told her that for the time being we were illegal immigrants and there would be procedures to carry out when the government offices opened again on Monday morning. I couldn't tell her how long it would all take.

By now the newshounds from the British media had discovered our whereabouts and several calls were being kept on hold. I had to tell Andy's mother when she rang that her son couldn't take the call because he was in the shower. After all, it was probably the best shower of his life and he was taking his time.

Previous spread The end of a dream. The damage inflicted on the balloon during the thunderstorm of several days previously is clearly visible.
Opposite A final visit by the Japanese military before *Cable & Wireless* disappeared without trace to the ocean floor.

Exhausted, but happy to
be alive – Andy and I at
the press conference at
Hamamatsu Air Force
base, Japan, soon after
being rescued.

When he emerged we had to line up for a seemingly endless permutation of group photographs so that all the air force personnel on duty had permanent records of themselves being there with us.

At one point there was an explosive bustle in the corridor as everyone rushed to watch the main news on the giant TV set mounted above the passage near our room. Several doctors and other officials beckoned us excitedly as the scenes of our rescue filmed by their own military flooded the screen, accompanied by a lengthy commentary apparently about what had happened earlier near their shores. Everyone bowed and shook our hands warmly as Dr No kept repeating, 'Headrine news. Headrine news.'

We acknowledged his excitement. 'Did they say who won the Australian Grand Prix?' I asked light-heartedly. It was meant to be a joke but someone was immediately dispatched to find out the information I required. A small fellow came scampering back up the passage. 'Eddy Irvine,' he enthused.

Eddy Irvine? He must be joking, I thought. He wasn't, though. Strange things happen in the world when you have been away from it for three weeks in a balloon.

'Jean-Louis Nicolle will be here soon,' the Japanese medical staff kept telling us. Nicolle was from Cable & Wireless in Tokyo and was there to vouch for us and take us the next morning for immigration procedures in Nagoya. As we walked out of the gates to the car that was to take us to the hotel, a gaggle of reporters were waiting, including several European crews. We were amazed at how quickly the media could mobilize their contacts. When we did arrive at the immigration office the next morning, the ITN team were there to greet us.

Long queues of foreign students were waiting in front of the windows, behind which sat some rather grim-looking men and women in navy-blue uniforms. It would be several hours before we were dealt with, we were told. ITN had brought a fixer with them and he scurried round the throng in an attempt to sniff out someone in authority. Soon he was back again with a silver-haired Japanese official sporting a suitable number of stars on his lapel. We all bowed and shook hands.

'Never in my thirty years here have I ever got permission to bring a television crew to witness immigration procedures,' crowed the fixer. We were then led up some stairs and along a passage to a large, bare room. Tables and chairs were hastily arranged. Three officials sat on one side of the makeshift desk, Andy and I on the other. We both completed the form placed in front of us, although we hesitated over the box headed 'Reason for visit'. I settled for 'Emergency abandonment of vessel in Pacific Ocean', which in retrospect seems rather pompous, if accurate. Our passports were stamped, everyone bowed again and shook hands, then we left.

The ITN crew stuck to us like leeches. They were kind enough to buy first-class tickets for us to travel with them on the bullet train to Tokyo. We made an incongruous sight in our Andy Pandy-style fleece dungarees. It was still all we had to wear apart from shirts, underpants and socks found for us by Jean-Louis. Once back in Tokyo, we were reunited with Russell Brice and Glenn Fairley, who had jumped straight on a plane to coordinate the salvage of our capsule. Unfortunately by the time they arrived the Japanese authorities had confirmed its demise. It was now at the bottom of the ocean near the Marianas Trench, the deepest place on earth.

We attended an impromptu press conference requested by our sponsor's subsidiary company. Rumours had just leaked in Japan that an unknown company called Cable & Wireless was about to make a hostile bid for a large Japanese telecommunications company. And then suddenly this huge balloon had landed in the Pacific off their shores. A colour picture of it graced the front page of twenty-five million newspapers circulated in Japan that day and it had the name of this unknown predator emblazoned all over it. Simon Cunningham, the boss of Cable & Wireless Japan, wouldn't confirm the rumours but you could forgive his wry smile when he contemplated the irony of the accidental and unexpected timing of such a massive PR coup. Awareness of his company had gone from virtually non-existent on 6 March to almost universal on 8 March.

I mentioned I liked sushi. Simon and his colleagues thought we deserved some, and we were entertained to a delicious dinner.

The next day we flew home. We had half expected to be offered Virgin Upper Class tickets, courtesy of that nice Mr Branson. It was a rather presumptuous thought, but then Richard had been to see many of his rivals off, if not back. It would have got him more of the publicity he brilliantly scoops at every turn. If the thought crossed his mind he was probably put off by previous remarks Andy had made when our permission to overfly China was withdrawn. 'I suppose it's all you can expect from upstart millionaires who want to come and compete in our sport,' he had gone on record as saying. Instead

To my nine-year-old son, Archie, it was now all a bit of a joke.

Some cuttings of the homecoming from the Prescot scrapbook.

COLIN AND FAMILY ENJOY EMOTIONAL HOMECOMING

Balloonist gets hero's welcome

Report by **Sarah Cole**   ◆

HEROIC Hampshire balloonist Colin Prescot flew into the arms of his family yesterday after his brave bid to circumnavigate the world.

Colin, his wife and children had an emotional reunion when he arrived at Heathrow Airport two days after his Cable and Wireless balloon was rescued from the ocean...

HERO: Colin Prescot with Susie and Archie yesterday.

DADDY'S HOME: Colin Prescot with daughter Pollyanna (above), the whole family (below) and balloon partner Andy Elson (below left).

"That was very frightening. It took us 90 minutes to sort it out and get out of it. When we finally got up to the top of the clouds Andy asked me if I wanted to look out at the clouds, but I said 'no thanks'."

Colin's wife, Susie, said she and the couple's children, Archie, nine, Pollyanna, seven, and Lara, 13, were relieved to have him home.

"We are really, really so excited to have him back. We have been so busy since they set off and our lives have changed. This morning the children asked if there was a fax from daddy and, of course, there wasn't because he was on his way home. It was a strange feeling."

Susie said their son was a passionate would-be astronaut and was hoping to join his father on his next voyage.

She added: "I've got a feeling I will be waving goodbye to both of them at some point. But I have told them they can't fly together."

Asked if he would let his son travel with him on his next attempt, Colin added: "We will see – perhaps next time."

The pilots said they were now looking forward to going home and were planning a huge party.

Record-breaker is back home safe

HERO balloonist Colin Prescot said he will think about another flight after his record-breaking attempt to circle the globe.

After flying into Heathrow from Japan on Tuesday evening after the failed attempt, Colin is getting back to normal at his home in Stockbridge in the Test Valley.

He told the Daily Echo: "It's wonderful to be home and see my family after such a long time. I feel absolutely fine and normal."

Colin will now spend some time with his wife Susie and three children Archie, 9, Polyanna, 7 and 13-year-old Lara before taking back over the reins of his successful company Flying Pictures – the world's biggest operator of hot-air balloons.

He said that if he goes again it would be with co-pilot Andy Elson, who shared the disappointment of the 18-day flight ending in a storm off the coast of Japan on Sunday morning.

"We have agreed to take a couple of weeks to think about another attempt," he said.

Colin agreed that the attempt would have been successful if they had been able to fly over China – which had refused permission after an attempt involving entrepreneur Richard Branson had violated its airspace without permission.

He said: "It was irritating to be first granted permission and then refused, but I have always respected the Chinese problem. They were not bloody-minded – people illegally entered their airspace. What Richard Branson did was not helpful, but I am not angry."

Colin admitted the low point of the trip was deciding to ditch. But he said: "It was not a difficult decision.

"Everything was going wrong with the weather. We were philosophical about it. What we did was the longest flight in history.

"We nearly doubled the endurance record and our rival balloonist Steve Fossett has said it will not be beaten."

REUNION: Colin greets his family at Heathrow Airport.

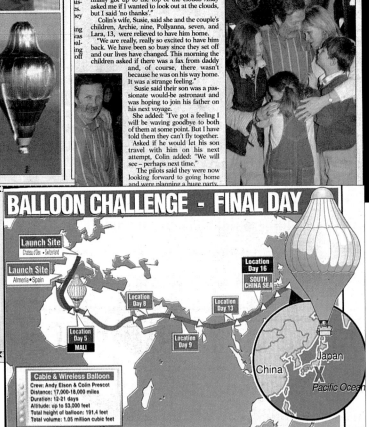

BALLOON CHALLENGE – FINAL DAY

Launch Site Château d'Oex • Switzerland

Launch Site Almeria • Spain

Location Day 5 MALI

Location Day 8

Location Day 9

Location Day 13

Location Day 16 SOUTH CHINA SEA

China

Japan

Pacific Ocean

Cable & Wireless Balloon
Crew: Andy Elson & Colin Prescot
Distance: 17,000-18,000 miles
Duration: 12-21 days
Altitude: up to 53,000 feet
Total height of balloon: 191.4 feet
Total volume: 1.05 million cubic feet

Left Family and colleagues at Heathrow Airport to welcome us back.
Below Andy and me at the Heathrow press conference. Andy is explaining that we met two of our three objectives – to survive, to get round the world and to still be friends at the end of it all.

we purchased two economy-class tickets on British Airways and waited for the flight to be called. By great good fortune Gordon Fowler, cabin services director at the airline and the husband of Susie's colleague at her company, had just left Tokyo the day before. He left word about us and we were immediately upgraded. We couldn't have been treated to a trip that was more in contrast to the spartan conditions of our previous eighteen days aloft.

When we came through customs at Heathrow's Terminal Four there was a huge welcoming committee with banners and champagne. The hugs I got from Susie and the children were the most special demonstration of reciprocated love I will ever know. Handshakes. Cheering. Press conference at a hotel. Party at the office. Television interviews. And then

home. Home at last. Just us. Susie, Lara, Archie and Polly. As I sank into the sofa by an open fire, a glass of cold Chardonnay in my hand, my heart was still beating with the sheer exhilaration and pace of events. Was that really me? Is it really all over?

The next day was strange. Susie had insisted I stay quietly at home for a few days. She and my colleagues at the office had been told of how three weeks incarcerated in a small space can play tricks on the mind. It was a well-researched subject. Three to five days after coming home, a deep sense of anticlimax hits you. After that the 'patient' should be closely observed in case full-scale depression sets in.

Well, it's all bollocks.

They got bored of watching me. I insisted on returning to work within two days – there was a lot of work waiting to be dealt with – and I'm still on a high many months after the event. I am sure that the difference between us and other prisoners of small

spaces is that we stayed in ours voluntarily. The hostages in Beirut and some long-term spacemen were either imprisoned against their will or under orders. There is a huge psychological difference.

I was also lucky that we were about to start the second phase of aerial sequences for the new James Bond film, *The World Is Not Enough*. This meant I could get immediately stuck into some more high-action stuff, although only in a supervisory role. I had been running the pre-planning of Flying Pictures' role in the movie before I left. Now that I was back Marc Wolff asked me if I would get involved again. There were some wizzy scenes to be filmed of skiers and microlight aircraft in the snowiest Alps for years. Much more tricky was the requirement for a vast column of circular saws that had to be hung under a helicopter, which would saw its way through jetties, pipelines and even a BMW. If this was not complicated enough it all had to be filmed at night. To do this our guys had to build two separate tables twenty-four feet high on which to land the skids so that the saws underneath fitted in between. David Arkell, our chief pilot who actually flew this contraption, very reasonably insisted on a co-pilot to talk him down since he could not even see the landing tables from his seat at the front of the helicopter.

The film set, which represented the oil wells in the Caspian Sea off Azerbaijan, was constructed at Hankley Common in Surrey. When I watched David set off into the night in his incredible, menacing machine (with petrol motors to drive the saws and laden with pyrotechnics), it was a sharp reminder that I had no monopoly on hazardous adventures.

Many people on the Bond film asked me if I was disappointed that we didn't make it all the way around the world in a balloon. I was not. When the Chinese withdrew their permission from all teams except Breitling, the conventional wisdom was that as the jet stream went straight through the vast country it would be near impossible to circumnavigate it in a balloon. The other teams gave up without even launching. We proved them wrong and we had the adventure of a lifetime. When Bertrand Piccard and Brian Jones completed their epic journey I was pleased. The record was ready to be captured and they deserved it. But if they had failed, I would not have been able to resist having another go, even though I should probably be moving on to something else.

Andy and I were awarded the Charles Green Salver, which is given annually for the outstanding balloon feat of the previous year. It was also awarded to Bertrand and Brian – the first time it had ever been given for two flights in the same year. In April we were invited to join the Queen and Prince Philip at Cameron Balloons in Bristol in celebrating the victorious flight of Bertrand and Brian. The citations included the view that only a few weeks ago it would have seemed inconceivable that our achievement could now be left in the shade by something even more extraordinary. Per Lindstrand had recently asked me if I still wanted to pursue the Edge of Space project. I told him that Andy and I had established

The Queen and the Duke of Edinburgh's visit to Bristol to congratulate Bertrand and Brian. 'Was it because of Branson that you had to fly round China?' Prince Philip asked us.

ourselves as a team in the same way as he had with Richard Branson and that it was more likely than not that I would want to continue on the same track. Andy was also very interested in flying to the edge of space, so we used the Queen's visit as the occasion to tell people that the two of us were now in the early stages of planning. It was an unrehearsed declaration, which was filmed by *National Geographic*, who were completing a documentary of our flight.

I met Steve Fossett for the first time in Colorado in May. He had flown in from California to be at a party Tim Cole was throwing for Andy and me at his home. We went to meet Steve at the local airport, where he showed us his new Citation jet, which he had just purchased for $17 million. As he stood at the bottom of the steps he bemoaned the fact that his year was ruined. First of all Piccard had stolen *his* record, he said. And then his new multimillion-dollar yacht had caught fire in New Zealand and needed extensive repairs. He had nothing to do over the summer. We sympathized but not that much.

Two years earlier Steve had been the architect of the $1 million prize offered by Budweiser for the first balloonists to circumnavigate the world. It came about when he was duck shooting with August Busch, the company's chairman. Busch wanted to sponsor Steve for his next attempt but Steve did not accept sponsorship. Instead he suggested that Budweiser offer the prize (presumably fully expecting to receive it himself), wanting to be rid of the pressures of sponsors' demands during his preparations and flight. Now that the prize had gone elsewhere he was sad that he hadn't even been invited to the ceremony.

Chris Bonington, the renowned British mountaineer, also flew in for the party in Colorado. He wanted to interview Steve for his forthcoming book about adventure. He was supremely irritated to see Andy and me there. He had already travelled considerable distances the week before to interview us at our respective homes.

When I got back from America I ran into Richard Branson at St Edward's, Oxford, where our respective children go to school. He had tried to telephone Andy and I through the satellite while we were flying. Now he was gracious enough to say he was sorry about the problems we had had by being banned from China. On 18 June Susie and I were to see him again.

All the teams of balloonists who had announced an attempt at the round-the-world record (even those that never took off) were invited for the weekend at the Forbes's Château de Balleroy in France. It was exactly twenty years since I had been there last.

Then we had honoured the three American balloonists who had made the first crossing of the Atlantic the previous year, 1978. Two of them, Ben Abruzzo and Maxie Anderson, had since been killed in separate ballooning accidents. Only Larry Newman could be there and he had been lucky to survive a horrendous hang-gliding accident some years earlier, which had left him seriously injured.

Richard Branson was given a special lifetime achievement award for his contribution to ballooning. The firework display was every bit as impressive as the one twenty years before. Instead of being synchronized to the *1812 Overture*, it was accompanied by *Tubular Bells*, the Mike Oldfield composition which made Richard seriously rich.

Over a glass of delicious champagne on the terrace I asked Brian Jones if he and Bertrand had had any alcohol on board *Breitling Orbiter 3*. 'No, not a drop,' was the instantaneous reply. There was a pause while several people around us took an interest in my reaction. 'That must have been boring,' I said at last, playing to the gallery. It was worth it just to see the look of shock and incomprehension on their faces, while Andy chuckled in the background.

At dinner I was asked if I knew the Branson team well. It was not an easy question to answer but I said I knew enough about them to give the China crisis as an example of the differences in their characters. 'I have known Per Lindstrand for twenty years and yet he never even mentioned it,' I explained. 'It was as though it had never happened. Richard Branson took the trouble to apologize to my face. Steve Fossett, on the other hand, cannot understand why we didn't go through anyway.' I knew Steve was listening. 'That's about right,' he said, 'why didn't you?'

In July I went to Nice to see Amelia Tarzi, the daughter of Safia who had inadvertently set me on course for my ballooning career all those years ago. Now a successful international lawyer and several years older than Safia was when she died, Amelia looked every inch as beautiful, elegant, exotic and chic as her mother did in 1976. As we drank coffee in the flower market of the Cours Saléya in Old Nice, her thirteen-year-old mongrel terrier, Rio, sat under the table swathed in bandages from a recent fight. I was touched that Amelia presented me with a crystal balloon on a gold chain for Susie. It was a special memento of her mother's, which she had kept for the twenty-three years since her death.

In August I returned to Alderney with the family for our holiday. Susie and I had a delicious meal washed down by Sancerre and claret at the First and Last Restaurant, which is well known to sailors who call in on the island. It is the first eatery they see when they stagger ashore after navigating one of the most notorious tides in the world. When the bill came this time Rita Gillmore and Sara Pittman, who run the restaurant, simply arrived with a flourish to say it was all on the house. Another restaurant, The Barn, at the far end of the island, stands in beautifully kept gardens tended by Francis Short. When we went for a light lunch there the following day, Francis told us he had been keeping a bottle of Taittinger at the back of the fridge for four months for when we next turned up. He produced it immediately.

I hadn't realized that the Channel Islands media had followed the flight of *Cable & Wireless* so religiously, starting every bulletin with 'Alderney balloonist Colin Prescot…' They justified this by the fact that I was the only balloonist to have flown from the island and that I spent 'a significant amount' of my time there. It was a surprise that so many people were so welcoming and everyone wanted to know all about the adventure.

Well, almost everyone.

Susie and I were invited for drinks one evening at Reynards, the jewellers in Victoria

Street. Jon Kay-Mouat, the President of the States of Alderney, was there. He had sent me a message of good wishes on behalf of the people of Alderney while I was in the air. I introduced myself and thanked him for his missive but he didn't appear to have a clue who I was. He had clearly never sent the message at all. When I explained that I was the balloonist who was trying to fly around the world, he simply said he thought I might be something to do with a balloon flight in France in which his wife had broken a rib. He shuffled off without as much as looking me in the eye. 'Oh well, you can't win them all,' Susie said, roaring with laughter.

For centuries people have got a 'buzz' out of living life on the edge. Many people have tried to work out why they do it. I firmly believe it is impossible to generalize. I have met and worked with many stuntmen over the years and they have been a very mixed bag of personalities. Some are noisy exhibitionists, others quiet, shy and modest. Many shun publicity altogether. In my case I have never sought to frighten myself, yet I have always known it is inevitable that I will. I don't like being frightened any more than the next man. I have a very low boredom threshold and the projects I have been involved in have always alleviated that boredom. When the opportunity arose to attempt to fly around the world I was excited by the complexity of the challenge. I believed I had the necessary qualities and I had not undertaken anything significant for some time. I was never good at managing my business and it had taken me eighteen years to realize that I needed someone else to help me. And yet it was more or less all that I had been doing in recent years. I probably felt the need to recharge my mental batteries, to do something for my own self-esteem. I was rejuvenated by the whole idea. At last, here was an opportunity to do something I was good at.

However, I also saw the proposed flight as a business opportunity. It was something out of which we had the chance to make a profit. I saw it as a risk-filled venture which we were qualified to take on. In that sense I was excited to have the opportunity to contribute something to the business and to my colleagues within it. But most of all it was a high-profile adventure which would give us all some fun.

As far as fame is concerned, it was never an issue for me until the Cable & Wireless adventure. Then I had my five minutes of it. Well, eighteen days perhaps. However, I was not around to witness most of it. Our sponsor calculated that the worldwide publicity of our adventure would have cost upwards of $90 million to buy. That was excluding documentaries, books and the astonishing twenty-two million visits, averaging more than ten minutes each, to the company's website devoted to our journey. When I came home there was some residual interest in our story. When I went to Boots the Chemist in Andover to replenish my washbag with all the things I had lost in the Pacific, the checkout lady recognized me. Wow, I thought.

That was more or less that, though. No one recognizes me now if I walk down the street and I am grateful for that. On the other hand, many people I know still keep coming up to me and saying what an amazing thing it was that I did. I don't contradict them and I admit that every time it happens it gives me a warm cocoon of pride. I always knew that I was viewed as someone a bit different. Many never could understand what made me tick. I was an eccentric, someone who seemed quite sane on the surface, someone who wore a suit and tie to work but someone who also did these extraordinary things. 'He can't seriously make a living out of all that nonsense?' people would say. To all except those who knew me well I was an enigma. Now I had done something which had attracted worldwide interest, something which people felt they could admire. And, yes, I savoured that.

It took only a couple of weeks after we landed for Bertrand and Brian to upstage us by flying through China and all the way round the world. I was genuinely pleased for them. They deserved it. Bertrand had been determined over several years and three attempts. It was he who had worked hardest to win permission to fly through China. If Andy and I had succeeded before them we might have started believing we were genuine heroes. The intoxication of the achievement of the so-called last great aviation record might just have gone a little bit to our heads. We might even have started saying things like 'We took off as pilots, flew as friends and landed as brothers.' (Give me a break, Bertrand.)

Robin Sebag, a friend of mine who lives a few kilometres up the valley in Switzerland from where *Breitling Orbiter 3* took off, wrote to me: 'We all know the wrong team won but you can't blame the Swiss for going mad. They haven't had a real hero here since William Tell.'

In the closing days of the twentieth century I received word that Andy and I were to be awarded the Gold Medal of the Royal Aero Club. It will be presented in London in April 2000 by the club's president, HRH the Duke of York. The Gold Medal has been awarded only forty times in the past century and among the recipients are Louis Blériot, the Wright brothers, Alcock and Brown, and Armstrong, Aldrin and Collins. I was as chuffed as hell about this and amused myself with the thought that it must be the first time it has ever been awarded for a failure. The citation did not express it like that: '…they established a world record for unrefuelled duration in any sub-orbital flying machine'. Put that way, it sounded rather impressive.

But there is also the downside. Indulging in stunts and adventures with varying degrees of risk to life and limb is undoubtedly very selfish. It has been tough on my family, who have had more than their share of worry. Susie once pleaded with me to come down from a horizontal bough of an oak tree eighteen feet above the ground, where I was hanging a swing for the children. 'If you fall down and break your neck, don't expect me to be looking after you, growing old and smelly in a wheelchair,' she said. She has never been keen on the more apparently dangerous of my projects. And yet she has been wonderfully supportive. She always knew how irritable I could get without a challenge on the horizon. When someone said to her, 'You must have been very pleased to get Colin back after his flight around the world,' I suspect she was only half joking when she replied, 'Well, I was at the time, but I must say it's wearing off now.'

And then there are the friends who got hurt or killed. Safia Tarzi was the first, of course – only weeks after my introduction to ballooning. There were others. Philip Hutchins was the winner of the first-ever Cross-Channel Balloon Race, in which I participated. He was a tremendous guy who combined a successful law practice with contributing enormously to the sport of ballooning. I shared with him the hilarious experience of watching Hans Buker attempting to jump the Spanish border in his vintage fire engine. Tragically, Philip was killed in Luxembourg in August 1982 while strapping himself into a chair beneath a balloon. An unexpected gust took him up to thirty feet before he was ready. He was ejected when the balloon reached the end of the rope which tethered him to the ground. When he hit the ground he suffered a heart attack and died instantly.

I came up with the idea of the Cloudhopper in 1979 as a fun machine for innocent pranks. Sadly, Frank Barnes was the only pilot in Britain to die at the controls of a balloon in more than twenty years. He was flying a Cloudhopper when he was killed in a collision with power lines. Coy Foster, a celebrated plastic surgeon and balloon enthusiast, had to rely on his colleagues to rebuild his face during several operations, after a raging on-board fire while he was ballooning in Texas. It was a miracle he

survived at all. He was also flying a Cloudhopper when the accident happened.

Nigel Rogoff, a top parachutist and leader of the RAF freefall team, had done several stunts for us over the years, the last dressed as a rabbit in Sainsbury's Flying Circus. Just before Christmas 1999 he hit the top of the stand of Aston Villa's football ground as he descended before a match. He fell forty feet on to the pitch. It was only because of his supreme fitness that he survived at all. He suffered severe internal injuries and had to have his left leg amputated above the knee. Eight months later he had still not been allowed to go home from his RAF convalescent home but he retained his sense of humour enough to change his e-mail address to ljsilver@…

Every time there is an accident my heart sinks. There is a period of great sadness and reflection. And then somehow I find myself taking a deep breath and carrying on as normal. There is nothing unusual about this. My colleagues Marc Wolff, Ian Ashpole and Robin Batchelor (aka the Birdman) all react the same way. There is no logic and no explanation.

And so we go on. I think we would all agree that if we had not had the laughs, the fun, the excitement, the adventure and the sheer *joie de vivre* we would all be a miserable bunch of so-and-sos. So many memories, so many great people, so many achievements. It was a privilege to be there.

I would never kid myself that there are not thousands of people who could have accomplished any one of my so-called feats, if they had just had the opportunity and the will to do so. There is nothing especially brave, clever or even all that novel about anything I have done.

The Right Stuff?

Nah.

CHAPTER TWENTY

GONE WITH THE WIND

WRITING HAS BEEN a new adventure, but the novelty has been wearing a bit thin of late. As they say in California, I'm outta here. Besides, I've had an idea.

INDEX

Numbers in **bold** refer to photographs.

INDEX

AUTHOR'S ACKNOWLEDGEMENTS

Thank you...

To Adrian Sington for commissioning this book.

To Katy Carrington for patiently putting up with my foibles and for so painstakingly coordinating the production of this epic (it ended up almost twice as long as it was supposed to).

To Richard Dawes for his good humour in editing the manuscript (and for not slashing it to pieces).

To Tessa Tennant, Christine Monk and Lucie Graves for pulling together all the photographs; to Linda Mitchell for printing out my endless stream of indecipherable notes; to everyone who supplied their pictures.

To Susie for leaving me to get on with it (yet again) and for insisting on only one phrase being removed from the text.

To Amelia Tarzi for helping me to reconstruct the story of her mother's life.

To Richard Branson for the foreword and to Mike Kendrick, my bitter rival of twenty years, for being big enough to arrange it.

To Trevor Wayman for the jacket design and Dan Newman for the internal layout.

To Sarah Bennie and Clare Powney for their infectious enthusiasm in marketing and promotion.

PICTURE ACKNOWLEDGEMENTS

All pictures featured in *To the Edge of Space* are taken from the author's personal collection, with the exception of the following:

Aerostat: 69; Allsport: 12-13, 198, 210 (*bottom*), 213, 216, 217 (*top and bottom*), 218 (*bottom, left and right*), 219, 220 (*inset*), 220-21, 223, 224, 229 (*bottom*), 230 (*bottom*), 234-35, 241, 265; Per-Olow W. Anderson: 77; David Arkell: 260 (*left and right*); Ian Ashpole: 56-57; by kind permission of Associated Newspapers/Solo Syndication: 86 (*top*); courtesy of Christopher Bailey: 122-23; Gordon Batchelor: 39; Robin Batchelor: 40, 41 (*main picture and top three insets*), 88-89, 97 (*bottom*), 98, 129, 130 (*bottom*); Bill Bennett: 131; Bettman/Corbis: 191; Lawrence Bickerton: 162, 163, 164, 165, 167; Peter Bish: 140; Patrick Bunce: 147 (*top and bottom*), 148, 149; Cameron Balloons Ltd: 218 (*top*), 261; Sue Carden: 176, 177, 178, 179; reproduced courtesy of Carlton International Media Ltd: 92; Corbis/Sygma: 49, 50; Peter Corns: 134-35, 155 (*top, left and right*); © The *Daily Telegraph*, 1979: 86 (*middle, right*); Terry Duffell: 42, 54-55, 128, 154, 155 (*bottom*), 180, 181, 182, 183; Andy Elson: 194, 195, 202, 228, 229 (*top*), 233, 244, 246; David Fanthorpe: 76; Eleanor Fein: 125; courtesy of Geoff Thompson: 242; Jean Louis Getaz: 62; © The *Guardian*/Peter Johns: 86 (*middle, left*); David Henderson: 6; courtesy of Henson Organisation: 102-103, 106; Hulton Deutsch Collection/Corbis: 190; Hulton Getty: 83, 87; J. Walter Thompson Company Limited: 22-23; David James: 118; Kyodo News: 250, 252-53, 254, 256; courtesy of London Weekend Television: 114-115; Christine Monk: 145, 259 (*bottom*); David Nowell: 157 (*inset*); Andy Parker: 2-3, 184-85, 187, 188, 199, 204-205; David Partridge: 141, 142; Chris Perrett: 31, 63, 192-93, 203, 266-67; Ian Pilinger: 170-71 (*main picture*); Alison Porteous: 41 (*bottom inset*); Colin Prescot/Andy Elson: 10-11, 225, 227 (*top*), 231, 232, 236-37, 238, 239, 243; Ronald Grant Archive: 101 (*top*); Skydive Sebastian: 211, 212; *Southern Daily Echo*: 258 (*top and bottom left*); States of Alderney: 158-59; courtesy of the *Sunday Mirror*/Jerry Young: 53 (*bottom*); Amelia Tarzi: 32-33, 34, 35 (*top and bottom*), 36, 37; Telegraph Colour Library: 14-15; Getty One Stone: 119 (*bottom*), 119 (*top*); courtesy of Trog: 86 (*bottom*); courtesy of Virgin: 8, 214; Simon Ward: 138, 150, 151; Jerry Young: 80, 84, 85, 87, 112-13, 137.